CONVERSATIONS
ON BEING JEWISH
IN TODAY'S WORLD

A
SHAAR
PRESS
PUBLICATION

Judaism

EMANUEL FELDMAN

ON JUDAISM

© *Copyright 1994 by* Rabbi Emanuel Feldman

First edition – First impression / November 1994
Second impression / June 2000
Third impression / November 2003

Published by **SHAAR PRESS**
Distributed by MESORAH PUBLICATIONS, LTD.
4401 Second Avenue / Brooklyn, N.Y 11232 / (718) 921-9000 / www.artscroll.com

Distributed in Israel by SIFRIATI / A. GITLER
10 Hashomer Street / Bnei Brak 51361

Distributed in Europe by LEHMANNS
Unit E, Viking Industrial Park / Rolling Mill Road / Jarow, Tyne and Wear NE32 3DP / England

Distributed in Australia and New Zealand by GOLDS BOOK & GIFT SHOP
36 William Street / Balaclava 3183, Vic., Australia

Distributed in South Africa by KOLLEL BOOKSHOP
Shop 8A Norwood Hypermarket / Norwood 2196, Johannesburg, South Africa

ISBN: 0-89906-034-X Hard Cover
ISBN: 0-89906-035-8 Paperback

Printed in the United States of America by Noble Book Press
Custom bound by Sefercraft, Inc. / 4401 Second Avenue / Brooklyn N.Y. 11232

table of contents

introduction

Jewish life today is in the grip of communal schizophrenia. The level of Jewish illiteracy and ignorance has reached new lows while, simultaneously, traditional Jewish learning and scholarship is growing ever stronger. The incidence of intermarriage and dropouts is alarming, but the incidence of returnees to classical Judaism gives one hope.

All this is a reflection of the fact that we are becoming two societies: those on the periphery of Judaism who are inexorably fading away, and a solid core that grows ever more intense and committed.

It is to both sides of this paradox that this book is directed. While making no claims to be a definitive study of Judaism, it explores certain major principles of Jewish belief and practice which can help persuade the diffident that our ancient faith continues to address their major needs as contemporary men and women. And for those who are returning to the ways of our people, it can serve as a source of significant ideas to help illuminate the way home.

To ensure a more effective discussion, I have deliberately chosen the colloquial style and have eschewed structured and tightly knit essays in favor of the more flexible and informal medium of a conversation between a seeking Jew and a Rabbi.

The ebb and flow of this form allows one to meander, to explore rivulets that appear suddenly out of nowhere, and to sense the eddies that move beneath the surface. Conversation, in a word, permits a far wider range of discourse.

Although each chapter is a self-contained unit, the order in which they appear reflects the path which is walked by many returnees to Judaism: the yearning to find one's roots (chapter 1) engenders questions about God (chapter 2) and prayer (chapter 3), which lead sequentially to the issues in the chapters that follow.

The author offers this work with the prayer that it will prove helpful to those who want to discover the depths of classical Judaism, and with the hope of demonstrating that this Judaism is not only a realistic alternative for today's Jew, but is in fact desirable and essential.

No book is an island unto itself. Numerous individuals are involved in the convoluted journey from the conception of the mind until the binding of the book.

My deepest appreciation goes to the principals and staff of Shaar Press, and especially to Rabbi Pinchas Stolper Senior Executive of the Orthodox Union — who first proposed the idea of this book to me, and who provided me throughout with a measure of their discipline and dedicated labor, without which no words of mine would have metamorphosed onto paper.

Most of this book was written in *Ir HaKodesh*, Jerusalem, where I had the daily benefit of the deep Torah learning, breadth of vision, and incisive analysis of my beloved brother, Rabbi Aharon Feldman. He took valuable time from his own writing and teaching duties to read much of the manuscript, to make cogent and wise suggestions, and he was a constant source of encouragement and inspiration during the course of the preparation of this work. To him I extend deep appreciation.

During the course of the writing, I benefited from the astute, sensitive, and insightful suggestions of Rabbi Nosson Scherman. His perceptive critiques, coupled with his unfailing patience and good humor, made my writing burdens much lighter.

I am especially thankful to my dear wife, Estelle, whose insights, fine editorial judgment, and keen discernment helped sharpen many areas of this work. Her gift for language and her sense of the magic of the written word were extremely beneficial to me, and for this, as well as for many other things, I am grateful.

There are a number of others who, at various stages of the writing process, were extremely helpful. Over and above all others, the membership of what is surely a most remarkable synagogue, Atlanta's Beth Jacob Congregation, served as a decades-long catalyst by their own intellectual curiosity and drive for Jewish growth.

These acknowledgments in no way implicate the acknowledgees in the errors and shortcomings of this book, for which the author retains full and exclusive rights and responsibilities.

As this volume sees the dawn of day, I express my humble thanks to the One Above who has allowed me the privilege to toil in His vineyards and to taste of His Goodness, in order to ללמוד וללמד לשמר ולעשות, *learn, teach, safeguard, and perform.*

Emanuel Feldman

Jerusalem/Atlanta, Georgia
Chanukah, 5755/November, 1994

on Judaism

teshuvah – the jew returns home

. . . in which is discussed . . . The adventure of returning
to roots / The meaning of
teshuvah / The courage to change / The yearning for higher
things / The nature of sin / Following the crowd / Separation
and union with God / Teshuvah as creation . . .

Rabbi: You told me on the phone that something was troubling you. I hope it's nothing terribly serious.

David: Well, it is serious, but it's not a domestic crisis or anything like that. I am still your typical American Jewish male, thirty years old, with a good wife, a child, and earning a livelihood.

R: So what's the problem?

D: It's something that has been troubling me for some time, but I don't think it's a run-of-the-mill situation.

R: Why don't you tell me about it?

D: I can't quite put my finger on it, but I am feeling a lack of satisfaction or achievement in my life. I have achieved some material things, but somehow that doesn't seem to be enough.

There's a certain nagging sense of discontent lurking in the background. I wouldn't call it unhappiness, at least not on the physical level. I'm a successful attorney, we have a nice home, we can afford more than most, we are healthy. But something inside is troubling me and I'm really not quite sure what it is. It's a certain unease about life in general. I'm not sure why I feel this way, or what's causing it. Day in and day out I get up in the morning, have breakfast, go to work, come home, say hello to my wife and child, eat, watch the news, maybe read a little bit and go to sleep. On Sunday I sleep late, read the paper, watch a lot of TV, and maybe go out with my wife. It's all okay, I suppose, but I keep thinking of that old song, "Is That All There Is?" There's a lot of rhythm in my life, but very little rhyme or reason. Even when I'm on a pleasure trip or on a vacation, I have the feeling that something is missing. It all seems to lack purpose. I keep asking myself, What is it all about? I mean, I should be looking forward to a successful life, and yet I keep feeling that life is passing me by, and that maybe I'm missing something important, but I'm not quite sure what it is.

R: I sympathize, and of course I am always glad to see you. But just where do I fit into this equation?

D: Well, the reason I wanted to see you is that lately I've been thinking that maybe my Jewishness is my problem.

R: Your Jewishness? How is that a problem?

Religion plays no part **D:** Don't misunderstand. I am proud to be a Jew, and I fight anti-Semitism wherever I see it. I love the State of Israel, and I give to the annual fund drives and all that. But the truth is that religion does not play a real part in my life. I keep thinking that maybe there are some answers in Judaism that will help me out of this rut.

R: So you decided to come see me. Well, perhaps the rut served some purpose.

D: I hope so. I've been thinking that maybe it's time for me
to begin learning a little bit about Judaism. Some of my
friends are observant Jews, and when I'm with them I realize
how little I really know about my religion.

R: Did you ever study Judaism on a serious level?

D: As I said, I'm a typical American Jew. I had a Bar Mitzvah,
and my Jewish education stopped there. I went on to high
school, to university, got a graduate degree, am thoroughly
familiar with the culture of the Western world — but as for
Judaism, I barely remember how to recite a blessing over the
Torah. And not only do I not know, I also do not observe many
Jewish practices. We light the Chanukah menorah, and we have
a family Seder and go to synagogue on the High Holidays, but
that's about it. I like Jewish food, but I realize that hardly qual-
ifies me as a good Jew. My tefillin, brand new and untouched,
are still in my drawer. My wife usually lights candles on Friday
night, but, to be honest, our Friday night is just like every other
night, except that we have gefilte fish and chicken.

R: So you're somewhat of a gastronomic Jew.

D: I suppose so. And I guess I'm not too proud of that.

R: Certainly we can try to learn more about God and Torah
and the Jewish people. But I hope you realize that even if
you learned all there was to know about Judaism, there is no
guarantee that what's eating at you will go away. I don't want
to proceed under false pretenses or with glib promises.

D: I am not asking for guarantees. But I would like to find out
more about these things.

R: Of course. My only condition is that I would undertake *To discover*
this study as long as the main goal of our discussions is to *the basics*
discover the basics of Judaism. This would be study and discussion for its own sake, and not just to make you feel better
inside. Chances are you will feel much more satisfied when
we are finished, and that would be a welcome by-product of
our discussions, but not the ultimate goal. Our purpose will be
to find out what we can about the basics of who we are and
where we come from.

Beyond this, I would want two commitments from you. First, that we will meet regularly, and second, that even if you find that your inner gnawing and unease is not abating, we will still continue our discussions.

D: I am ready to make that commitment, though I probably don't know what I'm getting into.

R: The worst that could happen is that you will have invested some time and that you'll emerge from it all with some new insights into your own Jewishness. Right now, the chances are that you know less than many Christians do about Judaism.

D: That's painful to hear, but you're probably right. Even though I am anxious to go ahead, I want you to know that I am a little nervous about where all this might lead.

R: I can appreciate that, but if you stay the course and don't quit on me, I can guarantee you one thing: you will know some basics about your heritage, and you'll be infinitely more comfortable with yourself as a Jew.

D: Where do we begin?

Excitement, challenge, adventure *R:* Before I answer that, let me make one thing clear. If you seriously want to embark on this journey, I am ready to accompany you — as long you realize that it is in fact a journey, with all that that implies: adventure, new ways of looking at things — sometimes unsettling new ways — a bit of danger from time to time, excitement, exhaustion, fear of the unknown, intellectual challenges, some occasional difficulties and discomfort, and some wonderful rewards. But you have to leave much of your luggage behind, by which I mean preconceived notions and clichés. If you understand all this, then I can try to help.

As to where to begin, Judaism is so vast that it's difficult to find a place that says, "Start here." I would suggest that we go about it in a relaxed, informal way, without a fixed curriculum, but that we set out to review some of the fundamentals of Jewish belief and practice, such as what we believe about God, how we view the physical aspects of life, what Torah and mitzvot are, how God and Jews relate to one another, what we mean by sanctity, what prayer is all about, what Shabbat and holidays represent, why the food laws are so significant, inter-personal relationships, how Jews relate to the rest of the world.

D: Sounds like more than fundamentals.

R: Well, everything in Judaism is both basic and profound.
  God is the perfect example: He can be viewed as the Being Whom we address in prayer — which is, of course, true — or He can be viewed in subtler and deeper ways as the Being beyond our comprehension. We will try to be neither too sim-plistic nor too esoteric. I'll let you take the lead and guide me into the areas that need exploration, and we'll feel our way. We'll talk about the main outlines and basic principles that are essential to our journey, but we won't enter every port or visit every fascinating site we encounter, because this will not, I assume, be your only trip. I think you will definitely want to come back to revisit the territory and examine it even more carefully. And, there are many reference works, as well as teachers and rabbis, to whom you can turn for a further and a deeper look.
  We'll have no special agenda for our meetings. We'll just have good conversations, and let the discussions weave and wend their way wherever they take us.

D: Am I going to emerge from all this as an Orthodox Jew?

R: There are worse fates in life, I assure you, but I will not try to convince you or persuade you of anything. I will address your questions as best as I can. What you do with the answers, how you conduct your personal life, is completely up to you. Obviously, I would be pleased to see you moving in the direction of more observance and Jewish awareness — I'm not particularly fond of labels like "Orthodox" or "Reform" — but our discussions will be open, honest, and straightforward, with no verbal legerdemain and no slogans — and you are free to challenge anything I say at any time.

D: How long do you think all this will take?

R: Obviously, we won't be talking forever, but with all due respect, that's like asking a piano teacher at the first lesson *The process of return* how long it will take to become a good pianist. Let's face it: there really is no end to the process of returning to one's roots — which is essentially what we will be doing. It is in fact a lifelong process. Ideally, it never should come to an end, because we're talking not only about learning some facts but also about learning about who we are, and about our relationship to God and to other people. One doesn't pick such things up in six easy lessons — or even in six hard lessons. Jewish learning is an ongoing process that takes place in a variety of ways.

D: You referred earlier to the "dangers" of the journey. What kind of dangers?

To challenge clichés   *R:* Several things. For one thing, I dare say that many of your cherished notions about Judaism are going to be challenged and overturned. You will be intellectually shaken up, which can be both exhilarating and painful.

You'll have to start out with a clean slate, be willing to shed the hackneyed prejudices, shibboleths, clichés, and dogmas of our day, and instead remain open to new ideas, new modes of thinking, new experiences. It is entirely possible that you may tentatively begin to change some old habits and adopt some new ones. Simple example: you may suddenly realize that you don't actually have to go out on the town every Saturday night, or watch television every Sunday. In general, you may find yourself viewing life from an entirely new perspective, because you will be introduced to different patterns of behavior.

The very ordinary act of eating, for example, might become different, with acknowledgments to God before and after food — not to mention that you will learn why certain foods are off limits. Time itself might take on new rhythms. There will be, quite literally, a new calendar for you to look at, with a Shabbat every seven days, and periodic Yom Tov festivals throughout the year. And you will find that the things we take for granted — such as the daily rising and setting of the sun, the monthly reappearance of the moon, the changing of the seasons — are all framed by prayer and an acknowledgment that Someone regulates time.

More importantly, we're going to be dealing with some crucial aspects of life itself. Some of the things we learn are bound to have an impact on your heart and emotions, not just your intellect. You may decide on your own, for example, to try out prayer, or to discover what the Shabbat experience is like.

So we are talking not about learning certain abstractions, but about a potential change in your attitudes and in your life. Transformation is what we are, in effect, talking about, and this is never easy. When a person begins to change and grow, whether it is Jewishly or in any other fundamental way, certain conflicts inevitably arise — with a spouse, with parents, friends, society, or within him or herself. People who begin observing Kashruth or Shabbat, for example, may find that their mental stability is questioned by other Jews, that they are accused of having joined a cult, of having hidden motives, or of trying to please a particular teacher or rabbi. In addition, certain inner doubts and uncertainties begin to surface from time to time. So studying Judaism is not like studying, say, world history, or any field of knowledge that does not relate to the self. All of the above is what I mean by a dangerous journey.

Growth and change

D: I wonder: perhaps I am getting into something that is over my head. Maybe I should just say good day, forget it, it was nice seeing you.

R: I think you'd be foolish not to open up the window on your Jewishness. You can only emerge a more complete person than before. Besides, why should you miss out on the adventure of moving into new realms of ideas? I realize that this can cause some anxiety, but one is not really a full human being unless one is seriously searching. You shouldn't want to go on like most people, doing the same tired old things, living the same hackneyed lives, behaving according to the rigid dogmas and rules of the society around us. It's refreshing to look at new ways of living.

Let me share an important idea with you. A *tzaddik* is not only a righteous man; he is also one who *becomes*, not just one who *is*. That is to say, he is not static, but dynamic; he is constantly developing, growing, reaching for higher things. In that sense, you have all the raw material of a *tzaddik*: you are reaching out for something more spiritual in your life, and this is a wonderful trait. And the truth is, you are not really able at this stage to say goodbye to your interest in your Judaism and drop the whole thing.

D: How can you be sure?

The inner yearning   *R:* Because by your own admission you still have some connection to other Jews, to Judaism as a religion, to the Bible, and to God. Otherwise you would not even bother to show up for Yom Kippur services, or to light the Chanukah menorah, or attend a Seder. And I suspect that your inner discontent probably stems from an inner yearning for higher things — a yearning that is unfulfilled.

This is what is amazing about us as a people: no matter how far we stray, we invariably retain some sort of attachment to Jewish roots — thin and tenuous and vague perhaps, but still an attachment. Even assimilated Jews can testify to that. Even if it's only a momentary resentment against some manifestation of anti-Semitism, or a moment of pride in the achievements of the State of Israel, or a flash of fear when Jews are threatened — that tiny flicker of identity with Judaism and with the Jewish people is never totally extinguished.

D: Yes, but do such Jews ever return to the fold?

R: Well, there's good news and there's bad news. The good news is that fairly significant numbers do return — tens of thousands of young people. For such people, the tenuous attachment was the first step in the climb back towards authentic Judaism. The bad news is that for the majority of Jews, the tenuous attachment is all there is. It is the last, fading connection to Judaism. Our task is somehow to kindle that spark and bring them back.

D: Are you discouraged?

R: Not at all. In fact, I am encouraged by what I see around me: a society profoundly materialistic — and profoundly miserable. I don't like to see the misery, but unfortunately the two go together like twins. We are living in a deeply unhappy society, and people try to escape this sadness and unease in a variety of useless ways, but primarily by overindulging in various instinctual pleasures that give immediate but very temporary gratification: food, drink, sex, drugs. The problem is that the hunger is in the inchoate longings of the soul, but we let our souls starve. Instead, we concentrate on feeding the body, and it just does not work. All that happens is that the senses get dulled and the appetites are never really satisfied. We'll discuss this more thoroughly when we discuss the Jewish concept of holiness.

D: And this encourages you?

R: Paradoxically, yes. I believe that this mad pursuit of pleasure — and Jews are not immune from it — is a barometer of the deep sense of emptiness that pervades the lives of people. It's a clear signal that within each Jew there is a yearning for something great and holy — a desire to be connected with sanctity, with religion, with Torah, and with God. This is a basic instinct, a spiritual thirst no different from the physical thirst for water. As a matter of fact, when the prophet Isaiah in Chapter 55 urges Jews to return to God, he declares, "All who are thirsty, go to the water . . ."

The pursuit of pleasure

Within each of us there is an elemental human need to seek an attachment to something transcendent. We may not articulate it, but each of us knows that we are finite, limited, ignorant, frail, weak. We are helpless in crisis and in the face of disaster. So it is not surprising that we should try to reach out and connect with a power stronger than we are, to an anchor that will root us to something permanent and eternal. We are, after all, more than just a vast assembly of nerve cells and their molecules.

This is not just theory. It has been well documented that the need to reach out to God — what we call religion — is one of the basic components of any human community. When we deny it, we are denying our spiritual components what they desperately crave and must have in order to exist. Most of us manage to repress this instinct for a while — with the resultant distress and inner dissatisfaction that we have been talking about.

I don't want to oversimplify, but this desire to connect with higher things really lies behind the return of so many

Jews today to Judaism. It's still only a trickle in terms of the total Jewish population, but it is nevertheless impressive. And that's why I am optimistic. Perhaps we are witnessing the first flowering of God's promise in *Deuteronomy* 30:2, in which we are told that at some future date "you will return unto the Lord your God . . ."

D: If the inner yearning is so universal, how is it that more Jews don't reach out to return to their faith? Why is it only a trickle?

Honesty vs. apathy **R:** Good point. I think it's because there are some special character traits which distinguish every returnee — traits which are not very common: honesty, fortitude, and courage. After all, you have to be honest and gutsy to say to yourself and to others, My past has not been perfect and I need to make a course correction.

Conversely, the returnees all lack certain other character traits: smugness, complacency, self-satisfaction. These are the great stumbling blocks to genuine return, or, to use the Hebrew term that I'll define in a few moments, *teshuvah.* The Torah often refers to such people as those whose "hearts are uncircumcised," meaning that there is an outer shell insulating their innermost yearnings, that they refuse to open themselves to any kind of sanctity. Smugness and self-centeredness are particularly deadly in the religious life.

D: What about the majority of Jews, the ones whose Jewishness consists of almost nothing? Are they going to disappear?

R: That's a very serious and painful problem. To the vast majority of Jews, their personal Jewishness is totally irrelevant. They scarcely give it a thought except in times of crisis. They are caught up in the noise and cacophony and speed and rush of our day. Some of them seem to be going through life in a stupor, like robots, thinking only in sound-bites — and that is not thinking.

Their only connection with their own heritage is that thin, tenuous thread of ethnicity I mentioned before — pride in the State of Israel, the fear of anti-Semitism, attending synagogue from time to time. That becomes the end-all and be-all of their

Judaism. This magnificent, majestic faith of ours gets diluted to nothing more than a Boy Scout code of behavior: support Israel and help old ladies cross the street. I am not against helping anyone cross the street, but there is more to this four-thousand-year-old religion of ours than nostalgia, gefilte fish, and being a pleasant person. I mean, you can be a pleasant atheist, too! Most Jews were never taught that there are certain demands made of us as Jews, that we have certain obligations.

A bright but uninformed Jewish college student once told me that what she most appreciates about Judaism is that it makes no demands on you, that it lets you live your life as you want to. This is pathetic nonsense, but so she was taught in her Sunday school.

There is a goal and a destiny to Jewish life. There is God, and prayer, and opportunities to connect with God; there is a sense of holiness to life, there is a guidebook called Torah, there are relationships to God and to other people. Judaism is not always comfortable. There is sacrifice, and there are things and issues for which you have to be prepared to give up your life. There is discipline and rigor. There is a way to behave and a way not to behave. There are boundary lines and limits. There are challenges every step of the way.

What I'm saying is that being Jewish is serious business. If all we have to sustain us are pap, platitudes, clichés, and sweet, humanistic sentiments, we will self-destruct as a people — or at best be left with a tiny number of committed Jews — while the rest of our people fall over the edge into the black hole of ignorance, Jewish illiteracy, intermarriage, assimilation, self-indulgence, and Jewish nothingness. Which is exactly what is happening to most of us. History is a graveyard of major cultures and civilizations that crashed into oblivion because their way of life lacked one essential ingredient: self-discipline. They knowingly allowed themselves to slide down the slippery slope of self-indulgence, physicality, and licentiousness. In many ways, this is what is happening to many of us today: our appetites and our pleasures dominate our thinking. Rigor, self-sacrifice, discipline — these are dirty words. I-want and I-desire and I-need are preferred to thou-shalt-not and thou-shalt.

Dangers of pap and platitudes

D: Are you suggesting that selfishness is a new invention?

R: Certainly not! The distaste for self-discipline is not a modern invention. It's as old as mankind. It began in the Garden of Eden, when Eve and Adam bit into the forbidden fruit, and it continues in the incident of the Golden Calf in *Exodus* 32. It underlies many of the historical deviations from classical Judaism. In fact, the major defections from Judaism in recent centuries, even on the part of the Jews who had fairly good grounding in Judaism, were also due in great measure to a refusal to give up the tasty fruit. The pity is that it is precisely the demands and the discipline that create the joy and warmth and delight of Judaism, but one has to be patient and stick around in order to experience it.

Is there future for Jews?

D: If so many of us are going overboard, what will our future be like? Is there hope for us as a people?

R: There is hope, yes. God will never utterly abandon us. This is the Biblical promise. There will be a Jewish people until the end of time. But what kind of a people, what kind of numbers and quality we will have — this depends on us, on you and your friends, and on me.

D: So what should we Jews do?

R: First, we need to understand that what is happening to us today is not because we Jews have made a deliberate decision to jump the ship of Judaism. It's not that we have tried the Torah and found it wanting; it's that most Jews have never tried the Torah. Jews today do not abandon Judaism with forethought. They simply follow the mob, take the line of least resistance, and because they don't recognize the cause of the gnawing within them, they drop out of Judaism. They leave after the entree, they don't stay for the full meal, and they never experience the satisfaction of being a Jew.

Let me say it again: the core reason for today's drop-out from Jewish life is Jewish ignorance, a lack of any Jewish knowledge beyond the most elementary level. And the only way to combat this hemorrhaging from our ranks is to take Jewish learning seriously. Most Jews feel that studying the Bible, or Hebrew, or learning Jewish practices, is for children

— as if it were some bitter medicine that only children have to take in order to become Bar or Bas Mitzvah. The fact is that we are the bearers of the most brilliant and profound religious and intellectual tradition the world has ever known, and yet we treat it as if it were some convenient fast food. That is the core reason behind our problems today.

The only solution is to address this basic issue by reading and learning and discussing and thinking about Jewishness — and by Jewishness I don't mean Jewish food, dance, or drama. It's time we Jews grew up and matured about our religion, and started concentrating on basics instead of on meaningless peripherals. Along the way, we might even find some things that quench our spiritual thirst.

D: You keep suggesting that people are dissatisfied with their lives, but most people I know seem fairly content.

R: I don't like to make broad generalities, but from where I sit
I see a significant number of people in relentless pursuit of fun and pleasure. Now, within innocent limits, this is not abnormal. But when it becomes frenetic and obsessive, it is a manifestation of an inner discontent. After all, if people remain hungry right after they gorge themselves on food, they are either not well or they are attempting to assuage their hunger with the wrong kind of food. Thinking people crave permanent and lasting spiritual sustenance, and they cannot be satisfied by temporary and evanescent fun and games — not all of it so innocent. The soul requires an attachment to something transcendent, something higher; it cries out for a change of direction, for a change in focus. How did Thoreau describe it? Most people "live lives of quiet desperation."

That's why I admire you for coming in today. It required a frank look into your own self, and a certain amount of courage. Unfortunately, most people just continue in the same *Fun and games* old way, convinced that more shopping, more clothes, a new car, a new house, a different vacation, a different spouse, new thrills, new sensations, new ways to feed the appetites will satiate the hunger. It is sad to behold, because these things give only momentary pleasure, and they quickly dissipate — everything new quickly turns old — and the people are as hungry and as thirsty and as troubled as they were before.

D: You did mention that large numbers are, in fact, returning to Judaism. I am curious: are they doing this successfully?

Course adjust-ments: teshuvah *R:* They are making an honest effort, and that's what matters. Success or failure is hard to gauge in such things. The important fact is that these people are not static but dynamic; they are making a move. We need to realize that the key to successful return is this very exciting truth: human beings can change no matter what kind of background they come from; no matter what their past history might be, they can turn their lives around. If they have a sincere and honest desire to connect with something transcendent, they can do it. Even though it's not an easy undertaking, and even though habits are difficult to dislodge, Judaism teaches us that a person has the power to make a course adjustment in his life.

I think this needs to be stressed: *teshuvah* is a function of free will. We reign over ourselves. We, not others, make the choices in our lives. When a person engages in *teshuvah*, that person is in effect saying, "I am free to choose my way of life."

To this it must be added — and this is most important — that God encourages and welcomes a return to Him, no matter what the person's behavior might have been. The door is always open, and behind the door, God waits patiently. But He alone doesn't open the door for us. In the final analysis, we have to push at the door again and again, and then somehow He helps us swing it open.

D: Rabbi, I don't want to mislead you, but I'm really not sure I'm ready to change my life. I'm simply curious about Judaism, and that's why I came in.

R: Let me repeat: no one is out to change your life. I am only describing what occasionally happens to Jews who begin to move back. The extent of your moving or not moving in any direction is up to you.

D: I find it interesting that in this whole discussion about returning, assimilation, ignorance, and human potential, you seem to be reluctant to discuss one word.

R: What word?

D: Sin. When you talk about people abandoning Judaism, not learning, not practicing, not behaving like Jews, pursuing *Sinning*
immediate gratification, overindulging their physical ap-
petites, aren't you really talking about sinning?

R: I haven't mentioned sin because I don't think it's the right
word for what has been taking place in our generation.
Genuine, classic, old-fashioned, hard-core sin really involves
rebellion against God, a deliberate throwing off of His yoke, a
conscious flight from His dominion and authority. We don't
experience that kind of sinning today. As I said before, today
we are experiencing a rejection based on lack of knowledge;
what plagues us is not sin but sheer ignorance, laziness, and
self-indulgence. Today's Jews are not sufficiently aware of God
to be able to sin against Him. Jewish tradition has a generic
name for such people: *tinokot shenishbu bein ha-akum* —
"children who have been captives among the idolaters" — and
who therefore are not responsible for their deeds or misdeeds,
because they never learned. The great classic sinners of old
who truly intended to rebel against God — these no longer
exist today.

D: You sound like you miss them.

R: The truth is that when there are great sinners, there are
great saints as well. And when the sinning is mediocre, the
righteousness is also mediocre. We live in mediocre times all
around. Sometimes I think it might be worthwhile to restore
the sinners of old if that would mean that we could also have
the saints of old.

D: This business of *teshuvah* — is that something that has *Teshuvah*
just come into vogue in contemporary times? Surely in *then*
classical Jewish times they didn't need *teshuvah,* because *and now*
everyone was observant.

R: Not so. We have both been using the term *teshuvah* — and
it is a fundamental and central idea in Judaism — so let's
define it. Literally, the word means "return," but it is more
than just a return to God, more than just repentance. It is a
deep, spiritual reawakening. It is the process that occurs when
a soul is stirred and wants to reconnect itself to sanctity. When

TESHUVAH: The Jew Returns Home □ 25

you think of *teshuvah* this way, you realize that it is not limited to those who have strayed from Judaism. Even those who have been observant and learned all their lives can do *teshuvah* in the sense that they can elevate themselves to higher levels of performance and spirituality. This can — in fact, should — occur even in an individual who is observant, prays regularly, and keeps the mitzvot. The halls of *teshuvah* are open to anyone, observant or not, who wishes to enter. Besides which, King Solomon says in *Ecclesiastes* 7:20, "There is no person on earth so righteous that he always does good and never sins."

This idea of *teshuvah* is really quite remarkable. When you get right down to it, when a person repents and says, "I made a mistake," God could respond, "Sorry, you abandoned Me, there is no coming back." After all, a convicted criminal can show remorse and throw himself on the mercy of the court, but he cannot make the crime disappear. Or God could say, "If you do come back, you come back stained; you are like an ex-convict with a record."

But instead, God wipes the slate clean: you have no record. On the contrary, in *Yoma* 86b, the Sages say that when real *teshuvah* takes place, not only does God wipe away the past, but past sins are transformed into merits. And in effect they also say, in *Berachot* 34b, that in God's eyes a true *baal teshuvah*/returnee is more precious that a perfectly righteous person.

D: Those are both very comforting ideas, but I confess that they are astounding. I don't comprehend them at all.

Separation and connection **R:** Well, they're not easy to grasp. Let's look at it from this perspective: what actually occurs when a person does not follow God's ways? In effect, he creates a disconnectedness between himself and God, a severing of the relationship, a clogging of the pipeline between them. The more he ignores God, the greater is the distance and the spiritual abyss that grows between them. It is similar to the estrangement that takes place when someone cavalierly and insensitively ignores the needs and wishes of a spouse or friend.

One day, this person — now far removed from God — wakes up and decides to move back, to come closer. He has a vast and difficult expanse to traverse. When you think about it, however, the greater the distance he must travel back, the more obstacles he has to overcome, the more arduous the journey — the greater is the honor and homage he proffers to God by humbling himself to return to Him.

What this means is that the very distance that once separated him from God now becomes the vehicle for honoring God. It's as if a person were to travel one thousand miles to catch a glimpse of the king's procession, just to be close to the king for an instant. This is a much more substantial gesture of loyalty than that of someone who had only to walk down the block to witness the same procession.

In other words, the farther a person has been from God, *The* the more honor he displays when he returns to Him. That's *journey* why God so cherishes the one who returns to Him after hav- *of return* ing strayed so long and so far — because the journey of return which he or she undertook was much more difficult than that of the righteous person. And that's why one's past transgressions — which created the distance in the first place and made the return trip so excruciatingly difficult — are now transmogrified into merits, because every inch traversed on that road back is a declaration of fealty and honor to God.

D: You're tempting me to go out and do some major sinning and create a huge distance between myself and God. That way I will be more cherished by Him when I decide to return.

R: Obviously, it doesn't work that way. In fact, a person who deliberately abandons God with the rationalization that he can always do *teshuvah* is actually denied the opportunity and the benefits of *teshuvah*, because his attitude proves that his repentance lacks sincerity.

What I'm doing here is simply clarifying three issues. First, how it is that no matter how far removed a person is, he can always begin moving back; second, why it is that God finds a *baal teshuvah* so precious; and third, how it is that the transgressions, by which I mean the distance, can be transformed into merits — that is, closeness to God.

D: Somehow I always took it as a matter of course — this idea of returning to God and Torah. But from this new perspective it really turns out to be an amazing idea, a real gift from God.

R: It is amazing — even more amazing than you would think.

The Talmud in *Pesachim* 54a and *Nedarim* 39b states that *teshuvah* is one of the seven special items God created before He created the world. The others were Torah, the Garden of Eden, Gehinnom, God's Holy Throne of Glory, the Holy Temple, and the name of the Messiah.

D: That is very suggestive and poetic, but what is it supposed to mean?

Teshuvah *R:* I think it clearly indicates that there is a basic connection
as creation between creation and *teshuvah*. Firstly, it shows that moving back towards God involves a personal form of re-creation of the self — because the returnee actually has to start afresh and throw off the past that has been pulling him away from God.

There's a deeper sense of creation, too. When you really get down to it, when a person, consciously or not, moves out of God's orbit and terminates his relationship with Him, the obvious corollary should be that God, on His side, should also terminate His relationship with that person. But God does not do that. On the contrary, He leaves open the possibility of *teshuvah* and return to Him. Instead of locking the door, He leaves it ajar. In effect, this is a re-creation of the man-God relationship, even if, for all intents and purposes, man's rebellion should have brought it to a permanent end.

Finally, the fact that *teshuvah* preceded Creation implies that without the possibility of repentance, humankind could not survive and Creation would have been doomed. In other words, the idea that *teshuvah* was put into place before the world was created really means this: in the very act of His creation, God inserted into the mechanism of the universe the possibility of a new creation in case the original creation covenant should ever be broken. This is a manifestation of the goodness of God: He wants to be close to His creatures and provide them with the potential to reciprocate that closeness, for only in this way will His creatures find true joy on this earth.

D: *Teshuvah* must be a pretty difficult process if it requires all this Divine intervention.

R: Let's face it: *teshuvah* requires a person to regret his past actions and behavior, to declare genuinely that he feels remorse, to accept the obligation to live a different kind of life. To humble himself like that is one of the most difficult things for a person to do. It needs some help from above, believe me.

D: You said before that *teshuvah* applies to righteous people as well as sinners. But surely the *teshuvah* of a pious, God-fearing person is much different from that of a person who has never known anything about Judaism or God or Torah, and has never in his life practiced anything of his ancestral religion. These two types of *teshuvah* must differ quite radically.

R: Quite true. An individual who is basically religious, observant and knowledgeable may feel that he is not praying with the proper intensity or devotion, or that he is not as fully conscious of God's presence throughout the day as he should be, or that he has grown casual in his observance of the mitzvot — and he resolves to make a more serious commitment to God. That was always the classic sense of *teshuvah*. Nowadays, however, the term by and large refers to those who have wandered far off the path of Torah and who now want to put their lives into reverse: they want to turn around and go in the opposite direction.

One of the key elements in classical *teshuvah* — the kind every Jew is required always to do, and particularly prior to Yom Kippur — is to renounce certain misdeeds of the past and to resolve not to repeat them. But today's returnee is not just renouncing a few misdeeds; he is renouncing his entire life until now. He is stating in effect that he wants to be a different person — which involves breaking habits and instincts, and changing his whole approach to life. It's like moving from one planet to another.

That's why I feel that today's returnee is truly heroic, *Heroic* because an entire new way of life has to be absorbed, a *returnees* great deal of new learning has to take place, a new way of looking at the world and at people and at one's own self. There is much to discover, it takes time, and the path is often convoluted and complex. Suddenly, relating to one's fellow human being takes on a new dimension. Suddenly, God is a new presence in one's life. Suddenly, the Torah's viewpoint has to be taken into account. And all the time, one has to battle instinct, inertia, habit, and the natural human urge not to change and not to move in new directions — plus the raised eyebrows and often outright opposition and antagonism of family and friends. This requires a huge amount of inner strength and conviction.

When you really get down to it, *teshuvah* today is a kind of death and rebirth: a demise of the past and a birth of a new life and a new creature. There is a severing with the previous "me" and the creation of a new "me" who has a new awareness, a new sensitivity, new ambitions and dreams and longings. Somehow, the connections to the new life become very powerful, and at the end of the trail, the rewards are enormous: a sense of having returned home and of being part of our majestic tradition, a sense of the grandeur and beauty and warmth of it all, the awareness of God's presence in one's daily life, the feeling of meaning and purpose that permeates one's self. Life becomes coherent and whole again. You begin to realize that there is more to living and more to the world than what we have been led to believe. There is the daily excitement and stimulation of listening and learning, of growth and discovery.

In a very real sense, Judaism answers the yearning of the thirsty Jew, and the emptiness is replaced by a sense of fulfillment and purpose. After all, the word *teshuvah* in Hebrew means not only "return." It also means "answer" or "response." You begin to respond to your inner yearnings, and then God responds to you. As I said before, I do feel that without Divine assistance, the whole complex process of return could not begin to take place.

D: So why doesn't God help all the Jews to return, and thus solve all our problems?

R: Because the first move must be ours. God, remember, has given us free will, the right to make our own choices in life — even the right not to choose Him, so if He forces us to return to Him, the decision is not ours and it lacks true worth.

But if we take the initiative and move a step towards Him, then He stretches out His hand and helps us along the way. The Talmud in *Shabbat* 104a tells us that "he who comes to be purified is given help."

D: Well, I've taken the initiative of coming to you. May I now expect His Divine assistance along the way?

R: Have no fear. I am confident that He can be trusted to do His part. He always has.

GOD – the jew wonders about god

David: I am confused about my Judaism. Ignorant is probably the more accurate word. And I don't even know where to begin.

Rabbi: You already have made a good beginning. You realize that you don't know, which is not only a beginning, but also the end purpose of all learning: to know that we do not know.

The truth is that you only become fully aware of how much you do not know after you have amassed a great deal of knowledge; that is, when we realize that knowledge is infinite, while we humans are not. So let's begin at the beginning.

D: But what is the beginning?

R: "*Bereshit bara Elohim*, In the beginning God created . . ."
Without that knowledge, nothing can begin — that first of
all there is a God, and that this God creates. As a matter of
fact, He is the only One Who can create. So before we get to
anything else, let us talk about God. That, of course, is not
easy to do, because we have to compress into words that
which is beyond words; we have to express in finite terms that
which is Infinite. But we must try, because God is literally the
beginning from which all else flows.

D: That's all well and good, but I'll tell you the truth, I have
never thought much about God. I have always sort of
accepted the general idea that there has to be Someone Who
made everything, but beyond that I have never worried about
it. But as to whether I actually believe in God, to the extent of
really knowing positively that He is out there and that He is
concerned with me and with how I live and with what I do, or
whether I believe enough in God in order to be able to pray to
Him, or change the way I live because of what someone tells
me is God's will — these are things I have never thought
about seriously. And it is a bit frightening. I am entering
unknown territory, uncharted waters.

R: In that respect, you are very much like most people. But
let's not be like most people; let's give it some thought.
Let's make a beginning.

D: Fine. What does Judaism tell us about God? What have *God alone*
Jews always believed about Him?

R: First and foremost, that God is first and foremost; that, He
is *echad*, which means that He is One, but not just in the
numerical sense. He is alone, unique, singular in every way.
We are commanded to reassert this fact every morning and
evening of our lives — in the *Shema Yisrael*, the central statement of Jewish faith — so that it becomes an integral part of
our very beings. There are no dual gods of light and gods of
darkness, or gods of good and gods of evil, as the ancients
believed. We do not believe in a trinity, even when this is
interpreted as three faces of one god. And God has no physical

form, cannot be personified, has no arms, no face, no mouth — and when the Torah does speak in such anthropomorphic terms, such as God's "outstretched arm" — it is simply using words that are familiar to the human experience, because they are the best available means of making certain concepts understood.

D: Or misunderstood.

R: True enough. The Torah speaks in the language of people, but finite language is inadequate to articulate infinite concepts, like the might or awe or love or providence or wrath or compassion of God. So the Torah utilizes terms like "God's right hand" or "eyes of God" — even though such expressions might mislead the ignorant.

The active God   But let us not digress. God is One, separate and apart from the world He created. And yet He is also part of His world, concerned with it and its inhabitants. He is unique and distinct from everything else, but He is also within the world He created. He did not set the clock of the universe in motion and then retire. He remains active, though hidden, and He listens and guides. He taps us on the spiritual shoulder from time to time to let us know that He is there. In the language of philosophy, this intimate aspect of God is called "immanence," while the distant aspect is called "transcendence." In the words of the daily *Amidah*, He is the *El hagadol hagibor vehanora*, "the great, mighty, awesome Supreme Being . . . Who performs lovingkindness . . . remembers the kindnesses of the Patriarchs and brings a redeemer to their children's children for His Name's sake, in love." That is to say, He is above us and is all-powerful, but at the same time He listens to us and He cares.

That word *echad*, "one," has far-reaching resonance beyond its literal meaning. For example, it means that there is unity in the entire universe, that all of creation is a demonstration of God's constant presence. It means that we ourselves are not separate from God, but that we too are — or at least can potentially be — at one with God, and not separate from Him.

D: What does that mean — that we can be "at one with God"? How does a mortal get to be at one with the Immortal?

R: It means that our goal should be to grow close to Him by conducting our lives as if He were literally standing by our side at every moment of the day or night, in whatever we do — which happens to be a religous truth, not just an "as if." There is a natural human tendency to think that we ourselves are gods, in the sense that we are not connected with the Creator, that we are a completely autonomous entity. *Deuteronomy* 8:11-18 puts it very vividly: success and prosperity can mislead people into forgetting that God is the Author of their good fortune, until they are tempted to proclaim, "My strength and the power of my hand made me all this wealth," and that all things were created not by God, but by their own might. One of the implications of *echad* is that this is not true; we are not independent creatures. *Echad* means that in ultimate terms, everything in the world is part of the great Unity which is God.

D: That's all very pretty. But what do you do with someone who has no appreciation for these things, who is not even sure whether or not he believes in God in the first place?

R: For a contemporary Jew seeking a way back to God, I think that the best antidote is to begin to perform some of the mitzvot. Belief in God is not necessarily the beginning — it can also be the end result. In your situation, perhaps you should "*behave* in God," and then belief in God will inevitably follow. By behaving in God, I mean to try to live in a certain Jewish way, to act in a certain Jewish way, which is the way of the mitzvah. *Doing as prelude*

The Sages relate a remarkable oral tradition about God's reaction to the sin of the Golden Calf. When God sees that His people are engaged in idolatry, He cries out, "Although they have abandoned Me, let them at least observe the mitzvot of My Torah" (*Yerushalmi Chagigah* 1:7)).

D: That is an amazing concept — because on the face of it, what good is it to observe the mitzvot if you don't believe in God? But I think I am getting your point.

R: Which is?

D: Which is that practicing the mitzvot can be a kind of prelude to a belief in God.

R: Right. What I am saying is this: God is the Author of the mitzvot, and we perform the mitzvot because they are His will. This is the source of the whole Torah. But at the same time, a deep belief in God can come about as a result of performing the commandments, studying about them, and living the Torah life. In the Jewish scheme of things, doing often leads to believing.

You have seen those signs on American highways, sometimes emblazoned on the sides of mountains: "Believe in the Lord and ye shall be saved." You will never see such signs in a Jewish land. For one thing, the concept of being saved is not a Jewish one — since only those who are otherwise damned need saving. We do not consider ourselves damned, and therefore our goal in life is not to achieve salvation, but to serve God in the fullest way possible, and to help bring God's ways to mankind. Belief is an element in this, and certainly a key and indispensable element, because in the final analysis our service to God is meaningless unless we believe in Him. But for those returning to the fold, it is possible to do mitzvot even if one is not yet certain about Who or What God is — or if one has never given much thought to the subject of God.

The belief pulse The idea is that one should not take his "belief pulse" too frequently. That's like constantly asking yourself if you are healthy, or if you love your spouse. Belief is a very subtle, slowly growing thing. It doesn't happen overnight, and sometimes a person has strong beliefs without realizing it. It is like a seed which grows imperceptibly, and before you know it, it is in full flower.

Becoming a believer is not just a matter of pressing the right buttons or doing the right exercises. It takes a lifetime, and the level of belief varies at different stages of a person's religious growth. A simple belief that there is a God is merely step one, but the totality of a Jew is much more complex than that. That's why you don't become a believer overnight. Things have a way of falling into place later in one's spiritual journey — and they do fall into place.

D: Just like that, effortlessly?

R: Nothing important happens effortlessly, but when you live a religious life, positive things begin to develop inside you without your being aware of it. That's because there is an inner logic to belief in God. Objectively speaking, it's not just a matter of blind faith, and that's why it can begin to develop within you when you at least open yourself to the concept. Because when you look at it objectively, belief in God is not at all illogical. To insist that the world and all its magnificent and complex parts are simply a result of chance creates more intellectual and logical problems, it seems to me, than does belief in God. The entire natural universe testifies that there is a God, as King David expresses it in Psalm 19: *Hashamayim mesaprim kevod El*, "the heavens declare the glory of God . . ."

D: Let's say I believe there is a God. Then what?

R: It may be relatively easy to believe that there *is* a God — that such a Being exists — but the next step is more complex: to have faith, trust, and reliance in that God. That is a bit different from simply believing that He exists.

When you have true faith in God, you are saying, for one thing, that the world has purpose and plan and design. We can see this plan and design in the physical universe: the perfect clockwork with which the seasons come and go, the sun rising and setting, the tides coming in and going out. There is an awesome complexity and beauty in the world; there is wonder and enchantment and power.

Take a fresh look at the vastness of the universe and all that it contains, its regularity and its creativity and its reproductive capacities; the panoply of living creatures, from man down to the tiniest flea; the exquisite beauty and dazzling singularity of a snow flake; the life-giving rains; the whiteness of clouds on a summer day, and the blackness of clouds before a storm; our human intelligence, our ability to create and imagine and think and build; the complexity of the human anatomy; the miracle of the human brain and the human eye; a universe teeming with life; the vastness of the solar system, which we are only now beginning to appreciate. Looking at all this, it's very difficult not to be convinced that behind it there is a Supreme Being. To assume that this intricately organized and delicately balanced universe happened at random, on its own — that it emerged from nothing — or even that there was once a creator who put it all into motion and then abandoned it and went into hiding for eternity — strains credulity.

I contend that not to have faith in the continued, ongoing Presence of God in spite of so much evidence is really to believe in the unbelievable. There is a Power that moves the universe. We see it all around us, but because we are accustomed to it, we become desensitized to it. Grass grows, leaves form, we grow, babies become adults — there is inexorable growth and change taking place constantly before our very eyes. And within us, as well. God is at work not only in the physical world but in other dimensions as well: the intellectual, emotional, and spiritual realms.

D: With all that evidence around, how is it that there are so many unbelievers in the world?

God not an abstraction **R:** I don't believe that there are so many unbelievers. What we do have are many people who simply don't think things through.

D: Or maybe they're afraid to think things through. Maybe they're afraid of the implications.

R: Quite true, because the implications — that there is a God, and that this God tells me how to live and what I may and may not do — this can seriously cramp a person's style.

But let's get back to the idea of one Creator. The corollary to all this is very crucial: that there is plan and design and purpose in the universe — and, because I am part of the universe, that there is plan and purpose and design in my life as well — although it is sometimes obscure and not readily apparent.

So while it is important to realize that there is a Creator, it is even more important to realize that God is still around and is still in charge. That's one of the differences between believing that there *is* a God as an abstraction, and believing in God as a constant reality.

D: I gather, then, that you believe in God rather strongly.

R: Wrong. As a great Jewish thinker once said: I don't believe in God; I know there is a God, just as I don't merely have faith in the laws of gravity. They are physical facts of life. But if we want to buttress our faith rationally, we can find support not only in the physical universe, but in the moral universe as well.

D: What is the moral universe?

R: I refer to a commonality of certain values by which the world is governed. For example, there is a universal repugnance in all societies and cultures about things like murder, theft, adultery, incest, lying, cheating. This is strange: in a world which invariably disagrees about everything, there is virtual unanimity about these things. Something deep within all of mankind is intuitively repelled by certain types of behavior. Even private cheating or personal immorality — behavior which does not affect others in any way — is instinctively condemned. This is very odd — unless it is a reflection of some Divine spark within all of mankind.

D: Well, it's not a proof, but it is a fascinating point.

R: And there are more such fascinating points, if not actual proofs, of God's existence. For example, the fact that you and I are sitting here as Jews discussing Jewish ideas is an indication of God's existence.

D: I didn't think our conversations had such cosmic significance. Perhaps we should be standing in honor of the occasion rather than just sitting comfortably.

R: Perhaps so. After all, every aspect of Torah study and Torah discussion has cosmic significance. What I mean is this: you and I have no rational reason for being alive as Jews after what our people has been through in the years since Sinai. And yet here we are. The very fact that the Jewish people continues to exist, despite everything, says something about the mysterious relationship between this people and a transcendent force which somehow wishes us to remain alive, and which maintains our existence.

By "transcendent force," of course, I mean God. Those familiar Biblical promises about the Jews being an eternal people, about our suffering and tragedies, but also about God never abandoning us — these take on tremendous meaning and power almost four thousand years after they were first

God and the Jews

uttered to Abraham. And with every passing generation they take on added power.

Remember, it was only a promise given to Abraham, yet Abraham and his children and children's children staked their very lives on that promise. Two thousand years after Abraham, as the Jews went into exile from their promised land, it may have seemed absurd. Imagine yourself as a Jew seeing Jerusalem destroyed by the Babylonians. You would surely say, "Yes, we have been kept alive since the times of Abraham; yes, we had kings like David and Solomon, and prophets like Moses and Isaiah and Jeremiah — but all that is over now. Our land is destroyed, our holy places pillaged, our people massacred, and here we are marching into slavery in chains. It is all over. We are history. The end."

The Biblical promise
And yet here we are today, two thousand years after the slave marches, thirty-seven centuries after Abraham, and only fifty years after a third of our people were slaughtered in this twentieth century, and we are alive, vital, dynamic and flourishing. There is something very strange and mysterious about the Jewish people.

Now, all this may not necessarily prove that a God exists — it may all be a fluke of history, it may all have happened by chance, it could all be attributed to random occurrences — but isn't it curious that no other people has benefited from such randomness and that no other people has lived through such a history?

Look, for example, at *Leviticus* 26:44. After the long list of terrible prophecies which will befall Israel if they abandon God, the Torah states unequivocally that God will never destroy us and that He will always maintain His covenant with us. The fact is that the Biblical promise is still very much alive today — and if the Bible is still alive, then is it not logical that the Author of that Bible is still alive as well?

D: Granted, these are very solid ideas, and rather persuasive. But they are still only indicators, not proofs.

R: True. But we need to keep these indicators in mind, because they are signposts pointing in a certain direction. At the very least, the indicators prevent us from permanently closing up the mind.

D: Fine. Let's take that as a given, and let's assume, as you say, that real, solid belief will come as I grow Jewishly. But once I achieve belief, then what?

R: Important point. Belief is not just another nice thing to keep in our briefcases. It entails obligations. Knowing that there is a God means that we cannot live our lives as we did before. If someone tells you that he or she believes in God, your first question should be, what are you doing about it? Because there are corollaries that go along with belief in God.

Corollaries of belief

D: Such as?

R: Such as trust in God.

D: But aren't belief and trust synonymous?

R: No. Belief in Hebrew is *emunah* — which is basically the same word as *amen*, an affirmation — in this case an affirmation of God's existence. Trust is *bitachon*, which goes further than belief. It means a trust in God, a sense that no matter what happens, there is a Divine plan at work in your life. You can believe in God's existence — have *emunah* — and still not trust that His hand is at work in every aspect of your life. But the reverse does not hold true: you cannot have *bitachon* without believing that God exists. *Emunah* is like the trunk of a tree, and *bitachon* is the fruit of the tree. There can be a trunk without fruit, but there can be no fruit without the trunk.

D: Why isn't it enough just to believe that God exists?

R: Unlike most commandments, the commandment to believe in God has a huge framework, almost a kind of continuum — ranging from minimal belief to maximal belief. In other words, there are degrees of belief. Some believe so powerfully that they accept whatever befalls them as a reflection of God's will. Others barely believe that God exists, and their entire Jewishness is expressed in a brief visit to a synagogue on Yom Kippur, or perhaps a *Brit Milah* for their son. In fact, sometimes people observe many, many commandments out of habit, without giving any thought to the belief that Someone commanded them. The spectrum of belief is very broad.

D: I am confused. Where does belief stop and trust begin?

Belief   *R:* One leads to the other. Belief must come first, because
and   obviously you cannot trust in something you do not
trust   believe exists. But it is possible to believe in the theoretical
existence of God and still rage at adversity and behave as if
your fate depended on your own efforts, or on chance, or on
the good or bad will of associates and competitors.

Trust, on the other hand, is very personal. When you trust
in God, you have the confidence and serenity to accept whatever befalls you as God's will. So you see, belief in God's
existence is the first step, but trust is the next step — and it is
not an easy one.

D: Is life easier when one develops trust?

R: Without doubt. Obviously, trust in God in itself doesn't
make everything turn out well; not everything in life turns
out to our liking, even if we do have trust. There are disap-
pointments, people get sick, hopes are dashed, tragedies
occur. What trust means is that we accept everything that happens — even things which make us unhappy — as being the
will of God. We accept the verdict as having come from a loving Father. We bear the burden, we know that God lives and
that He loves us, we know that we do not always understand
— and we go on from there. It is infinitely easier to accept
adversity if we are confident there is a good reason and purpose behind it.

D: That sounds like blind faith. Am I supposed to believe and
trust even in the face of things that are not just or fair? I
thought Judaism was a rational religion. This is totally irrational.

R: It is no more irrational than trusting another person to tell
the truth, or accepting someone's check. Are you not trusting that he has enough money in the bank to cover his check?
All of society is based on interpersonal trust.

D: Yes, but in the case of God, you want me to trust in Him
even after He has hurt me or caused me to suffer. I
would not take anyone's check after his earlier checks
had bounced.

R: Quite true. But Jewish history demonstrates that although on the surface it may appear that God's checks occasionally bounce, the long-term story is that, if I may say so, He has excellent credit and that nothing of His really bounces. And obviously, when it comes to God, we are talking about trusting not just another human being with human frailties, but about trusting the One Who created the world; Who, we believe, listens to us; to Whom we pray; Who is the Author of all history; Who made the mountains and the oceans and the deserts and the stormwinds. This is trust on a different level, on a higher plateau.

This new kind of trust means that even though we are hurting, we continue to believe in Him and to trust in Him — because we know that He is the Author of all mankind, and furthermore, that He is concerned with us as individuals. It means that life is not a series of random occurrences, but is like the pieces of a mammoth jigsaw puzzle which a Supreme Intelligence is putting together. So what happens to us — good or bad — is part of a vast plan. We count for something. We matter. Our life experiences make a difference, and perhaps some day we will be able to understand their significance. Granted, this degree of trust and total acceptance is the highest end of the spectrum, and not everyone attains it. But when we reach it, we have achieved serenity.

Acceptance and serenity

D: Serenity is a goal devoutly to be wished for, but it seems very much out of reach. I hope it is not a substitute for blind acceptance.

R: Don't denigrate blind acceptance. It, too, results from great faith and trust, and it doesn't happen on its own. You can't simply wake up one bright morning and say, "From now on, I will enter the mode of blind acceptance." I realize that "blind acceptance" is not something that today's society is comfortable with, but we must understand that it is part of the package of serenity — which really means the ability to say the following to yourself: "It's all right not to know the answers to everything. It's fine that there are certain things that I will never comprehend, and although I will continue probing and inquiring, I recognize that there are certain mysteries in this world that are beyond me." The culminating step in the climb towards inner trust is to recognize that the universe is filled with mystery, both on the cosmic and on the personal level. It means knowing that God is present always and in all situations. That He Listens. That He is concerned. That He takes care of us daily, that He in fact yearns for us to turn to Him. That He is the only true reality in the world and that, compared to Him, all else is just mirage and shadow and make-believe. When we realize that the Creator of this immense universe, Who made the planets and the galaxies and the mountain ranges and the oceans, Who makes the grass grow — that this Creator is also concerned with us, and listens to us, and encourages us to speak with Him — this is a tremendous source of wonder and inner peace.

Surrender and serenity

This is the kind of surrender that we call serenity. And it is a surrender that can only come after much struggle, intellectual and emotional exertion, thinking, study, rigorous intellectual discipline — and prayer. And after all that, we become like a child, trusting in our Father Who is God. And all of this is a result of *emunah* and *bitachon*, belief and trust. It is a solid anchor in a turbulent universe.

And there's more: true belief can help us see a pattern and a purpose in our lives. We really begin to sense that God is truly in control. Sometimes we see it only in retrospect, after things have happened to us. You may remember that scene in *Exodus* 33 where Moses asks God to show him His ways, so that he, a human being, will understand how God directs the universe. It's an amazing moment. God replies by ordering Moses to get down into the cleft of the rock, and as God passes by, Moses will be granted the opportunity to see God. Moses gets down. God passes by. What does Moses see? The Torah tells us that Moses only sees the back of God. That is, he could only see God after God had passed by, meaning that God's work is often so hidden that we understand it only in retrospect, long after it has taken place.

D: Do people actually achieve this kind of knowledge, this serenity?

R: They do, but as I said before, it doesn't come easily. It is worth the effort and the struggle, however, because one of the wonderful by-products of a belief in God is the element of trust in Him. The believing Jew believes so fiercely and trusts so powerfully that nothing that befalls him affects his belief and trust in God — even if it causes him suffering. It's what Job has in mind when he says in that famous thirteenth chapter: "Though You slay me, I will trust in You." This kind of total belief and trust and acceptance — the way a child trusts a parent — is what gives profound serenity to a human being.

D: Where can I buy such serenity?

R: Well, it's not for sale. It's not something that just happens on its own. It is the result of a long period of thought, study, prayer, and service of God in a thousand different ways. And after all the labor, ultimately it is a gift that God bestows upon you. But it's a gift that has to be earned.

Don't think that trust in God is a guarantee that nothing will ever go sour in your life. As a matter of fact, if things are always smooth you never have an opportunity to put your belief and trust into practice. But it does mean that whatever life has in store for you — good or bad — you will be able to handle it and accept it, because you know that there is a good God Who is directing all things. This is why I say that belief in God is not just a nice abstraction. It also has some very positive implications for daily life.

D: Most people think that belief in God is something that you either have or don't have. I never heard the idea that you have to work at it.

R: Believe me, you have to work at it constantly. Look at the first of the Ten Commandments: "I am the Lord your God Who took you out of the land of Egypt." If this is a commandment, what are we being commanded to do? In the other commandments, we are told to honor parents, or to observe Shabbat, or not to take God's Name in vain, or not to murder or steal or commit adultery. There is, in fact, a classic dispute between Maimonides and Baal Halachot Gedolot if this first commandment is to be considered one of the 613 commandments.

Ten commandments

D: It seems to be stating a fact, a kind of preamble.

R: Exactly — that and more. Beneath its surface factuality, it demands that we keep working towards a belief in God. It wants us to remember constantly, as we go through the various activities of each day, that God is the Creator. By keeping this always in mind, and by doing everything with this in mind — not only prayer and Torah study, but also the ordinary, mundane things of life — we fulfill this first commandment, and our belief and trust in God grows and develops and matures. That's why Maimonides calls it the commandment to believe.

D: Once a person achieves *emunah* and *bitachon* and the serenity that goes along with them, is that all there is? Has he then "arrived" religiously?

Attendant responsibilities *R:* No, there is much more. Because in addition to the benefits that we receive, there are obligations we must accept. When God made a covenant with us — and He repeated it several times with the Patriarchs, and again at Sinai — He promised to be our God and our protector, and to shepherd us safely through history until the end of time. But every covenant, every agreement, has two sides to it: He will be our God, but we have to be His people.

D: Well, that doesn't sound too bad. What's so difficult about being His people when we have His promise to take care of us?

R: It is certainly not too bad. It is, in fact, very good, provided we keep our end of the covenant. Because, you see, when we abandon our part of the agreement to be His people as the Torah defines, He is absolved from His part; that is, His part of the agreement becomes null and void. That, too, is in the spiritual covenant that governs our relationship with God. So you see that belief in God is not only a privilege; it also carries obligations.

D: I was afraid you were coming to that.

R: You were right. We call it *ol Malchut Shamayim,* "the yoke of the Kingdom of Heaven," the idea that we are "harnessed" to perform a higher duty, that we are creatures of discipline and self-control and purpose.

Truth to tell, life without obligations is not very interesting or enjoyable. When you get right down to it, such a life has no meaning — either for individuals or for nations. History is a graveyard of once-great cultures that crash-landed into oblivion because their way of life lacked one essential ingredient of civilization: discipline. They consciously and willingly and with eyes wide open allowed themselves to slide down the slippery slope of becoming self-indulgent animals.

As I keep reminding you, even in Paradise there are do's and don't's, as witness Adam and Eve in the Garden of Eden. There, too, they are told what they may and may not do. What I am saying here is that the obligations we have — the mitzvot — are not for God's benefit but for our own benefit. Because, as I have been suggesting all along, the performance of God's mitzvot actually enhances life, enriches it, gives it meaning and purpose, invigorates and stimulates the body and the soul.

D: That's not a bad deal: God agrees to be our God and take care of us, on the condition that we do our part and serve Him — and it turns out that doing our part is actually beneficial to us. So we end up benefiting from both sides of the contract. It's hard to refuse such a bargain.

A two-sided contract

R: Right. It's all for our benefit — if we keep our part. If we don't, then it can be a rather lonely time for us. But there's a catch to this covenant: we cannot get out of it. There is no escape clause. We're in it for life, figuratively and literally. If we stay in it, we are rewarded with a life of satisfaction, joy, purpose, and meaning.

D: You keep saying "He." Is God a He, a She, an It, or what?

R: I don't want to get caught up in any semantic issues. (In this regard you might say that I am anti-semantic.) Human language simply cannot encompass the terminology with which to refer to God, so we use human pronouns. The "He" represents God in certain masculine manifestations — but obviously, God has no gender. In fact, when Jewish tradition speaks of God's Presence, it uses a feminine word, *Shechinah* — which represents God in certain feminine manifestations. The Jewish mystical writers discuss this in greater depth. One of the key words for God in Hebrew is not at all gender-related: it is *HaMakom*, "The Place," which, according to some scholars, is based on *Exodus* 33:21, where God says to Moses, "Behold, there is a *makom* (place) near Me . . ."

D: That's an odd name for God.

R: What it means is that God is not inside the world, or even the entire universe, as we normally think. The world is not the place in which God can be found, because if God could be contained within the bounds of the world, that would mean He has limits — which cannot be true of God, Who is limitless and eternal and larger than anything He created. Just the reverse: God is the all-encompassing Place in which the world can be found. That is, the universe is in God, not the other way around.

God cares and listens   In any case, despite God's might and power, He cares about His creatures, listens to their prayers, and is concerned with each individual human being — and about each individual blade of grass as well. I mentioned before that in the daily *Amidah* we describe God as "great, mighty, awesome." What's fascinating is that in the next breath we refer to Him as *gomel chasadim tovim*, the One Who "performs beneficial kindnesses . . ." That means that God is the life-force of the universe and of everything in it. He did not simply create the world and place us in it and then tell us to fend for ourselves. God's essence is goodness. Because He is good, He does not abandon us on this planet Earth, but instead gives us a guide by which to live. This is the Torah, through which God speaks to us — a map with which we can negotiate the difficult terrain of life. More: it guarantees us a life of meaning and purpose. In fact, He created us out of a sense of goodness, because His goodness, by definition, needs to expand, needs to have an object, and therefore He expends it on others.

D: That's all well and good — no pun intended — but I want to ask an obvious question. If God is good, and goodness is His essence, then why is there so much that is not good in the world — earthquakes, typhoons, floods, tornadoes — and all of those "acts of God" that kill and destroy, in the supposedly perfect natural universe? What about the death of innocent children? Or sickness and suffering and tragedy? We see these things around us all the time. How do you reconcile this with a God Who is supposed to be good?

R: That is not only an obvious question, but a good question — a question about the good. And there is no easy answer to it. Let's spell it out. On the one hand, the universe runs like clockwork: the sun rises and sets at a predetermined moment each and every day. The seasons come on time. Summers are warm, winters are cold. The planets move about in an orderly, regular pattern. The tides rise and fall predictably, and the moon waxes and wanes according to an exquisitely precise schedule.

D: All true. But on the other hand, some aspects of the universe seem totally chaotic and capricious. Storms, plagues, natural disasters of all kinds — they all seem to happen at random, as if there were no one in charge. It is difficult to reconcile the clockwork and the chaos, and to accept that one God is the Source of all this.

R: Granted, in the world there is joy and suffering, laughter and weeping, growth and decay, life and, inevitably, death.

Clockwork, chaos, and the hiding God

This is why it is called the eternal question. It has many variations, such as: Why do the righteous suffer, why do the evil prosper? In *Exodus* 32, when Moses asks God to reveal His essence to him, as we mentioned earlier, what is it that Moses wants to know? Amazing: our tradition tells us that Moses asks God to reveal to him the answer to this very question: Why do the righteous suffer? If God is just, where is justice? If God is good, where is goodness? An entire book of the Bible — *Job* — is based on this theme. And the Mishnah touches on it directly when it says: "It is not in our power to explain either the tranquility of the wicked or the suffering of the righteous (*Avot* 4:19).

And yet, two ideas can help light the way. One is that God is a hiding God and does not reveal His existence or His eternal plan to us. God is here with us, but His Presence is not always evident. Our constant task is to unveil Him, to find Him, even in the darkness. When the Psalmist in 16:8 says, "I place God before me always," he means "always" in the sense of "all ways" and constantly: we are to strive to see God's Presence even when God seems completely hidden.

The second idea is that we believe that this world is only part of the story, that this is but the entranceway leading to the world-to-come — as the Sages say in *Avot* 4:21 — and that in that world, the scales are righted. So, you see, we don't know the full story yet — not of success and not of earthquakes.

Part *of the* *story*   Bear in mind also that underneath all the apparent chaos, there is a discernible pattern in the world. Evil does occasionally seem to triumph, but only on the surface. Hitler is defeated; Stalin is defeated; fascism and Communism do go under. Right may seem to be defeated by might, but in the historical sweep of things, right does not go under. And the mere sight of Jewish revival around the world — the vigorous new interest in Jewish roots and Jewish learning in Israel and elsewhere — is itself an indication of God's guiding hand. So belief is not a blind leap in the dark. There are some very good, rational underpinnings for belief in God.

D: Does God want us to believe in Him?

R: Of course. It's the first of the Ten Commandments.

D: Why?

R: Because by believing in Him, by knowing that He exists, our lives are enriched and enhanced. We become more complete human beings, happier and more fulfilled. It is not for His benefit but for ours that God wants us to believe in Him, as an expression of His love for us.

D: Fine. Accepted. But if so, why does God make it so difficult to believe in Him? Why does He play hide-and-seek with us? Why doesn't He show everyone clearly that He is God?

R: How would you propose that He do that?

D: Simple. He could show us clearly, in a hundred different ways, that He exists. For example, the moment we sin, we get punished. The moment we perform a mitzvah, we get rewarded. That way, everyone would know that God is God.

R: That wouldn't work.

D: Why?

R: Because God wants our belief to be hard won and significant rather than automatic and trivial. He wants us to believe in Him precisely when it is possible not to; to trust in Him precisely when it is difficult to do so. He wants us to do His mitzvot not because we have no choice — we'll be struck by lightning if we don't — but out of free choice. When you have no alternative but to serve God, that service is less valuable. A mundane illustration: what is more meaningful — a gift you receive from someone who was forced to give it to you, or a gift from someone who gives it to you because he wants to?

D: The answer is obvious.

R: This is what God is doing. He would rather we serve Him   *Free choice* because we want to, rather than because we have to. He would rather we believe in Him because we freely choose to, rather than because we are forced to. In other words, God does not want His subjects to be automatons. Service from a robot is meaningless. When a human being, confronted with an array of conflicting choices, pulled in all directions, tempted to abandon God, nevertheless chooses to believe and practice and study and observe and trust and pray — even though he could have gone off in other directions — that is valuable in the eyes of God. That enhances God in the eyes of the individual, and it enhances the individual.

D: You're talking about free will.

R: Exactly. This is a cardinal principle of Judaism. We can freely choose our paths. God wants us to follow His path but does not force us to do so. And if we were immediately punished or rewarded for our deeds, or if God made it impossible not to believe in Him, that would be tantamount to removing our freedom of choice. God deliberately hides within the enveloping cloud.

D: Maybe we should give up and not try to understand anything about God or His ways.

R: Not at all. The greatness of the human mind is that it constantly attempts to comprehend — by asking, probing, exploring. This is as it should be. If you really think about it, everything in our daily experience has the potential to remind us about God. Whether it be the blade of grass we walk upon, the trees we see, the leaf on the sidewalk, the clouds, the miracles of electricity, or of sight and smell and touch, or our every heartbeat and breath — there is really nothing that does not remind us of God's presence. But of course, one has to be sensitized and attuned to see it. God performs miracles for us every day — in our daily prayer we acknowledge His "miracles that are with us every day" — but we don't always see them because our senses have become dulled. That's why Isaiah in 40:26 says, "Lift up your eyes on high and see, Who has created these?"

D: And we become sensitized and attuned through study and prayer, and so forth.

Entering the mystery

R: You are getting the idea. But even as we sensitize ourselves, we have to remember that there are certain things which we may never comprehend. That should not deter us: we must keep probing anyway. And praying for depth and wisdom. And for humility. Especially humility, because if we attain true humility, we will not be disappointed if it turns out that there are certain things in life we are not able to comprehend.

For example, the very concepts of infinity, eternity, and immortality are beyond human understanding. Something that has no beginning and no end? Something that goes on forever, endlessly? These are concepts beyond our full comprehension, because they are beyond our experience. That's one reason why it is not possible for us fully to understand the nature of God. We are mortal and finite, and we are trying to grasp the meaning of the immortal and the infinite. We are bound not only by the physical force of gravity which pulls us down and ties us to the earth, but also by a spiritual kind of gravity which anchors us to our physical selves and to the material world.

Therefore we cannot fathom the essence of God. When God tells Moses to climb into the cleft of the rock while He passes by, He says, "My face may not be seen." That very mysterious thirty-third chapter of *Exodus* suggests that humans are only capable of perceiving a kind of "shadow" of the Creator, but not His full visage and essence. And it also means that although Moses comprehends more about God than any mortal before or since, even his knowledge is limited, because he too is only mortal. This is the thick cloud that envelops him when he goes up to Sinai — and which certainly envelops us as well.

D: And yet, despite the enveloping cloud, Moses continues to climb upward. It does not seem to disturb Him.

R: This is exactly how it should be with us. The fact that Moses may never fully comprehend as much as he would like to comprehend about God does not deter him from continuing to learn as much as he can. And it shouldn't deter us, even though we are hardly on the level of a Moses.

D: In effect, though, what you are saying is that there are no answers to the mysteries of life, to the eternal questions about suffering, death and tragedy. Will we ever understand?

R: Perhaps some day. Because there *are* answers, but they are beyond our present understanding.

D: But why can't we see God as clearly as the people in the Bible did?

R: Simply because we are not on their level of perception. They were granted the gifts of prophecy and revelation so that they could accept the Torah and develop the legacy that they would pass on to future generations. *Measure for measure*

Furthermore, when Jews fail to earn the clarity of God's continued Presence and Revelation, He deliberately makes Himself unseen and hides Himself. The Torah tells us quite clearly that if we become distant from Him and His teachings, He too will become distant from us — He will "hide His face from us" (*Deuteronomy* 31:17). It is measure for measure. To the extent that we abandon Him, He abandons us. Which means that He withdraws certain providential aspects of His relationship with us, which makes it more difficult to sense His Presence. He may even allow things to run on their own temporarily, without the Captain, so to speak. And you know what happens to a ship when the captain is absent. It may float for a while, but soon enough it runs aground. There's no greater punishment which He can inflict upon the world. When this *hester panim*, as it's called in Hebrew, takes place, chaos and confusion rule, and very little makes sense.

D: Sounds like today. But how long will His hiddenness, this *hester panim*, last? Is not God allowing His creation to disintegrate? Will things ever get a little clearer, or at least a bit less murky?

R: Those are difficult questions. The best way to strip away the veil is to attach ourselves to His teachings, to the study of His Torah, and to prayer. Then, gradually, our hearts open up and God penetrates our being. Then we realize that there are aspects of life which reason alone cannot comprehend. Sometimes we sense the reason in our hearts rather than in our heads. In a super-rational way. And this is not unreasonable.

D: No, but it's not rational.

Beyond our minds *R:* Must everything be subject to human reason? Some things are beyond reason. Not everything in the world is purely rational. Even the scientist in his laboratory is aware of mysteries and has to resort to intuitions, to presuppositions, to hypotheses, to gut feelings, and to other non-rational tools.

D: That is true in a way. But I thought Judaism was such a rational religion.

R: It is rational, but only up to a point. We have the most profound intellectual tradition in the world. We honor the mind, we emphasize study and learning as no other civilization in the world. To us, Torah study is the highest form of worship, and it is the greatest mitzvah. The Talmud is a very subtle and precise system, with great stress on analysis, logic, careful thinking. And Torah makes no unnatural demands upon us. But remember, we are not talking about mathematics, but about religion — which by definition deals with matters that are far beyond human comprehension. Think about it: if we are unable to understand fully the essence or nature of God, then how can we expect fully to understand the ways in which He runs His universe?

The point is that a believing Jew believes that God is One, and whether or not he comprehends His ways, he still believes. (By the way, did it ever occur to you that we never question God when things go well?) As for the contradictions — God, is after all, God. He is not required to make sense to our mortal non-sense, and to behave according to the criteria which we mortals establish. This would be nice, but a bit too easy. Listen to what the Rebbe of Kotzk once said: "I would not under any circumstances crown a Divine King over me whose ways can be understood by simple creatures of flesh and blood." In other words, if we were capable of understanding everything about God, then He ceases to be God; He becomes like an ordinary president or prime minister whose constituents can second-guess him, repudiate his policies, and vote him out of office.

D: But a lot of people refuse to believe in God precisely because they don't understand.

R: And a lot of people make the mistake of assuming that whatever our minds cannot fathom does not exist. This is a major fallacy. It is making God over in man's image. And, by the way, this helps us understand why the Torah is so very rigorous in its denunciation of those who would make images of what they conceive to be God. The reason is that although it is a perfectly natural human instinct to want to be able to touch, concretize, and make tangible and palpable — and fully understandable — that which we worship, when we do so, we place limits on that which is without limits, we localize and make temporal that which is universal and transcendent.

God in man's image

For example, the pagan habit of creating figurines to represent the deities is not necessarily primitive or unsophisticated, but rather an expression of this instinct. Thus also the Greeks: they were a highly intelligent people who gave the world philosophy, drama, poetry, architecture, science, and an appreciation of physical beauty. Western civilization was born in Greece. But they too had gods of this and gods of that. This was not due to naivete, but to a natural turning away from abstractions. The classical Christian depictions of sons and mothers of god; their traditional practice of offering prayers at the statues of Mary or of Joseph or at depictions of the crucifixion — all these stem from a similar need for explicit and tangible objects of worship. When patriots virtually worship the flag, it is an expression of the same common need.

Because this desire is so deeply rooted within mankind, and because it leads to the image-worship which is the antithesis of Judaism, the Torah takes great pains to warn us against submitting to it. "Thou shalt make thyself no carved image" (*Exodus* 20:3-5). Think about it: a Torah which is spare and terse in its words, and uses just two words to prohibit theft or adultery or incest, uses forty-four words in two separate verses to prohibit the making of images. And this prohibition is found elsewhere in the Torah as well.

D: Why? Why all this concern about carved images?

A demanding God

R: Perhaps it is because it is a cardinal sin to attempt to limit the limitless, to try to bring down to our level something which by definition is far above our level. Humans would like to turn God into just another human — perhaps a bit more powerful, stronger, wiser — but basically on our level. That would make things very convenient. For if God is human, then when He is too demanding, He can be replaced, or changed, or eliminated, or ignored. We are created somewhat like God, with certain powers and abilities to create on our own — "in His image" — but occasionally we get the wrong impression and refuse to surrender our instincts and desires and needs and gratifications because, in our feverish imaginings, we begin to think that we ourselves are really God. We want to have a god, but we want our gods pulled down from their heights so that they are not far above us but alongside us, clearly seen, watched, defined — and limited. And we like our gods humanized — literally given a human face — and thus made less awesome, less fearsome, less commanding, and less demanding. Isn't that what we have done to our political leaders? This was one of the underlying motifs in the story of the Golden Calf in the thirty-second chapter of *Exodus*.

D: In other words, we want to have our cake and eat it too — or have our God and ignore Him.

R: Yes, left to our own desires; we would rather not be told *Partner*
what to do, how to live, how to behave. So along comes *of God*
the Torah and says: Listen, you are the culmination
of God's Creation, the last in the order of Creation, in which
everything was prepared for you in advance of your appearance. God has placed you in charge of His earth, but
there is one condition: You must be subservient to Him. If you
serve yourself, you will become a slave. Paradoxically, you
become a partner with the Creator Himself when you serve
Him and when you surrender yourself to Him. Creating
images, figurines, statues of deities, is man's way of bringing
God down to size — human size. This instinct is the root
cause of sin — for sin is really the refusal to accept a Master,
and the desire to diminish if not eliminate the Power of the
Master. That is why the Torah is relentless in its war on all
kinds of idolatry.

D: But it is interesting — even though everyone tries to make
God tangible, they still want to have some kind of god.

R: The fact is that faith and belief are universal needs. All
men in all periods yearn to believe in something beyond
themselves. And therefore every civilization has created its
own system of deities of one sort or another, even those who
worshipped stone figurines. They were all ways of expressing
this natural human yearning to reach out to something beyond
the self.

The object of this yearning need not be an idol; it can be
an idea — as witness the Communist movement, which
claimed to be atheistic but yet had its own pantheon of beliefs
and gods. Until very recently, almost every town square in
Russia was bedecked with statues or huge posters of Lenin,
the chief god of the Communist pantheon. It is part of our
nature to try to reach out to something beyond our selves,
because deep down we sense our own mortality and weakness. That explains why in our time people without religion
are in such need of heroes. The John Kennedys and the John
Waynes ride high for a while, and when they fall, new heroes
are erected in their place. We may huff and puff, but deep
within us we know that we are merely flesh and blood, and so
we try to make contact with that which we consider eternal

and immortal. The sadness is that this natural human need can easily be turned towards the wrong gods.

D: That is an interesting perspective — that this need for a god is so universal that in itself it is a testimony to the presence of God.

Longing to touch God   *R:* Exactly so. It's as if in each human soul there is a built in mechanism which longs to be in touch with its beginning point, which is God. For some, this desire for God is side-tracked into idolatry or into worship of ideas or people, but the essential yearning for something beyond the mere self is never snuffed out.

This may explain why there is deep disquiet and discontent within so many people — almost a desperation. We talked about this during our first meeting. They attempt to satisfy this discontent by purchasing new gadgets, or by constantly going on trips, or by seeking new adventures and thrills. But they do not realize that all this stems from a deep and genuine inner longing for something beyond themselves, and that this thirst cannot be slaked by material things, because it stems essentially from a spiritual source. It is a search for an anchor in life, for truth, for a source from which we came.

D: I wonder sometimes if anyone can really prove the existence of God. It's not a matter of two plus two equals four. If God is so far above our understanding, it is to be expected that we will never arrive at a belief in God through our rational faculties alone.

R: Nevertheless, with all the difficulties and questions, I do think it is much more reasonable to accept the existence of a Supreme Being than to deny it. Acceptance of the idea, granted, does engender some important questions. But the alternative is to say that there is no God at all, that everything is simply random and blind chance and coincidence — that the blade of grass or the snowflake, much less the intricate living things and the complex universe, all happened by themselves. This is intellectually untenable.

But even though our understanding is limited, there is hope. At the end of the daily *Aleinu* prayer we recite the passage from the fourteenth chapter of the prophet Zechariah: *Bayom hahu yihye Hashem echad uhshemo echad*, "On that day, God will be One, and His Name will be One." That means that at the end of days all the mysteries will be revealed, and we will realize that those things which, to our finite minds, seem irreconcilable, not understandable, and completely contradictory to the idea of a just God — that these will some day — "in that day" — be finally seen as one, not as contradictions that seem to split God into two opposite aspects. Everything will be perceived to be unified and whole, without contradictions.

Our present view of God is not a unified one, not a complete one. It is shattered and fractured into tiny pieces, and our own finitude, our temporal limitations, permit us to see only a small part of what God does, a fleeting glimpse of the whole picture. Because we cannot perceive the patterns of His conduct, we assume that there are contradictions and an absence of justice. Our vision is obstructed because of our mortality. But on the day of the final redemption, says Zechariah, not only will God be One in the sense that He will be accepted by the entire world as the Creator; God will be One in the sense that we will finally see Him whole and not in pieces, complete and not fragmented, so that we will finally realize that everything is part of one entity. *Obstructed vision*

In fact, our tradition tells us that at the end of days, mankind will no longer recite the blessing *Dayan Ha'emet* — "the true Judge" — which we recite when tragedy occurs. Instead, we will recite *Hatov V'hameitiv*, "Who is good and Who performs good" — which is the blessing of joy and good tidings, because then we will finally understand how everything is for the ultimate good. In that day, history will be like a multicolored kaleidoscope whose jumbled pieces will all settle into one beautiful and symmetrical whole.

One more point, but a crucial one: ultimately, all indicators and proofs of God's existence are dry and arid. By themselves they mean little. What God wants is action based on our belief in Him. He wants to imprint that belief in our hearts and emotions, not just in our intellects. Note that the term for Jewish law is halachah, which connotes walking or moving along a path, from the word for "go" or "walk," *haloch*. Halachah implies action, movement as opposed to passivity. If belief remains only in the mind, it remains sterile and barren. If it moves into the emotions, into the affect, and is translated into attitudes and action, then it plays a daily role in our lives. Perhaps that's why the first of the Ten Commandments stresses that "I am your God." Not just *a* God or *the* God, but *your* God, Who is concerned with you, and to Whom you can turn at all times. We belong to God, but God also belongs to us — and that, it seems to me, is a very comforting thought.

D: Not only comforting, but also demanding.

R: Definitely so. Privileges cannot exist without responsibilities. Our relationship with God works in both ways: we are to love Him, but He already loves us. We are to have faith and trust in Him, but He already has faith and trust in us.

D: I can understand God loving us. But God having trust in us? This is strange.

R: There's an odd comment in *Deuteronomy* 32:4 about God. It describes Him as *El Emunah*, "the God of Faith." Faith in whom? Say the Sages: in His people Israel. He has faith that we will follow Him, cleave to Him despite everything, just as He cleaves to us despite everything. In a fascinating insight, the Sages in *Berachot* 6a say that God wears tefillin, just as we do — with one major difference. In our tefillin there is written the passage "*Shema Yisrael* . . . Hear O Israel, the Lord Who is our God, that Lord is One." In God's tefillin, there is written *Mi k'amcha Yisrael* . . . "Who is like Thy people Israel, one nation on earth" (*I Chronicles* 17:21).

Shema: absorb and understand

D: Speaking of the *Shema*, in all of our discussion today about God, we haven't touched on that statement at all.

R: Quite right. The *Shema Yisrael* is the central statement of Jewish faith and belief, the first words taught to a child and the last words on the lips of the Jew as he departs this world: *Shema Yisrael*, "Hear O Israel, the Lord Who is our God, that Lord is One." The very first word in that declaration of faith, *Shema*, means not only to hear or listen. It also means "to understand." In other words, the act of listening is not an act in which only the ear participates; the mind and the heart also participate. In a way, the *Shema* says that if your final goal is to understand something about God, the first step is to learn to listen and hear and understand and absorb.

Of course, there is more to the *Shema* than that. God is singular and unique, but simply to state that is insufficient. As we said earlier, the word *echad* in Hebrew, normally translated as "one," is not merely a number. *Echad* connotes "source" or "root" — that from which all else extends. It also connotes a unity.

The very next sentence of the *Shema* commands us to love God completely, without reservations, and to be committed to Him with all our being — intellectually, emotionally, physically, financially, spiritually.

That is to say, God's oneness is not only a characteristic of Himself: God's adherents are also required to serve Him in a way of "oneness." That is, we are to serve Him not in a fragmented, piecemeal way. Not half-heartedly, but wholly, totally, completely — which is what is meant by *bechal lev-av'cha*, "with all your heart." Just as He is whole and complete, so must our service of Him be whole and complete. The key way to serve Him, this credo goes on to say, is to study His words, to make them part of us, to teach them to our children, to discuss them constantly — as we are doing right now — to wear them next to our minds and hearts in our tefillin, to place them on our doorposts. This is what is meant by the *Shema*'s exhortation, "Teach them thoroughly to your children, and speak of them . . ."

Without reservation

D: In other words, the Torah is supposed to be all-encompassing.

R: Precisely. You literally have to surround yourself with it.

Internally, you have to fill yourself with it, and externally you have to place reminders all around you — visually, verbally, intellectually — in every way. And in this way you will ultimately begin to comprehend something about God.

The best way to understand the mysteries of God is to listen, study His Torah, engage in serious prayer, and do the mitzvot. By going in this path, we learn to allow God to continue His work within us, to keep our souls open to His influences and impulses, and to surrender our selves to Him. That is the most productive way. Probably the least productive method is to get into endless, theoretical discussions.

D: Like ours?

R: We may be theoretical, but we're certainly not endless.
And if this remains merely theory, it would perhaps be interesting and stimulating, but ultimately, yes, it would remain sterile. However, Torah life has to start somewhere — and it usually starts with discussion — but it cannot end there. Discussion is important mainly because once the mind is opened up, surprising things can happen to a person.

D: Like what?

R: Like finding yourself gradually moving towards Torah living. If a person isn't careful, a theoretical discussion can lead to practical Jewish living.

D: Shall I be careful?

R: Not too careful, please.

pRayer – the jew Reaches towaRds God

*. . . **in which is discussed** . . . The lonely God and the lonely Jew / God as the Giver / Spontaneous and fixed prayer / Public and private prayer / Petitionary and other kinds of prayer / Praying in Hebrew and in other languages / Does prayer change God's mind? / If He knows everything, why bother asking? / Does He really listen? / And other fascinating aspects of reaching up and out to our Creator . . .*

Rabbi: I haven't seen you in a few weeks. What have you been doing with yourself?

David: Well, I have tried to pray in shul.

R: "Tried"? That sounds ominous. I gather it was not successful?

D: Right.

R: I'm not too surprised.

D: I'm surprised to hear you say that you are not surprised.

R: Well, it's just that you apparently walked into a synagogue some Shabbat morning, without any mental or spiritual preparation at all, and expected the heavens to open up. It just does not work that way. You have to go in very tentatively, carefully, not expect a major religious experience, listen carefully, and keep your heart and mind open. And you have to do that over and over again, constantly, week after week. If you know it's going to take time, you won't get frustrated and discouraged. Like anything else worthwhile, you can't expect to succeed without an investment of energy, thought, and practice — and maybe even a little discomfort.

D: Sounds like hard work.

R: You are right on the mark, because the traditional term for prayer is *avodah*, which means "worship" and "service" — but also means "work." "Worship of God" is *avodat Hashem* in Hebrew — literally, "work of God." The ancient rabbis used to get spiritually ready for prayer one hour before, and wind down for an hour after prayer. To maintain sincerity, to concentrate on what you are doing, to remain open to the words and their implications — none of this occurs on its own.

This is the point: Judaism is an extremely rewarding way of living. It is satisfying, comforting and fulfilling, and it has everything you require for a life of meaning and joy and serenity. "Serve God with gladness, come before Him with joyous song," says Psalm 100. But it does not happen effortlessly. We've talked about this before.

D: Yes, and I'm trying to ignore it, hoping I will be the exception and that all these wonderful things will fall into my lap without my having to do very much, but now I give up. So guide me, please. Tell me what I have to do.

R: First of all, you tell me: what was the problem in the synagogue?

D: For one thing, I was uncomfortable.

R: That in itself is not a bad thing.

D: I felt isolated, alone, all by myself. I was sitting with many people, but they were all strangers.

R: I agree that people should be friendly, should offer you a prayer book, find you a place to sit, make you feel at home. *Conversing with God*
But once prayer starts, that is a matter between you and God.

Whether or not you know the people around you is totally beside the point. The synagogue is not a social club, and praying is not a social activity. The synagogue is the place in which we talk to God. And God talks to us. Period.

Keep in mind that when you are most lonely, that is the most effective moment to approach God. The sense of loneliness, the feeling of vulnerability and dependence, is what helps us to reach out to God. That is when we realize that we need Him for help, consolation, support. That is when we best pour out our hearts to Him, when no one else in the world exists but God. So a bit of discomfort and loneliness is not at all a bad thing.

D: Logically, it follows from what you say that private prayer is better than public prayer. When I pray in the privacy of my room, I am literally alone. If this is so important, why bother with public worship at all?

R: A valid point. But nothing overrides participation with the community of Israel in its prayers to God. Let me present *Private and public prayer: the intimate and the communal*
four brief reasons why.

First, every *minyan,* or quorum, required for public worship, even if it consists only of the minimum ten, represents the entire Jewish people. During public worship, the individual Jew subsumes himself under this entity and becomes part of the past, present, and future of all Israel. That's one reason that the words of prayer are always in the plural — "we," not "I" — whether we pray in public or in private, because no Jew really stands before God as a mere individual; he or she is always part of the historic community of Israel. The fact is that even when the individual prays alone and offers up his or her own personal and private supplication to God, he or she is still contained under the whole — except that in the public setting it reaches a zenith that simply cannot be replicated in private prayer.

Second, worship of God by the community is a sign of respect and honor for Him. *Berov am hadrat melech*, says *Proverbs* 14: 28: "The glory of the King is in the multitude of the people." A public declaration of fealty to the king is more meaningful to the king than is a private one.

Third, and connected with this idea, is the fact that certain prayers can only be recited in public. *Kaddish*, for example, which is the ultimate hymn of praise to God, cannot be recited in private. Nor can the repetition of the silent *Amidah* and its special congregational responses, like *kedushah*. Nor can the formal Torah reading or the Priestly Blessing by the *Kohanim* take place without the public quorum.

Fourth, communal prayer brings with it a significant added benefit: once we pray with a unit of Jews, the collective spiritual strength of that unit adds a power to the worship that cannot be achieved by one's own self. So while private prayer is certainly acceptable, the virtues of communal prayer override it.

Alone before God **D:** Isn't that a contradiction? On the one hand you say that we are supposed to feel alone before God, and on the other you say that worship ideally should be within the community.

R: It's not really a contradiction, only a fascinating polarity.

Jewish tradition holds on to the opposing polarities without letting either one go. For example, within the set liturgy there are places where spontaneous, personal prayer is encouraged. And the *Amidah* is first recited silently in the synagogue — in effect, privately and personally — and then is repeated aloud — in effect, communally. That is to say, even in public worship we maintain the elements of intimacy with God, of privacy with Him.

One manifestation of this occurs when men and women sit separately in shul. Men and women become symbolically alone, separate from the other gender. The prohibition against conversation and idle chit-chat during prayer is another manifestation — because it is not only disrespectful and disturbing, but it also destroys the idea of maintaining a sense of aloneness and privacy within the context of the community. In synagogue, I am to be alone with my God; the only conversation I am permitted to have is with my God and with no one else.

By the way, God is also alone. There is no one else like Him. And the Jewish people is alone, set apart from the world. In *Numbers* 23:9, we are referrred to as an *am levadad yishkon*, "a people that will dwell in solitude . . ."

That's one reason that the times set for the three daily prayers correspond to the times set aside for the ancient sacrificial service in the Temple — which were public offerings. *Why three daily prayers?* Our present-day *shacharit* service corresponds to the daily morning *tamid* offering; our *minchah* corresponds to the afternoon offering; and although there were no formal sacrifices during the night, our *maariv* service corresponds to the part of the offerings which lay on the altar all night long until the morning. And on Shabbat and Yom Tov, our additional *musaf* prayer corresponds to the *musaf* offering in the Temple. This confluence is in keeping with the prophet Hosea's statement in 14:3, "We will repay the bulls (of sacrifice) with (the prayers of) our lips" — *uneshalmah parim sefateinu* — which means that Jewish prayer after the destruction of the Temple is a surrogate — a kind of proxy — for the absent Temple service.

Incidentally, the connection between the Temple sacrifices and prayer is not just chronological. It is also conceptual. A sacrifice was required to be without blemish; so is prayer. A sacrifice required proper intention and concentration on the part of the one who offered it; so does prayer. A sacrifice represented something of value which the individual gave of himself; so does prayer.

D: Okay, you've explained that it's good to feel alone in prayer, plus the significance of communal prayer. Fine. But alone or not, in synagogue or at home, my praying just does not seem to work.

R: How can you know if your prayer "works" or not? The purpose of prayer is to connect with God, to have a conversation with Him. Sometimes it's when we are most certain that our prayer is failing that it is most successful. I think what gets in the way is the preconceived notions we have about prayer.

PRAYER: The Jew Reaches Towards God □ 67

D: Such as?

R: First of all, we need to recognize that prayer is not easy, especially when it has not been part of our daily lives. Look at it objectively: suddenly we find ourselves speaking to the Creator of the world, addressing Him directly as *Atah*, "You." No other religious act is quite like this. We are standing directly before God, spiritually naked, in full view of Him Who knows us best. It is quite an awesome moment when you think about it: the sudden realization that we are talking to the Master Himself, to the King of Kings. And we are not asking Him for trifles. We would like peace, life, wisdom, health — and, by the way, could He send along the Messiah to redeem the Jewish people and the world from its suffering and misery?

D: It is rather frightening when you put it that way. Should I feel frightened when I pray?

Awe *R:* It would be perfectly natural to have a sense of fear, awe,
and reverence — that which in Hebrew we call *yir'at*
love *Shamayim,* literally, "fear of Heaven." But there is another aspect of prayer — and it softens the element of fear. That is the idea that God welcomes this encounter, encourages it. He wants to talk with us, wants to become part of our lives. Knowing that God loves us gives us a sense of peace and serenity, and prevents us from becoming so fearful that we cannot pray at all. I know this is easier said than done, but remember that we are praying for one reason: to reach out to God. And while this thought alone can unnerve us, remember that God is the loving Father Who cares for us and holds out a helping hand to us. So relax when you pray. Reach out for the serenity it provides.

This means that attitude is very important. Some people go into prayer with a chip on their spiritual shoulders: "Okay, here I am, what are You going to do for me?" It is important to enter the mode of prayer — alone or in synagogue — with no preconceptions and no prejudgments(which is the pristine meaning of prejudice). And remember — don't take your pulse constantly. Don't keep asking yourself, How am I doing, am I being inspired, am I being uplifted?

There is something else as well. Be an active participant. Don't be passive. Concentrate. Think. Make a spiritual, emotional, and intellectual effort to reach out to God. Allow the influences of the words, the melodies, the chants, the atmosphere of prayer, to penetrate your being. Look at the translation of the words, and at the explanatory notes in your Siddur — it's important to use a good Siddur with good commentary — and stimulate your heart and your mind.

D: You mention thinking and the mind. But isn't prayer a matter of heart and emotions?

R: No question about it. But Jewish prayer involves the mind as well. In fact, our prayer book contains readings from the Mishnah and Talmud which are purely intellectual and unemotional. And on Mondays, Thursdays and Shabbat, the central portion of the service is the reading and study of the weekly Torah portion. This is because in Judaism, study of Torah is itself a form of worship of God, because through the study of God's words we achieve a certain closeness to Him. In the formal prayer service we thus exercise several aspects of our being: not only the heart and the emotions, but also the mind and the intellect. Don't make the error of thinking that the heart and mind are two separate faculties. They actually work in concert. That's why I say that in order to pray well, one has to utilize both mental and spiritual qualities.

Emotion and intellect

D: Well, all that is easier said than done, but I could try it. It is certainly a goal worth reaching for.

R: These are only practical hints, because so many newcomers to prayer come to it with an attitude that makes things even more difficult, and makes it almost impossible to succeed. The key is to know that God cares for you, welcomes you, wants to hear your prayers.

D: A basic question bothers me: if I have no particular needs at the moment, why should I pray in the first place? What's in it for me? Just to recite praises to God seems relatively pointless.

I need nothing; why pray?

R: You raise some good issues, and we'll get to them all. But
I must say that you just made quite a statement: "What's
in it for me?" That is typically Western. "Me" is the key, and
what the "Me" can get out of anything is the subtext. I am
struck by this because one of the underpinnings of all of
Judaism — and particularly of Jewish prayer — is that while
the Torah respects the "Me" — the personhood of every individual — the key to Judaism is to learn to be subservient to a
higher order, to a Commander who commands. That sounds
foreign to Western ears.

This is particularly true of prayer — because one of the
key elements of successful prayer (and by "successful" I don't
mean that it gets good results, but that it truly affects the soul
and reaches God) is to realize how vulnerable we are, how
great God is, and that He — not we — is the Master of the universe. This concept is true of many mitzvot: Shabbat, for
example, is also designed to impress upon us that we are not
the master. That may be why the Talmud in *Berachot* 10b says
that a person should not stand on a high place and pray. It is
better to pray from a low place, as the Psalmist says in 130:1:
"Out of the depths I call You. . ." — because a low place
suggests the idea of total subservience to the Master.

Freedom
and
subser-
vience

The concept of subservience to anyone, even to God, is
very hard for us — raised on the doctrines of personal freedom and independence to do as we like — to absorb, but it is
the single major essential component of Jewish prayer. The
added benefit we ultimately derive from this concept is that
once it becomes part of us, we become much better human
beings.

The delicious surprise of it all is that despite the fact that
He is the Commander and the Master, God nevertheless
desires our prayers and wants us to reach out to Him.

D: Why? It doesn't make sense. Does God need us?

R: First, some ground rules. Any question about Judaism is
acceptable, but how you ask the question is important.
Whenever you feel that something doesn't make sense, just
add two little words: "to me," so that now you would be saying, "It doesn't make sense to me." Or, better said, "I don't
understand it."

Now to your question. The great, all-powerful God wants *Does He* to hear from us not because He needs us, not because it makes *need* Him "feel good" when we address Him, but because we need *prayer?* Him and it is good for us to reach out to Him. That's why in Judaism there is a blessing for practically everything in the universe. When we see the first flowers in the spring, there is a blessing acknowledging God as the One Who created the trees and the creatures to give us pleasure and joy. When we see the ocean, or a mountain range, or a desert, or thunder and lightning, we acknowledge God as their Author. There is a special blessing when we hear good tidings, when we acquire something of significance. Even when we hear news of a close relative's death, we recite a blessing acknowledging God's judgment as based on truth and justice. It goes without saying that there are blessings for food and drink. We even thank God after performing our bodily functions — by which we express our gratitude for the miracle of our complex bodies. All this is designed to make us constantly aware of God. This adds a new dimension to our lives.

When God wants to hear from us, it is because He wants to help us create a bridge to Him. It is part of His essence, part of His goodness, that He wants to give us whatever He can. So when we reach out to Him, He uses that bridge to reach out to us as well.

But do not misunderstand: even though He does not need our worship, it is very precious to Him. For example, Psalm 22:4 says something that is heavy with meaning: "The Holy One, Blessed Be He, is enthroned on the praises of Israel," suggesting that His Holy Throne is formed from our prayers, and that it is our prayers which hold Him aloft for all the world to see. And the Talmud in *Yevamot* 64a states that God greatly desires the prayers of the righteous, and that the world is so set up that Israel's prayers are an essential component of God's relationship to His world.

There is also a very suggestive Midrashic comment which *Actualizing* Rashi cites at *Genesis* 2:5. The verse describes the world just *the poten-* prior to Adam's creation: ". . . the herb of the field had not yet *tial good* sprouted, for God had not sent rain upon the earth, and there was no man to work the soil." The Midrash suggests that this means that rain could not water the earth until man prayed for the rain. That is to say, without prayer, all growth would have remained only potential, not actual. Only Adam's prayer actualizes the potential. This is a metaphor for the power of prayer in general, and explains why God desires it: it makes it possible for Him to actualize the potential good within His universe.

D: Occasionally it occurs to me that we "noodge" God an awful lot. We bother Him for every tiny thing.

R: Listen, I can't speak for God, but our tradition teaches us that God is pleased when He is "noodged," and displeased when He is not. Remember that one of the major characteristics of God is that He is a *noten*, a Giver. By asking God for something, we make it possible for Him to fulfill His "Giver" aspect.

D: So it turns out that there is something in it for me after all.

R: In effect, yes, but that's not the goal. We perform mitzvot not because we benefit from them but because they are the Will of God in the Torah. It is important to remember, incidentally, that according to Maimonides and others, prayer is not an option but a Torah obligation, and, like any mitzvah, we have to engage in it whether or not we feel like it.

D: But how can something as personal and as inherently emotional as prayer be a commandment? Can such things be legislated? How can I be forced to pray when I am not in the mood?

Legislating prayer **R:** First, even if there were no commandment to pray, we would still do so, because by our very nature we must reach out to a higher power — not necessarily to ask for things, but simply to make a spiritual connection. In fact, the Mishnah in *Bava Kamma* 2a refers to a human being by the strange term *mav'eh*, which the Talmud tells us is derived from the word *ba'ah*, "to pray." That is to say, man is defined by his essence, which is that he is a praying creature. Whether we realize it or not, the soul deep within us is constantly seeking contact with God. Our spiritual selves can no more do without prayer than our bodies can do without water.

D: If man is defined by his essence, which is prayer, and this is *mav'eh*, how come the Torah calls man "Adam" and not *mav'eh*? Does the Torah not consider man as essentially a praying creature? Their names really ought to be Mav'eh and Eve in the Garden.

R: The two names illustrate the dichotomy within man. He is born as Adam, a creature more related to the *adamah*, or earth, than to heaven. Part of his mission is to elevate himself, to refine his instincts, and to adjust his sights upward until prayer becomes his essence.

What I am saying is this: man originates from earth, but his destiny is to connect earth with heaven to the point that his highest aspirations becomes synonymous with his self. He is born as Adam, but he can become *mav'eh*.

Despite this internal urge to pray, there is a fascinating disagreement between two giants of Jewish thought as to whether or not the act of prayer fulfills a Biblical obligation. Maimonides maintains that it does, basing himself on the Talmud in *Taanit* 2a, which says that *Deuteronomy* 11:13, "to serve Him (*l'avdo*) with all your heart," means that we are required by Torah law to worship Him. The term *avodah*, as we saw earlier, refers to Divine service or worship. As a matter of fact, in his Book of the Commandments, Maimonides lists prayer as the fifth of the 613 commandments (*Sefer HaMitzvot*, 5). Nachmanides, on the other hand, while agreeing that prayer is not an option, does not consider it a Biblical commandment, but rather a rabbinically ordained one. According to him, the only time there is a Torah obligation to pray is when there is an emergency, because at moments of great crisis it is a mitzvah to think first of God and to recognize that only He can truly help us.

D: What you're saying makes eminent good sense and is important, but it still leaves me frustrated. There are a number of things that bother me about prayer, regardless of whether it is Biblical or rabbinic. For example, what about spontaneity in prayer? Supposing I am just interested in saying a prayer to God? Perhaps I am frightened, or sick, or in desperate need of something. Am I not allowed to pray for that, using my own words, or must all my prayers be read out of the

Spontaneous and regular prayer: kavannah

book, using words that someone else wrote, and repeating the same things every day — things that have no meaning for me in my present circumstances?

R: What you ask is very important, and therefore the answers are crucial to an understanding of what Jewish prayer is all about. So I ask you to please listen carefully.

Service of the heart   First, we must realize that the key ingredient of prayer, whether it is read from a book or is completely spontaneous, is that it must emanate from the heart, and that it requires *kavannah*. That means a sense of direction as to the object of prayer — "know before Whom you stand," as the Talmud in *Berachot* 28b reminds us — as well as concentration and inwardness on the part of the individual. As a matter of fact, the Talmud in *Taanit* 2a, which I cited earlier, asks a question about that familiar phrase in the *Shema* which commands us to "serve Him with all your heart." What does this mean? They respond that this refers to prayer — which is known as *avodah shebalev,* "service which is in the heart." Prayer without heart is not prayer, but simply a recitation and a mumbling of words. On a deeper level, prayer has an impact on the heart: the more we pray, the closer do we come to God.

Obviously, we can pray at any time of the day or night, for anything, in any language, at any time the mood strikes us. That is fine, desirable, wonderful. But remember that the reverse is not true. If we are not in the mood to pray, we still have to pray. If we are not in need of anything, we still have to pray. If we are not sick or not in desperate circumstances, we still have to reach out to God. In fact, it's not that we must; it's that our own souls require it.

Think about it: if we pray only when we are in the mood, then prayer becomes nothing more than a selfish act: I do it only when I feel like it, when it helps me. That's like saying, "I'll give charity only when I'm in the mood, I'll fast on Yom Kippur only when I am in the mood." It's like telling a loved one, "Don't show up until I need you." This is why there are things like legislation, and regulations, and time limitations in connection with prayer: to make certain that we stay in regular contact with God. And as I indicated earlier, the daily prayer cycle is conjoined to the daily sacrificial cycle in the Temple. Just as that cycle was not optional but mandatory, so is daily prayer not optional but mandatory.

It is important to remember one crucial idea, and that, too, will help answer your question. Prayer is not some divine candy-dispensing machine, and God is more than just our agent in heaven whose function it is to satisfy our requests for goodies. Prayer is actually an expression of the yearning of our soul to be in close contact with its own Source and Creator.

D: You mean that it's improper to ask God for anything?

R: Not at all. Petitionary prayer is perfectly legitimate, and God welcomes it. But it is only one of several types of prayer. The problem is that because we think in English, our Judaic concepts are affected by Anglicized thinking. In English, the term "pray" suggests asking for something. "Entreaty," "request," and "supplication" are the typical synonyms: "Give me that coat, I pray you." So let's put Jewish prayer into perspective by defining some terms.

Strictly speaking, "prayer," *tefillah* in Hebrew, refers only to the *Amidah* — also called the *Shemoneh-esrei* — the silent, standing prayer which consists of nineteen blessings on weekdays, and seven on Shabbat and Yom Tov. The balance of the formal liturgy in our prayer book — which actually comprises the bulk of the prayer book as we know it — is not actually prayer, but material which accompanies prayer — such as the *Shema*, and the Psalms, and readings from our sacred books.

The silent *tefillah* is divided into three parts: praise, *The silent* petition, and thanksgiving. That the central and largest *prayer* portion of this silent prayer is petitionary clearly demonstrates that it is certainly legitimate to ask God for anything at all — particularly since any request underscores our dependence on Him.

But in the rest of the prayer book, over ninety percent asks for nothing for ourselves. Most of it is filled with praise and recognition of the Almighty. That's because some of the chief purposes of prayer are: a) to remind ourselves that there is a God; b) to help us realize *that* we need, and that God fills those needs; c) to help us understand *what* it is that we truly need.

D: I'm not quite certain what you mean by that. How does prayer show us what we need?

R: Solid, intense, regular prayer sensitizes us to life and its purposes. It helps give us a new perspective on things. And when we attain new perspectives, we begin to realize that what we need is not so much a new car as new understanding of Torah; not so much a new house as new insights into other people; not so much to become a millionaire as to become a *mentsch*, a fine, Jewish human being. That's what I mean by understanding *what* we need.

And it should be obvious that we have many needs — not only spiritual ones — and that God supplies and fills those needs for us. In effect, prayer teaches us to declare unabashedly that we are incomplete without God and that we need Him. Every aspect of prayer, petitionary or not, helps us recognize our impotence as against God's omnipotence, our insignificance as against God's significance. And, most importantly, the fact that despite our insignificance, God still wants to listen to us.

Robotic *D:* All that is fine theory, but I am troubled by the fact that
prayer from time to time I see people during prayer who seem just to be mumbling words. There is certainly no outward sign at all that they are aware that they are talking to God.

R: I will not defend rote service of God, but we must realize that one of the great challenges of the religious life is to do things in a fresh way when they are constantly repeated — such as when one has to recite the same *Amidah* three times a day, for example. That's why real prayer requires much more than the mere recitation of words. It takes concentration and effort.

The same holds true for any mitzvah, particularly those which are repeated each day, such as tefillin, or being aware of the mezuzah and its message, or blessings before and after meals, or the simple act of giving charity. These all require special concentration because they are done so frequently and thus tend to become routine, spiritless acts. Daily prayer, if one is not careful, is the most susceptible to inattention and to automatic behavior.

But let's not be too harsh on people who seem to be

praying like robots; let's assume that something spiritual is happening inside that we cannot see. After all, only God knows what takes place within the human heart. By the same token, a person who shows every outward sign of talking to God could, for all we know, have his mind on something else entirely. The point is that we simply cannot know if a person is or is not performing a mitzvah with the proper reverence and intention. And it really is not our concern. That is a matter between the individual and God.

D: Sometimes I wonder if it isn't better to pray only occasionally and not on a regular, scheduled basis. At least then there might be a sense of freshness about it.

R: The problem of rote is a real one, but your suggestion is not the answer. It is crucial to maintain daily contact with God; the soul demands it and needs it, just as the body needs food and water. We do not have the right to deprive our souls of this daily sustenance. If we feed the soul only occasionally, it will atrophy and dry up and wither away. Furthermore, the Jew who prays regularly, even by rote, can more easily bring himself back to genuine prayer than the Jew who rarely prays. Once the soul loses regular contact with God, it is very difficult to bring it back. Even bad prayer is better than no prayer at all. And the reality is, as we discussed before, that if we pray only when we feel that we are in the proper frame of mind and spiritual mood, the chances are that we will pray very infrequently. Prayer — and mitzvot in general — thrive on frequency. They are our spiritual muscles. They should not be allowed to become flaccid and flabby from lack of use.

Regular contact

Incidentally, there are ways in which one can combat rote and bring to prayer more *kavannah*, or inwardness — by which I mean full concentration of mind and heart. One can make a beginning, for example, by making a special effort to concentrate on one particular portion of the service each day, without neglecting, of course, the rest of the prayers. How to go about this would require further discussion with a halachic authority.

D: This will take some intellectual digesting. There are things here that had never crossed my mind.

R: Before you begin digesting, there is something else you must understand about regular, fixed prayer: its very regularity helps set the stage for good, spontaneous prayer. It helps us attune ourselves and open ourselves up to God. Without the discipline of obligatory prayer, we would never be able to engage in spontaneous prayer. In other words, the person who converses with God regularly will experience deeper and more frequent spontaneous prayer than the person who never reaches out to God. The second person is a stranger to God, an occasional guest, while the first one is a familiar figure, more comfortable with God because He speaks to Him every day.

Imagine this scenario: a person who does not pray regularly experiences a major crisis such as illness or a severe business downturn. Will he instinctively reach for his Siddur or his book of *Tehillim*? Highly unlikely. But someone who prays every day, perfunctorily perhaps, will pour out his heart in his next scheduled *Amidah*. He is pre-programmed, if you will, to speak to God and will use every opportunity — formal and spontaneous prayer — to plead for his current need. What I'm saying is that the one who *davens* regularly develops a heightened sensitivity towards God and creates a reciprocal sensitivity from God towards him. At the very least, when he knocks at God's door, God does not wonder who this stranger is . . .

When you get right down to it, *tefillah*, *davening*, prayer — whatever term you use — is really a fellowship with God, a kind of communion with Him. It is an interaction, a dialogue on a very profound level.

D: You keep using terms like "conversation" and "dialogue," but isn't it a one-way monologue, with us doing all the talking? We don't really hear the other end of the dialogue, do we?

From man to God, from God to man *R:* Even if God seems to be silent, it is still a dialogue, because He does in fact hear and respond to every knock on His door. Prayer, when you think about it, is in a certain way the parallel of prophecy, except that it runs in a different direction. Prophecy is the avenue from God to man; prayer is the avenue from man to God. In prophecy, God speaks to man and man listens silently; in prayer man speaks to God, and God listens silently. But even though there is physical silence, there is in each instance a response.

When you think about it, prayer is really quite astounding: for a brief moment in time, finite man reaches out and touches the Infinite God, and the Infinite God reaches out and touches finite man. The two dimensions — mortality and immortality, earth and heaven, physical and spiritual — meet each other and become as one. Prayer is the bridge we cross towards the realm of God, and at the other end of the bridge God comes forward to welcome us into His domain for a spiritual colloquy.

So you are right — spontaneity is important in prayer, but it is deepened and enriched when it is buttressed by regular and daily contact with God. Such discipline actually helps us heighten our sensitivity to God, and warms up our frozen emotions and allows them to gush forth spontaneously even in the midst of the formalized liturgy. If we reserve our contact with God for the occasional volcanic outburst of religious emotion, we will rarely reach up to Him, and we will end up the losers. Spontaneity is a supplement to regular prayer, not a substitute. Prayer is not like some long-running show that we drop into when we have nothing better to do.

D: But what about mouthing other people's words? What kind of meaning can it have when what I am saying to God was written and prepared by someone else?

R: You are overlooking one important fact: when you read the prayer book, you are not merely reciting these words. Yes, we say them, but in a deeper sense, we are *listening* to these words, as if we were listening to great music. These words — most of them are from the Psalms — are not mere words, nor were they written by ordinary people. They were written by prophets and saintly men, and they are the music of the soul as it addresses God. Yes, we recite them aloud, we whisper them, we read them, but in actuality we are tuning in to these words. And these set words teach us how to pray and what to pray for. They are a model of ideal prayer.

Why repeat someone else's words?

D: Why don't Jews take the best of both worlds — come together as a group, but allow each individual to pray what is in his heart? That way, we'd get both public and private prayer at the same time.

R: That is a unique idea, and in fact public Jewish prayer does leave room for private meditation and contemplation of God. But bear in mind that by reciting — by which I mean listening — to the fixed liturgy, something very special occurs within us: we remove ourselves from our selves and step into the community. We become subsumed under the whole and become part of the corporate entity.

As we said earlier, that's one reason that the daily prescribed times of Jewish worship are connected with the specific times set aside for the public Temple offering service each day. The collective community, *Klall Yisrael*, prays together in the same way and at the same time, using the same words.

Entering the eternity of Israel   Think of it: all Israel saying the *Shema Yisrael* or the *Amidah* or the *Ashrei* together at the very same time. The individual himself, as individual, says nothing. He surrenders his personal identity for a moment and does not even bring forth his own words. Instead, he articulates the spirit of the Jewish people as expressed in the liturgy. In this way, the Jew enters the collective, eternal spiritual entity of the Jewish people. In effect, he takes his private, individual self and, through the established prayers, puts it into the service of the wider community of the Jewish people. This is literally selfless prayer, a total surrender of the self before the Creator. For these few moments he asks nothing for himself. He recognizes only God's existence and his own dependence upon Him, his own subservience to Him. Can you think of a more unselfish form of conversing with God? By submerging himself into the historic entity of *am Yisrael*, he moves into another level of existence: a continuum of eternity and timelessness. When we learn to worship God in this way, we have learned how to pray as a Jew. This is why liturgical, textual prayer is so significant.

As I said, there is room — even during public worship — for private, spontaneous, personal requests. It is always possible for every individual to speak to God in his or her own way, at any time. But *tefillah* goes beyond the petitionary, personal aspect, and moves off into a more profound realm where time, timelessness, Jewish history, Jewish future, and God and His relationship to the Jewish people all coalesce at that one magnificent moment when we reach up to God.

It's not a matter of "repeating someone else's words." Yes, they are by and large the words of the Psalms of David, but those are not ordinary words. They are the very soul of the Jewish people. And as we participate in them, we slowly become part of the eternal dialogue between God and Israel. David and the other authors of our prayers were prophets and poets and religious geniuses — finely tuned Divine instruments. Anyone who has ever listened carefully to our worship service cannot fail to notice the careful architecture of the entire service: the preciseness of the *Amidah*; the rhythm of the Psalms; the precisely calibrated sections of the service which touch both the emotions and the intellect; the grace and vigor and power and resonance and sensitivity of the words and concepts.

As for repeating the same words every day, that is no more repetitive than listening to a magnificent symphony every day and finding new things in it each time we hear it. *The music of repetition* There is a unique structure to the prayers — from the acknowledgment of God when we first open our eyes in the morning, to the blessings upon arising, to the awareness of His presence through the Psalms, to the statement of faith in the *Shema*, to the various acknowledgments of God in the *Amidah* and its various supplications for life, wisdom, forgiveness, knowledge, health, return to Zion, through the denouement of the closing entreaty for the fulfillment of the Biblical promise of mankind's ultimate acceptance of the One God.

A long service is like a great work of art, a beautiful piece of music. It provides ascent and descent, moments of drama and moments for reflection and meditation. It provides an opportunity for the kind of thinking that you cannot do during the routine of daily life. For a brief moment in time, you are filled with spirituality and your soul leaps upward. This is called *deveikut*, cleaving to God, a moment when our soul and the spirit of God are united as one. At such rare moments, our entire being loses contact with the physical universe and clings spiritually to its Creator. Do you know what the medium is which can bring on such an exalted state? That oft-maligned, fixed, set, regular prayer book.

How to approach God There is one other aspect of fixed liturgy: it teaches us how to approach God. Our set prayers are models of worship, the way a Rembrandt is a model of painting, or Bach is a model of music. Because of this I am amused at the "liturgy committees" of modern Temples which write "original" prayers and make emendations to classical prayers, abbreviate them, "improve" them. It's as if we were to take laymen who know nothing about music — who never played an instrument, never studied music, cannot even read it, but who have a vague "feeling" for music and enjoy it — and appoint them to a committee to abbreviate or improve Bach or Beethoven. Actually, I am not amused but saddened by this, because it displays a total misunderstanding of what prayer is all about.

The fixed words in the Siddur set a mood that allows us to come into contact with God. Real contact does not happen every time we pray. It takes diligence, care, study, attention, concentration. The laws of prayer; the fixed times for specific services; the desirability of praying always in the same location in synagogue or at home; the whispering of the words, or the silent readings, or the proclaiming aloud; the various postures of prayer — standing, sitting, bowing, facing Jerusalem; the cadence of the text; the petitions and the praises — all are designed to help establish this mood and to achieve the ultimate goal of opening ourselves up to God and, in some mysterious way, communicating with Him. This takes constant practice, the way the musician practices daily, or the athlete. For it to succeed — and by success I mean to establish a genuine dialogue with God — it has to be done regularly, frequently, faithfully.

Granted, there is a tension between spontaneity and regularity, between an essentially emotional act and rules and regulations, between a pouring out of the soul to our Maker and a formal liturgy that sets the words out before us. But remember what it is that we're trying to do when we pray: we are trying to reach out to the great King of Kings. We cannot reach such a goal all on our own, without some assistance. A set liturgy directs us, guides us, gives us the tools, puts us in a frame of mind to be touched by God. And, by the way, the set liturgy makes everyone equal before God — because even the most inarticulate, unexpressive person now has an eloquent instrument with which to reach out to God.

D: But why do there have to be so many praises and halleluyahs? It all seems so repetitive and needless. Does God require all this flattery?

Does God require this flattery?

R: Firstly, a careful analysis of the praises — they are primarily from the Psalms — demonstrates that they are not merely repetitive. These are profound poems and hymns which have numerous layers of meaning. God does not require them; we require them. In actuality, they are the explosion of the soul at the shock of recognition of Who God really is. Once we realize who we are, and Who God is, and all the wondrous things He does, there can be no other response but this. What seems like repetitiveness is in fact the sounding of the great themes and grand motifs of the God-human relationship.

In adddition, these hymns establish the tone of prayer, which, as we have seen, is one of submission, surrender, vulnerability, dependence, and acknowledgment of God — called *ol Malchut Shamayim* in Hebrew, accepting the "yoke of the Kingdom of Heaven." Far from flattery or sycophancy, they are all expressions of our awe and wonder at the works and power of the Holy One. They help strip us of the arrogance and self-centeredness which, as we saw earlier, are the great barriers between us and God. And that in turn helps make us able to communicate to God and open to His influences. They soften our hard exteriors so that God can penetrate our hearts and guide us.

D: Speaking of praising God, I have always been puzzled by that formula when we recite a blessing: "Blessed art Thou, Lord our God, King of the universe," which is repeated so many hundreds of times for food, for commandments, and during general prayer. Who are we to bless God? Isn't it the other way around — that God should be blessing us?

R: Good question. The fact is that we are all victimized by the limits of translation. The Hebrew word which begins all these blessings is *baruch*, which has always been translated as "blessed," and which is connected with the word *berachah*, "blessing." But its meaning is far more profound. It bears the same root as the term for a natural spring of water, *bereichah*, which is to say that *baruch* connotes an ever-flowing, endless, and ever-increasing source. It also is connected to the word for "knee," *berech*, which implies bending at the knee, or submission. Thus, when we address God by this term, we are not blessing Him. Instead, we are acknowledging that He is the Source of everything, and that we submit our entire beings to Him. *Baruch* thus describes God as both "Source" and "One-to-Whom-we-submit." Admittedly, an endless and increasing source of goodness is a blessing in fact, but not in the sense that everyone reads the words "Blessed art Thou."

And while we're on the subject of blessings, let me point out something else quite fascinating. In the longer ones, which we recite prior to the performance of a mitzvah, there seems to be a lack of certainty about how to address God. The first part of each *berachah* addresses Him in the second person: "You." But the last half of each *berachah* uses the third person, "He," for we say, "Who has sanctified us with *His* commandments . . ." Surely the framers of the blessings, who weighed each word and syllable so carefully, did this deliberately. What did they have in mind?

What they tried to do was to express the dual nature of God's relationship with us: that He is close and yet distant; part of our world and yet above it; open yet concealed; clearly evident, and yet mysterious and hidden; immanent yet transcendent. The clear, open, immanent aspect of God is found in the first part of the *berachah*; the distant, concealed, transcendent aspect is found in the second part.

But we are digressing. All this discussion should not distract us from focusing on the ultimate essence of prayer. Three times a day we withdraw from our mundane pursuits in order to be alone with God. Three times a day we remind ourselves of our dependence on Him — and simultaneously of the great miracle that permits us to communicate with Him in the first place. We knock on God's door, so to speak, not to obtain a piece of chocolate, but to obtain a new perspective on ourselves, to discover who we really are and what we should become. By admitting God into our hearts, souls and minds, we are able to find our real selves. We ask His help in attaining a holy life, so that we will make the right decisions and not be tempted to abandon eternal things for temporary gain; and we pray for help to push back the underbrush and enable us to see that which is very obvious, but to which we are purblind: the hand of God in the ordinary events of the day. Prayer clarifies and refines reality, and helps us see things as they are. It helps us understand what matters and what does not matter. Once this occurs, we begin to behave differently, and ultimately we become better human beings: more decent, more honest, more compassionate — more like God wants us to be.

Keep in mind one other important point: as crucial as words are, and as much as they are the vehicles which articulate our soul's conversation with God, words are only the instrument of prayer. Ultimately, prayer goes beyond mere words. It is the resonance of the words that is crucial — what the words convey, the tone they set, the mood they establish, the feelings they engender. This is the key to real prayer. It helps us open the window to God and make ourselves accessible and reachable: I am here, God, I am open to You, I await Your subtle, hidden, unfelt but profound influence on how I live my day. Affect me, touch me, allow me to make the decisions that are right and best for me, for my loved ones, for my community, for the world, for the Jewish people, for You. Through the words and emotions of prayer, the window opens up; the rules surrounding them, the times of the prayers, their structure — all these help to keep that daily window open.

D: You seem to be saying that in prayer it is not so much that we have an influence on God, but that we open ourselves up to allow God to have an influence upon us. This puts an entirely different perspective on prayer.

R: Exactly. That's another reason Jewish prayer is called *avodah shebalev*, "the service which is in the heart." That is, prayer performs a function within the heart. It affects our heart, our spirit, and helps us realize our complete dependence upon God for our every need. Prayer is really soul-talk.

Why Hebrew? **D:** I'll have to give that more thought. By the way, we did not discuss why prayer has to be in Hebrew. Does not God understand all languages?

R: Of course, and the Talmud in *Sotah* 33a permits prayer in any language. But Hebrew is the preferred language of prayer, for a number of good reasons. Firstly, it is God's language, as Nachmanides demonstrates in his comment on *Exodus* 30:13. It is the language of the Creation, the language of the Torah, the language of Moses, the Prophets, and King David the Psalmist. It carries in it the soul of the Jewish people, our entire heritage and destiny. That's why we call it *Lashon Hakodesh*, the Holy Tongue. Clearly, anyone would want to pray to God in the language which He Himself sanctified and used as the vehicle to communicate His teachings to us.

Further, every Hebrew letter has meaning beyond its sound. Each letter has a numerical value, which undergirds every Biblical word with a mysterious cosmic force. The mystical sages tell us that God used these letters to create the world, because they are the raw material of Creation.

Even the shapes of the letters are significant. The *aleph* is formed in a certain way in order to express a certain idea. The shapes of the *bet* and *gimmel* express other concepts. Hebrew is more than just another language.

Certainly the prayers can be read in translation, but there is a huge difference between the subtlety and the spiritual resonance of, say, *Shema Yisrael* in the original Hebrew, and "Hear O Israel" in English. Even though the translation may be as accurate as possible, it cannot possibly capture all the nuances of the original, and therefore the impact upon the soul is considerably diminished in any language other than Hebrew. If the problem of translation exists in ordinary literature, how much more so in the emotional, subtle, spiritual realm of reaching out to God and into one's own self.

In addition, Hebrew connects us with past generations of Jews, all of whom uttered these very same words for thousands of years. So the answer is that yes, one can pray in any language, but the most powerful language of prayer is Hebrew.

D: Why use words at all? Why cannot prayer simply be thought? Must prayer be verbalized?

R: Good point. But words are what distinguish us from the beasts, and we use our most distinctive quality to reach Him — the quality which defines our humanness. Furthermore, when we read that God breathed the breath of life into Adam, that means that God actually gave him the power of speech. Therefore, when we seek God, it is appropriate that we utilize the very "breath" which He breathed into us.

D: All this helps me understand something that's been both- *God knows* ering me for a long time. I've often wondered: since God *everything;* knows everything and is aware of everything, why do we have *why ask* to ask Him for anything? Surely He knows what we need long *Him for* before we know it. But now I'm beginning to see that I've *anything?* been missing the point. When I pray for something, it's not that I'm informing God of something new; it's that I am open- ing up my soul for His presence to enter and to do for my life whatever He deems best. Simply to express this need to God is important: to know that I am in need, and to know that God is the One who answers needs. And even when I am not in need, just to be with Him and to communicate with Him on a very deep level. This is the point of prayer.

R: Very well said. You have been listening well.

D: And I think this may answer another key question that has *Does* been troubling me. Does prayer make God change His *prayer* mind? I'm not as clear about this, but I suspect that the *change* answer lies somewhere in the things we've been discussing. *God's*

R: This is a more difficult problem, but, as you say, the *mind?* answer is inherent in the things we have been talking about. God does not change His mind per se. But when, for example, we pray on Rosh Hashanah for life and peace and health, we are in fact saying to God that we wish to open our- selves up to Him. We want life so that we can serve Him, not merely in order to eat a few more steak dinners; we want health so that we can carry forth His work in the world, not merely in order that we should be able to do more fishing; we want prosperity so that we can afford to serve Him and help others to do so, not just to amass new possessions. In the deepest sense, when we ask for such things, the unstated and unwritten understanding is that we wish to continue our service of God in all of its ramifications, or, if we have not been serving Him at all, to begin serving Him in some small way. We're not asking Him to change His mind, but to change us so that we can become worthy of His blessings.

Take, for example, the story of Passover. The Israelites are told to slaughter a lamb and to smear the blood on their doorposts, and when the Angel of Death smites the Egyptians, he will pass over the homes of the Israelite and they will be saved. Now, if God wants to save the Israelites, why does He not just save them? Why must they go through this entire procedure?

Changing the individual   The answer is that God wants them to become worthy of being saved. They follow His instructions and commandments, which in itself sanctifies them and makes them worthy of being saved. They have become different from what they were before they fulfilled the commandment.

Let's use a more vivid example: when a person is ill, there are several possible heavenly scenarios: a) God has decreed that he shall not be healed; b) God has visited sickness upon him in order to humble him, to remind him that there is a God and that he is not the master.

In the second scenario, God wants him to pray as a manifestation of his new humbling. Thus, when he recovers, it is because God's purpose has been fulfilled, and there is no change of mind. In the first scenario, if the person recovers, it is because he has transformed himself into a new person. It is as if the decree was pronounced upon a different person; the man now praying for his life has changed and is not the same individual who was sentenced. That is, God's decree is sometimes conditional: if there is sincere contrition and prayer, the decree is rescinded; there is a reprieve and a pardon. But it all depends on the person.

Here, too, prayer does not change God's mind; it changes the individual, gives him a healthier perspective on life, and now that he has changed, the decree upon him can also change. In other words, prayer has influenced the individual himself and transformed him into a different person from what he was before he prayed. The decree no longer applies to him. This is the natural result of prayer.

There is yet another way to look at this problem of change of mind. God so created the universe that He made man His partner in governing the world. That is, He so willed it that man's deeds and strides — or mincing steps — toward perfection should have an impact upon God's actions. God wants to be prayed to, and genuine prayer has an effect on the course of events, cosmic and individual, for God so set things up in the first place. Thus, we find Abraham praying for the residents of Sodom; Isaac, on behalf of Rebecca; Jacob, that he be saved from the murderous Esau; Moses, on behalf of the Jewish people. And, of course, there is the magnificent supplication and outpouring of Hannah, the mother of Samuel the Prophet, at the beginning of *I Samuel*, which is, in fact, the epitome and model of all Jewish prayer.

In the final analysis, though, prayer does not always achieve the results man would like. God is under no obligation to answer all of our requests in the way we want Him to.

D: But does not God hear all of our prayers?

R: Yes. Our tradition refers to Him as *Shome'a Tefillah* — "He Who hears prayer." But He does not always respond in ways that please us, or that we can readily understand. God has a mission and a purpose for each one of us, and He will not grant requests which will interfere with that purpose. God answers each individual in the manner that is best for him or her. It may be that what we think we need is really not what is best calculated to carry out the mission He has ordained for us.

Does He listen?

Remember, incidentally, that even when He chooses not to respond in obvious ways, when we engage in prayer we are not only communicating with God above, but also acknowledging His Presence at significant moments of the day. We recite the *shacharit* service just when we arise from our long sleep at night, and even before we partake of food; *minchah* is in the middle of the working day, from which we break away to acknowledge God's presence; *maariv* takes place after the sun goes down and darkness has set in, and we are about to take leave of the waking world for many hours.

Staying in touch with the self   Beyond acknowledging God's Presence, prayer helps us stay in touch with our own selves within. During prayer we withdraw from the daily struggle of living. We step back and look at life from the perspective of eternity. When we really pray properly, some of the issues in our lives which so occupy us and tear away at us turn out to be much less crucial than we had imagined. We begin to see life in a new way, and we learn to distinguish the significant from the trivial, and what really matters from what doesn't. One of the great things that genuine prayer does for us is to provide us with a fresh point of view.

D: I suppose, when you get right down to it, that this whole area of prayer is so mysterious and so awesome that one has to pray to God and ask Him to help us understand what prayer is all about.

R: Yes, and you can do that spontaneously, in any language you like, at any time. Remember, that was one of the great prayers of Moses himself in *Exodus* 32: he wanted to know the essence of God, and he prayed to God to reveal Himself fully to him.

D: There is a lot of work to do before I can learn to pray properly. Maybe I'll begin by following the example of Moses and pray that I should be able to pray.

tORAh – the jew leARns god's wisdom

. . . in which is discussed . . . The origin of the Torah / Revelation and human reason / The bridge from heaven to earth / The Ten Commandments and the 613 / Who interprets Torah today? / Oral and written Torah / The shape of tefillin / Torah and personal freedom / To penetrate the mind of God / Why Torah study is the supreme commandment / Three pathways to God / God reading His blueprint / The joys of Torah study / The ongoing encounter . . .

David: You've been using the word "Torah" constantly, taking for granted that I know precisely what you mean by it, but I think it's time to discuss the whole concept in a little more depth. I'm not quite sure that I understand what Torah really is, what we mean when we say that God gave the Torah to the Jewish people, and why study of the Torah seems to be such a major principle of Judaism.

Rabbi: That's a tall order, but you are certainly on the mark, so let's make an effort to clarify those issues. We'll look at the most important idea first — the origin of the Torah

— because that's obviously the foundation on which classical Judaism rests.

Origin of Torah   To put a very complex matter simply, and to get directly to the heart of the matter, let me say that if Torah is not the word of God, then it really has no claims upon us to follow it. Why should we sacrifice anything, even our comfort, much less our very lives, for something written by other human beings, even great ones — who lived thousands of years ago? I wouldn't give up my life for Shakespeare or for Aristotle. But if, as Jews have always firmly believed, it is the Word of God and the Will of God, we are seriously obligated to obey it, study it, and live by it. And we can be called upon to make great sacrifices for it.

D: That is a very neat formulation. But obviously not all Jews see it quite that way.

R: Let's face it: most Jews, except the committed ones, don't think about it at all. And certain segments of American Judaism have attempted to have it both ways: it is the word of God, but then again, maybe it is not; it is the word of God, but only those sections which do not inconvenience us; it is the word of God, but only those parts that we can understand. And, of course, there are those who reject entirely the idea of Torah as the Word of God, but consider it to have been written by very wise men whom we respect, but since we in our day are also wise, we can change, adjust, and calibrate it according to our own needs.

The sad fact is, however, that those groups that have been unable to come to terms with the Divine origin of the Torah are having a difficult time in stemming assimilation and intermarriage within their ranks, and are experiencing serious problems in holding on to their young people. It is an indisputable fact that an alarming number of these young people are abandoning Judaism entirely and drifting off into assimilation and intermarriage, or, at best, complete indifference to Judaism. I don't think this is a coincidence.

D: Why do you say that?

R: Because every single study shows that the less one believes in the Divinity of the Torah — the less observant one is, the less conscious one is of one's Jewishness — the greater the incidence of assimilation and intermarriage. This should come as no shock to anyone. I take no joy or comfort in watching this tragedy unfold before our very eyes, but the fact is that it is taking place.

I suspect that many of the young generation perceive in these philosophies a certain intellectual inconsistency and flabbiness, a kind of consumer-oriented religion in which the customer is always right and in which contemporary fashion rather than eternal truths dictate the teachings of the religion. I also sense a yearning for a religious life with more mystery and passion and heart and emotion, which these groups have been unable to supply. It is hard to get excited about a hybrid religion that is a kind of half-divine centaur — half God and half human. And certainly it is difficult to work up passion or sacrifice for a completely man-made religion which takes its religious cues from the daily paper. So they drop out entirely, or, here and there, wander into cults like "Jews for Jesus" or so-called "Jewish-Christians." A surprising number are even moving over into the Orthodox camp — that is to say, back to classical Judaism — where they find a Judaism that is profound, mysterious, challenging, intellectually consistent and emotionally satisfying.

But I don't want to go too far afield. I am only illustrating *Revelation* that if we really want to understand who we are as Jews, we really need to come to grips with the idea of Revelation and of Torah as the Word of God. After all, we're talking about the Eternal Constitution of the Jews, not just an *ad hoc* code of conduct.

D: Agreed. Let's start from the beginning. What do we mean when we say that the Torah is the Word of God?

R: There are many implications to that concept, but first let's look at some basics. The classic Hebrew term is *Torah min haShamayim,* literally "Torah from Heaven," Divine Revelation. That is to say that God revealed His Torah to us at Sinai through the awesome Revelation so vividly described in *Exodus* 19:

> . . . *there was thunder and lightning and a heavy cloud on the mountain, and the sound of the shofar was very powerful, and the entire people that was in the camp*

shuddered . . . all of Mount Sinai was smoking because God had descended upon it in the fire; its smoke ascended like the smoke of the furnace, and the entire mountain shuddered exceedingly. The sound of the shofar grew continually much stronger . . .

At this magnificent moment in history, God shares with His people Israel His own essence that is embodied in the Ten Commandments — which themselves are representative of the entire Torah. Through the agency of the Torah, God invites us to attach our lives to Him, and thus to give ourselves joy, tranquility, and fulfillment. He tells us explicitly in the Torah, especially in *Deuteronomy* (11:26-28; chapters 27 and 28; 30:15), that to live by the Torah's guidelines is to have life; to reject them is to reject God and to spell doom for ourselves as individuals and as a people.

I am running away with my thoughts, because *Torah min haShamayim* is so basic to us as Jews, but this is the core of it.

D: Is this one of those aspects of Judaism that must be accepted on faith alone?

The claims of Moses **R:** It is a matter of faith and belief, yes, because I am not able to prove to you conclusively that the Torah is from heaven. Nevertheless, it is faith buttressed by a great deal of compelling reason and logic. For example, it makes excellent sense that God should want to reveal His Torah to us. He is, after all, our Creator, and He is also the very embodiment of goodness. It follows, therefore, that He would not have created us and placed us on this earth to fend for ourselves without some guidelines for survival. This would have been the very opposite of goodness. His Torah is that primer for survival — and obviously more than mere survival, because it teaches us how to transform life on this earth into something worthwhile and joyous.

D: That may be so, but not necessarily. Besides, wouldn't one expect the Torah to claim authority for itself by basing itself on a Revelation from God?

R: True, but here too there is a basis in reason. Note that the Torah tells us that there were some two to three million witnesses to this claim — six hundred thousand men between the ages of twenty and sixty, plus women, older and younger men, and children. Moses doesn't come down from the mountain claiming that secret, mysterious things happened to him while he was up there all by himself. He doesn't ask them simply to take his word for it. The very Torah which Moses brings to the people states that the Revelation was witnessed by all the people. Certainly if this claim were false, any one of them — all of them — would have risen up to call Moses a liar!

Furthermore, Moses dares make a claim, in *Deuteronomy* 4:32, that would have been foolhardy were he fabricating the concept of Revelation. He states that no nation other than the Jews has ever claimed, or will ever claim, to have received God's word directly from Him in public. This statement is subject to empirical examination — and the fact is that what he said then remains true even until today: no other religion has ever made this kind of claim.

This is why I say that Divine Revelation, which is by definition miraculous, and the claim that it took place before multitudes and not before a few select people, is not a matter of faith alone but is supported by reason.

Make no mistake about it. The citation from *Exodus* which I cited earlier is more than just a vivid description of a historical event. It also shows why the sound of God's voice speaking directly to us created a profound and permanent effect on the soul of the Jewish people. Granted, we do not claim to understand precisely what is meant by "sound" and "voice" in regard to God — human language and words are inadequate vehicles with which to convey what actually took place — but suffice it to say that it was an unmistakable experience of communication and connectedness from the Divine realm to the human realm. This experience was so shattering and so profound that it entered our spiritual genes, so to speak, and made it possible for the Jewish people to believe in God and in the Divinity of the Torah forever.

The human encounter with God

The fact is that this Divine Revelation at Sinai is the most significant event in the history of mankind. Consider: God appears before the entire people Israel and through Moses presents the Torah to them. In a very real sense, this is an event as momentous as Creation itself, because when you think it through, the ultimate purpose of Creation is that mankind should live by the values of the Torah; and when God finally decides to give this Torah to mankind via the Jewish people, that event represents the climax and completion of Creation itself.

There is more: not only is the event itself staggering, overwhelming and unprecedented, but the very fact of God's Revelation to us demonstrates that there can be a direct Divine-human encounter, that God is concerned with His creatures and does communicate with us. This in itself is a basis of our belief in God, and it underlies the entire concept of prayer: God listens, God is concerned, God responds.

Only the Ten Command-ments

D: I have always been under the impression that the Divinity of the Torah applies only to the Ten Commandments.

R: Not so. The Ten Commandments contain the essence of the Torah, and its main principles. But all of the 613 commandments — these ten plus the other 603 — stem from God and are of equal holiness.

D: Well, let's grant that I do believe in the Divine origin of the Torah. Then what? What are the implications for my life?

R: Well, for one thing, if you believe in the Divinity of the Torah, it has a powerful hold on you. It is God speaking to you in your daily life. With this awareness, you can hardly turn your back on God, or ignore Him, or be dilatory about doing His will. And since God Who gave the Torah does not change, and truth does not change, it follows that the Torah which He gave us also does not change. This is why the Torah describes itself as *chukat olam*, "an everlasting statute." We all understand that "Thou shalt not kill" does not change. In the same way, all the commandments are eternal. And it specifically forbids us to add laws to it or to subtract from it, as in *Deuteronomy* 4:2, 13:1 and 29:28. One does not add or subtract from that which is already perfect.

D: But times change, situations change: how is Torah, even though it is eternal, applied to new conditions?

R: The Written Torah itself has its own mechanism which *Torah* allows for the Torah to be applied to every generation and to *and* every new and changing situation. This is done by duly qualified *change* sages and scholars who are empowered to apply the principles of the Torah to every conceivable scenario. *Deuteronomy* 17:11 specifically says that we are to follow their decisions, "according to the teaching that they will teach you, and according to the judgment that they will say to you, you shall do . . ."

D: Just who are these people? Does every rabbi today have the right to make his own interpretations?

R: Not at all. Only those world-class scholars who are universally recognized for their learning, piety, and unimpeachable integrity, who devote their entire lives to the study of both the Written and the Oral Torah, who are loyal to its precepts, who are profoundly familiar with its principles of halachic interpretation, who are intellectually brilliant, and who are spiritual giants, have the authority in every generation to rule on fundamental matters of Jewish law and Jewish practice. Maimonides, for example, was such a person in his time. The Gaon of Vilna, Rabbi Joseph Caro — and the Chazon Ish and Rabbi Moshe Feinstein in contemporary times — all were such people who were universally recognized by world-class Torah scholars as being a kind of unofficial Jewish Supreme Court. These and other sages were given the right by that verse in *Deuteronomy* 17 to apply and interpret the laws of the Torah.

Their works and legal opinions and decisions are preserved in what is called the Responsa literature — responses that they wrote to questions and problems submitted to them by individuals and communities — and they serve as a further basis for applying the Torah to every conceivable scenario. This is an ongoing process up to and including this very day. What is the Jewish attitude towards abortion, or towards surrogate motherhood? What about so-called mercy killings, or brain death? May a Jew hold shares in a company which is engaged in selling weapons of destruction? The list goes on and on, and the decisors of our day are prepared to deal with every new eventuality from the perspective and principles of Torah law.

The
Oral Torah

D: You referred a minute ago to Oral Torah, but you'll have to explain what you mean by that.

R: It is in effect the twin of the Written Torah as the fundamental source of authority in Judaism. Without the Oral Torah, we cannot possibly know what the Written Torah really means. They go hand in glove and are really inseparable. For example, the Written Torah, on the face of it, clearly prohibits work on the Shabbat. But when you examine it, it turns out to be ambiguous. What is the definition of work? So the Oral Torah — which came down to us together with the Written Torah — defines this for us.

Or when *Exodus* 16:29 says, "No man shall leave his place on the seventh day," what does that mean? Are we forbidden to leave our houses, or cities, or rooms on the Sabbath? Or when we are commanded that "thou shalt bind [the words of the Torah] for a sign upon thy hand and for frontlets between thy eyes, and thou shalt write them on the doorposts of thy house and thy gate," how do we know that these refer to the tefillin and the mezuzah? And how do we derive the square shape and black color of tefillin, or the content of mezuzot? Only because the oral tradition tells us. I like to think of the Oral Torah as the soul and spirit of the Written Torah, for without it, the Written Torah would remain incomprehensible and unworkable.

That a complementary law system was well known is clear from some of the prophets, who refer to certain details not found in the Written Torah. *Jeremiah* 17:21-22 refers to the prohibitions about carrying on Shabbat, which are not mentioned in the Written Torah, but which emanate directly from the Oral Torah. Similarly, *I Samuel* 8:11 mentions certain laws regarding the Israelite king which are found only in the oral tradition. Another example: there is no specific written prohibition in the Torah concerning doing business on Shabbat, but *Nehemiah* 10:32 refers to it as part of "God's Torah given to Moses . . ." And *Nehemiah* 13:15-17 lists a number of Shabbat restrictions that are not found in the Written Torah.

Let me be more specific. The Oral Torah is that body of traditional learning, interpretation and exposition which originates at Sinai and continues in an unbroken oral chain until it is finally recorded in the form of Mishnah and Gemara — which together are called "Talmud." This Oral Torah was communicated by God to Moses at Sinai as a supplement to the Written Torah, and in each subsequent generation the duly constituted religious and rabbinic authorities applied the teachings of the Written and Oral Torah to the ever-changing conditions of life and society. The end result was that the Oral Torah, because of its intrinsic fluidity, kept the Written Torah from becoming a frozen, distant book, and instead maintained it as a living, breathing organism. By the way, the punctuation and pronunciation of the words of the Torah — and according to some opinions, even the cantillation notes of the public Torah chanting — are part of the Oral Torah.

This means that the concept of *Torah min haShamayim* applies to the Oral Torah as well as to the Written. It is a good idea to study Maimonides' Introduction to the Talmud — which is available in English — in which he details the transmission of the Oral Torah through forty generations — from the times of Moses until Ravina and Rav Ashi of the fifth century C.E., the redactors of the Talmud.

D: And when we say "Torah," what precisely do we mean by that term?

Meaning of Torah

R: Important point. "Torah" literally means "teaching," or "instruction," or "doctrine." In its most narrow sense, Torah refers to the Pentateuch, which we call the *Chumash,* or the Five Books of Moses. In a wider sense, the Written Torah includes all the Biblical books after the Five Books — from *Joshua* all the way through *Chronicles.* There are twenty-four books in all, divided into three segments: Torah, Prophets, and Writings — (in Hebrew: *Torah, Neviim, Ketuvim*) whose acronym in Hebrew is *TaNaKh.* And in a still wider sense, Torah includes the entire Oral Torah — by which I mean the Talmud, which consists of Mishnah and Gemara. These last three terms, by the way, each mean the same thing: "learning" or "study."

The Mishnah, which was essentially oral but was committed to writing in the second century of the Common Era, is a type of code of Jewish law which tells us what is prohibited and permitted, and how and when to perform the various mitzvot.

Mishnah and Gemara

Every individual Mishnah engenders a comprehensive discussion and analysis. This is found in the Gemara, which consists basically of the discussions of the Sages who lived in Palestine and Babylonia between the second and fifth centuries. But because this is a record of the debates and dialogues which took place in their learned schools (and were ultimately reduced to writing in the fifth century of the Common Era) the analysis frequently veers off into history, instructional narratives and philosophic observations. It is not an easy study; it requires intense concentration and intellectual discipline. But it is probably one of the most fascinating and absorbing studies that mankind has ever known.

Foundation of Jewish law Mishnah and Gemara — that is to say, the Talmud — constitute the foundation for all of Jewish law — which is known by the term halachah, "the way," or "the going" with God. One cannot fully comprehend Jewish law and its history and development without at least a working knowledge of Talmud in the original.

The Talmudic period is followed by the age of the Jewish law codes, the greatest embodiment of which is the classic "Mishnah Torah" of Maimonides, who lived in the twelfth century. In this monumental code, he gleans from the vast amalgam of Torah and Talmud and law codes which preceded him, the essential practices which a Jew is to follow.

D: This discussion we're having right now — is this part of Torah?

R: Definitely. In essence, what this means is that while we believe in the Revelation of God and Torah at Sinai, Torah in its broadest sense is not a finished system, but is an ongoing search for eternal truth, a search that continues in every generation. Torah is thus the oldest book we know, and also the most contemporary and immediate. The students and teachers of Torah in every generation transform it from a closed book into an open book, into a living tradition. And God looks at every student of Torah as if that student were standing once again at Sinai accepting the Commandments. So you can see how and why the study of Torah is pervasive in Judaism — in fact its dominant feature. No facet of life, intellectual or emotional, is untouched by Torah.

D: This is what frightens me about it. If it is so all-embracing, what happens to personal autonomy? Are we left with any freedom at all?

R: "Personal autonomy" is a term that needs some refining, *Personal* and would bring us into another discussion altogether. But *freedom* if you are asking if in Judaism we have the right to make our own decisions without regard to a higher authority, I must tell you that in Judaism only God is autonomous.

The truth is, however, that living the Torah life provides real freedom in its genuine sense. Genuine freedom means not being enslaved to one's own instincts or to the dictates of the society around us. It does not confer license to do as we please, or endorse complete absence of discipline. It means having a vision and a purpose and following it. That's what the Mishnah in *Avot* 6:2 means when it says that "one is not free unless he labors in Torah." This is alluded to by the similarity between the Hebrew word for "engraved" in Exodus 32:16, which says that the letters of the Commandments were "engraved (*charut*) on the tablets," and the word for "freedom," *cherut*. Both words are spelled חרות, only the vowels are different. The implication is that the tablets contained not only the engraved words of the Commandments, but also the idea of true freedom.

In any case, even when we live by Torah we retain a large degree of autonomy. Even though no laws or commandments of the Torah can be tampered with or changed, there remains nevertheless a broad framework for our own judgment and decision making. In fact, the major characteristic of the Talmud is its relentless questioning and probing. Nothing is taken for granted — except the existence of God and the Divinity of the Torah.

But let us not get caught up in questions like personal free- *To* dom or autonomy, interesting as they are. The real issue in *penetrate* study of Torah is the effort to penetrate heaven — to know and *heaven* ascertain God's Will. This transcends all other questions; it even goes beyond the issue of knowing the background and the rationale behind the laws. What really matters is: How does God want us to live our lives on this earth? How does He want us to relate to other human beings, to other non-human creatures, to the physical world which surrounds us? When these become overriding concerns, a Jew who immerses himself in study of Torah becomes not only a learned Jew, but a different Jew entirely. Because when the mind is occupied with such matters, wondrous things occur — not only to the mind, but to the entire person as well.

D: Speaking of the mind, I have heard that the study of Torah is considered to be the most important commandment of all. Why does Judaism place such heavy emphasis on studying this Torah?

R: Before I answer, let me make your question even stronger. You probably don't realize that countless thousands of Jews throughout the world — laborers, businessmen, professionals — are engaged in regular, daily, ongoing study of Torah in one form or another. They study Mishnah or Talmud or Bible or the Codes daily in groups or alone — early in the morning, before they go off to their work, or every night, or during their lunch breaks. And I mean daily, including Shabbat and Yom Tov. This takes place in every major Jewish community in the world: in London and Paris and Amsterdam and Johannesburg and Melbourne and Washington and New York and Los Angeles and Chicago and Denver and Miami and Baltimore and Atlanta and Boston. And it goes without saying that in Jerusalem alone — not to mention the rest of Israel — there are thousands of such groups, literally. So we can expand your question and ask: What motivates all these people from various backgrounds — physicians and mathematicians and grocers and plumbers and writers and teachers and scientists and rabbis and poets and businessmen and mechanics and engineers — to devote so much energy and time and love — to the study of Torah?

D: Now that's a very good question. Why?

Emphasis *R:* For one thing, study of Torah is a specific commandment
on Torah in *Deuteronomy* 6:6, which we recite daily in the *Shema*:
study *veshinantam levanecha,* "thou shalt teach them thoroughly to thy children . . ." — which directs us to transmit Torah to the next generation; *vedibarta bam . . .* "and thou shalt speak of

them [the words of the Torah] while you sit in your home, while you walk on the way, when you retire and when you arise" — which directs us to study the Torah ourselves. This need to devote ourselves to knowing the Torah, to work at it, to strive to comprehend it, to give it first priority, is repeated over and over again throughout the Bible. The very first chapter of *Joshua* repeats the motif: *vehagita bo yomam valaylah,* "thou shalt occupy thyself in it day and night."

Beyond this, when a Jew opens his mind and heart to Torah study, he is opening up his mind to God's will and to God's wisdom — which by itself would be sufficient to explain why we place such emphasis on studying it. And it is obvious that without Torah study we would quite simply not know how to behave as Jews. It is only through study of God's word that we discover what God expects of us.

And there is something else as well: our history demonstrates that the moment study of Torah is neglected, assimilation of the Jewish people into its surroundings makes its inroad. Without fail, every Jewish community in history that did not teach and study Torah as its first priority gradually disappeared from the scene.

Beyond all the good, rational reasons, Torah is the mysterious bridge which connects the Jew and God, across which they interact and communicate, and by means of which God fulfills His covenant with His people to sustain them and protect them. *The mysterious bridge*

It is therefore no surprise that Torah study is so central with us. It is the first blessing a newborn child receives: "May he grow up to Torah, the wedding canopy, and to good deeds." The lullabyes of Jewish mothers through the ages sang of Torah as the *beste sechorah,* "the best merchandise." The prayer book is filled with petitions to God to help us understand His Torah. No wonder R. Akiva in the Talmud, in *Berachot* 61b, states that to expect a Jew to live without Torah is like expecting a fish to live without water. That's because the fact is that the Torah is the essence of the Jewish people, our very life and soul, and without it we literally have no existence. This magnificent Divine-human encounter is summed up by the Zohar at *Leviticus, Acharei,* 73a: "The Holy One Blessed Is He, Israel, and the Torah are all one." That has many layers of meaning, but at the very simplest level it states that all three components are irrevocably intertwined.

This explains why, in a traditional Jewish community, the one who is looked up to and most admired is the scholar of Torah — not the entertainer, or the athlete, or the very wealthy man. Which, by the way, says a great deal for the traditional Jewish community, because a people is distinguished by what it reveres and looks up to.

I doubt that very many of those thousands who are devoting their time to exploring Torah would give you precisely this answer, but it is this which lies at the bottom of it. They are in fact engaged in discovering the essence of Judaism, which is to say, the essence of themselves.

D: In other words, the commandment to study Torah is more than just another "thou-shalt." Torah study seems to be the commandment par excellence.

R: Quite true. Because in addition to what we said before, study of Torah represents one of three major pathways to God. One path is through the heart and the emotions, which is best exemplified by prayer — as we have already discussed. Another is through action, the performance of mitzvot: observing Shabbat and Yom Tov, kashruth, giving *tzedakah*, posting the mezuzah, doing kindness, donning tefillin. A third path is through the human intellect, through our ability to think and question and analyze. This is best exemplifed by study of Torah.

But Torah is more than just study, intellect, and analysis. Torah requires action, doing, performing of commandments. Torah study in the abstract without Torah living is without meaning. And this is not all: Torah also requires the heart, the affect, the feelings and emotions. It becomes part of us and reaches us not only through the mind. If we do not open our hearts to Torah, we will never know it.

Three paths to God It turns out, therefore, that Torah combines within itself the three pathways to God: heart, action, and intellect. So what you heard is quite accurate. Our Sages do say that of all the mitzvot and of all the approaches to God, the study of Torah is the mitzvah par excellence, that it outweighs them all: *Talmud Torah keneged kulam* (Peah 1:1; Shabbat 127a).

I hope it's becoming clear why Torah study is so unique. When we study Torah, we are not studying an abstract and arcane text of the ancient world. We are studying the way in which God wants us to live on this earth. And in a very real way, by careful study of Torah we are, in a manner of speaking, entering into the "mind" of God. This is no small achievement.

Which explains why the study of Torah is unlike all other mitzvot. With other mitzvot, such as placing a mezuzah on the doorpost, or observing the Shabbat, the mitzvah is completed once we perform the act. Even the mitzvah of *gemilut chasadim*, doing acts of lovingkindness, has its own built-in limits. For example, in giving charity, you are not required to give more than a fifth of your earnings. And, of course, if there is no one for whom you can do *chesed*, you cannot possibly do this mitzvah.

Torah study, however, is the only actional mitzvah which has no beginning and no end. It is constant, ongoing, and requires no other participant but you. And as long as you are alive, you are under the obligation to study — by day and by night, in sickness and in health — always. It demands your best energies, and demands them constantly, not merely occasionally. This is precisely how Maimonides puts it: "Every Israelite is under an obligation to study Torah, be he rich or poor, healthy or sick, young or old or infirm, in fulfillment of *Joshua* 1:8: 'Thou shalt speak therein day and night.'"

The limitless commandment

D: If the obligation to study Torah is so all-pervasive, when does a religious Jew have time to earn a living — or even to perform any of the other commandments?

R: The obligation to study is constant and ongoing, but one is absolved from this obligation in order to perform the necessary functions of life such as earning a livelihood, or serving God, or praying, or observing the commandments. I am merely stressing that, all other things being equal, the study of Torah is paramount and takes precedence.

D: If study of Torah outweighs all other mitzvot, isn't that really saying that some mitzvot are more important than others? But you keep saying they all have the same value.

God studies his own blueprint

R: In general, we do not weigh the value of mitzvot; we are supposed to give them all equal weight. But Torah study is obviously in a category by itself. For example, there is a startling image in the Talmud (*Avodah Zara* 3b; *Bava Metzia* 86a) that portrays God Himself as studying Torah: "one-third of the day He studies Bible and Mishnah . . ." We don't know precisely what that means, but it does hint at the identity between Torah and God.

This echoes that other very well-known and suggestive tradition — that Torah is the blueprint God used when He created the universe (*Zohar* II, p. 161a, *Terumah*). And a number of other sources (*Chagigah* 13b; *Zevachim* 116a; *Shabbat* 88b; *Bereishit Rabba* 1:4) repeat this remarkable idea that the Torah existed before the Creation of the world .

So Torah is clearly much more than God's Divine roadmap for us. It is in fact the foundation stone of the universe; it is His spirit in the form of words and sentences; it is idea wrapped in physical garb.

In other words, Torah study is a commandment unlike any other, because one is studying *Torat chaim*, "the Torah of life." Quite literally it is life-giving to the world, to the Jewish people as a whole, and to the individual Jew. In fact, a Torah scroll is treated as if it were a living creature: we stand up before it and give it reverence; if it should fall in our presence we are required to fast and do penitence; if it is destroyed, those witnessing it have to rend their garments, just as they do when they witness a human death; a destroyed or useless scroll is buried, as is a human being. All this is because both the Torah and living creatures are vehicles for spirituality.

By the way, one of the striking side benefits of Torah study is that it brings genuine joy to an individual. Did you know, for example, that a person who is sitting *shiv'ah* in mourning for a loved one is forbidden to study Torah — precisely because Torah study engenders joy, which is unbecoming during the week of mourning? Isn't that remarkable? Music is forbidden during the mourning period — and so is Torah study! For the same reason, study of Torah is forbidden on the national day of mourning which is Tishah B'Av, the Ninth of Av, when the entire community of Israel mourns the destruction of the Holy Temples.

The fact is that a true Torah scholar is a joyous person. *The joys* Psalm 19 says it magnificently: *of Torah*

> *The Torah of God is complete, soothing the soul; the testimony of God is trusting, giving wisdom to the foolish; the laws of God are straight, giving joy to the heart; the commandments of God are clear, enlightening the eyes.*

D: If study of Torah is the paramount mitzvah, it is more important than the practice of the mitzvot. But I thought that the key to Judaism was practice of the mitzvot.

R: An excellent point. In fact, you touch on a famous discussion in the Talmud. In *Kiddushin* 40b, the Sages discuss the relative merit of study versus practice. R. Tarfon maintains that practice is greater, while R. Akiva holds that study is greater. The Sages come down finally on the side of R. Akiva — that study is greater, but only because it leads to practice. Maimonides codifies this in his Laws of Talmud Torah 3:3, where he says: "There is no mitzvah among all the mitzvot which is equal to the study of Torah; the study of Torah outweighs them all because study leads to action; therefore, study precedes action in every place."

D: But that's illogical! If Torah study outweighs them all because it leads to action, then Torah study is *less important* than what it leads to. Action should be more important than Torah, because how to act seems to be the ultimate purpose of Torah study.

R: Again a fine point. Action, as R. Tarfon claims, is really most important, since the ultimate purpose of Creation is to carry out God's word in the finite reality of this world, and thus to elevate and sanctify the physical. But you can't do this fully without mastering Torah first. Clearly there is a tension here, because when you have a personal mitzvah obligation that only you and no one else can do, you are required to interrupt your study of Torah in order to do that mitzvah. *Talmud Torah keneged kulam* really means that the sanctity of Torah is greater, because we are in direct contact with God when we study His "mind." Nevertheless, we have to forgo this sanctity in order to implement the purpose of Creation through our deeds.

In practical terms, study and practice go hand in glove and are virtually inseparable. A true scholar of Torah not only studies, but practices what he studies; and a truly pious Jew not only practices, but studies what he practices.

What emerges from all this is that Torah study is more than the mere accumulation of knowledge. For one thing, because it is God's word, it cannot help but have a major impact on our behavior, character, and outlook on life. The Sages say that God gave us Torah and mitzvot in order to elevate us and purify us (*Bereishit Rabbah* 44:1). Its values become internalized within us, and it has the power to change individuals, families, communities, and entire societies. Jews have always found that something remarkable happens when we study Torah and allow its ways and its values to become a part of ourselves: we begin imperceptively to approach life in a different way.

D: Listen, I try to be a good person and to do the right thing, but not because I am forced to do so. Just because the Torah says to love thy neighbor, and just because a person studies the Torah, do you really think that's going to make a hateful man change his nature?

Magic on the soul

R: Being a "good person" and doing the "right thing" are generalities. Judaism is primarily an actional religion, not merely theoretical. It seeks to transform good intentions into good deeds; that is, to transform the ordinary into something sacred. You may by nature be a good person, but study of Torah will help you to actualize it, and tell you how to channel your good intentions into good deeds — how and when to give charity, how and when to visit the sick, how and when to attend the dead, how and when to help the downtrodden. We will discuss this in greater detail when we talk about interpersonal relationships.

As for the person who is by nature hateful, if he allows himself to be exposed to Torah long enough, he will find himself gradually changing. Each mitzvah, each word of Torah, is holy, and as such it works its own special magic on the soul.

D: Really? How?

R: For one thing, the Torah and its mitzvot constantly remind us of God. A person who is always aware of God's presence will not readily steal, or plunder, or think exclusively of himself. I am not suggesting that every observant Jew is perfect. But certainly there is less crime and less immorality among observant Jews than elsewhere. Just ask the police if they are kept busy in observant Jewish neighborhoods. That's because Torah creates within us a quality of self-discipline without which a person cannot possibly function effectively as a human being. Further, it maintains our identity and unity as a people. How long do you think the Jewish people would have survived without Torah and its mitzvot?

Over and above all this, when you get right down to it, study of Torah is a form of worship of God. And if I may say so, it's a kind of conversation between the Jew and God which began at Sinai and goes on into eternity. All this affects us as individuals.

D: That's all very pretty, but if I may say so, if this is a true conversation how do I get to hear God's end of the conversation? Sometimes it's rather hard to make out.

R: It's not always apparent, but in the very words of the Torah is His conversation. In His own hidden way, God responds to each individual through the Torah, and the amount of response we hear from Him depends on the amount of effort we put into Torah practice and study. What I mean is that when our minds become preoccupied and caught up with Torah and its ideas, it stands to reason that the mind itself becomes sanctified. Trivialities and foolishness slowly get filtered out, so that we are no longer dominated by them. The mind gradually becomes a repository for holy things. It becomes a kind of holy vessel which is now able to absorb thoughts and concepts and ideas which previously had been foreign to it. In other words, as the mind is saturated with Torah, the common, the ordinary, and the unsacred are crowded out, and suddenly there is space into which God's presence can enter.

All this affects not only our ability to understand Torah and the will of God, but it also affects our ordinary, mundane thoughts and activities. It is indirect, but in a very real way this is God conversing with us, responding to us, making contact with us. We begin to think differently, react differently, behave differently.

D: I suppose that in time I will understand that a little better, although it is a striking idea. But let me be frank with you: it all seems so overwhelming. I'm perfectly willing to concede that Torah is very likely the word of God — though I probably could not defend that position logically — but I'm not sure I'm quite ready to make Torah study that pervasive in my personal life.

The *R:* I can understand that you are not ready to give it a great
Jewish deal of time. But you must understand that without some
crown continuing study and learning, even a minimal few minutes each day, your Jewish life will atrophy and dry up.

D: What happens if I find out I'm not cut out for serious study?

R: You don't have to set out to become the world's greatest Judaic scholar. One small step at a time is sufficient. Slow, steady, gradual learning is the key to growing as a Jew. And bear in mind that in Judaism, Torah learning is not reserved just for the privileged few or for an intellectual elite. Judaism allows everyone to become part of the aristocracy of the learned, and learning is in fact open to everyone. The greatest compliment Jewish tradition gives to Moses is to call him "Moshe Rabbeinu," "Moses our teacher" — the one who transmits Torah to all of Israel, not just to the few. The Jewish community is blessed with many outstanding teachers who are ready to transmit the Torah to anyone who wants to listen. Torah, remember, is compared to water: just as water is free to everyone, so is Torah free to everyone. But be humble, because just as water flows to the lowest point, so Torah enters the hearts of those who are humble before God.

Maimonides, in his Laws of Talmud Torah 3:1, cites the classic statement of our Sages that God gave Israel three crowns: those of priesthood, of kingship, and of Torah. The crown of priesthood was given to Aaron, and the crown of kingship, to David — which means that priesthood and kingship come only through inheritance. But the crown of Torah, continues Maimonides, is availabe to all Israel equally. As he puts it, "The crown of Torah — let anyone who desires it come and take it." *Deuteronomy* 33:4 says it this way: "Moses commanded us a Torah, an inheritance of the congregation of Jacob": the entire community has a right to it. This is what is meant by our being "a kingdom of priests and a holy nation." In this respect, everyone can be a priest, everyone can be holy, and everyone can be learned. One just has to want it strongly enough, and be willing to give it the time and energy it requires.

I see you squirming a bit, so let me quickly add that although we are required to study Torah, we are not required to know all of Torah. We are only asked to expend our best efforts. When we meet our Maker, says the Talmud in *Shabbat* 31b, we will be asked several key questions about how we lived our lives on this earth. One of the questions will deal with our study of Torah. Interestingly enough, we will not be asked how much of Torah we know, but simply, "Did you set aside a regular time for the study of Torah?" *"Did you try?"*

One has to begin gradually. Don't be fearful of how much remains to be done. All learning is cumulative. If you do it steadily, with discipline and perseverance and, yes, without anxiety, you will be astonished at the amount of progress you can make in a relatively short time.

And it is a very exciting project: to unlock the sources of our faith, which is the world's greatest religious and intellectual tradition — to learn about its origins, to understand the principles which undergird them, to be exposed to God's wisdom, to enter the mind of God.

The best way to do this is to set up an unbreakable and irrevocable schedule which locks you into Torah study each day and each evening — even if it is only for twenty minutes each session. Through regular and faithful study you begin to sense some progress.

This is not to say that Torah is a simple matter. Not at all. In its advanced levels, it requires intense concentration, deep and rigorous analysis — all in an effort to understand what it is that the Torah — and God — require of us. Study of Torah, remember, is not merely a study of history or philosophy, or a how-to manual. When all is said and done, it means that we *The mysterious encounter* attempt to enter God's mind, so to speak, and to discover how He wants us to live our lives. It is in a very real sense a dynamic, ongoing encounter between us and our Creator.

D: You claim that through study of Torah I can gain an understanding both of God and of what it means to be a Jew. But so many texts have no practical bearing on life. For example, I've read that the Talmud discusses property damages. What does my ox goring your cow have to do with the mind of God, or understanding what it means to be a Jew, or what God wants from me?

R: A great deal. For example, by learning the laws of damages, you gain an insight into the value of another person's property, the care you must take not to injure another person, and your accountability and responsibility for negligence. All this is part of God's plan for the world and for each individual.

Esoteric **D:** What about something really esoteric, like mikveh, or
matters animal sacrifices?

R: Here, too, the same idea applies. Mikveh introduces you to significant concepts which we never hear about in modern times: holiness, sanctity, defilement, purity. And the sacrificial system gives us insights into the worship of God, how to subject ourselves to God, to recognize God's providential care for us, to focus on Him as the Creator, and, obviously, to be willing to sacrifice, to give up things for Him, and ultimately to be able to surrender the self before God.

In every facet of Torah study we gain new insights into the details which comprise our relationship to God and to other human beings. And above all else, we have God's promise that the Torah is not too difficult for us to grasp. *Deuteronomy* 30:14 says that Torah "is very near to you, in your mouth and in your heart to do it." I don't think God's promise is to be taken lightly.

D: I don't take it lightly, but I am still puzzled by some questions. You say that the study of Torah is the overriding mitzvah. But it seems to me that we would have to study Torah even if it were not a commandment, because apparently it is the only way one can understand God and one's own Jewishness.

R: That is certainly true. But by making it a requirement, the
  Torah underscores its centrality, and tells us that it is not
merely a nice, optional thing to do, but something we need to
do even if we don't notice any immediate benefits, and even if
we are not in the mood for it. That's why, by the way, the
Torah reading each Shabbat and Yom Tov takes place right in
the middle of the worship. Because Torah is central to our connection with God. "Thou shalt ponder over it day and night,"
says the Book of *Joshua,* echoing what we say in the *Shema
Yisrael:* ". . . when thou liest down and when thou risest up."
It frames and surrounds our lives.
   The point is that Torah study is not only a means to an
end, but is an end in itself — and perhaps this is why it is the
mitzvah par excellence. In one sense, the study of Torah is
like a doorway which we open into the great palace of the
King. But in another sense, (study of) Torah is the great
palace itself.

D: It does seems awesome in its scope — but I would like to
  begin somewhere. Where would you suggest?

R: Anywhere your heart pulls you. It could be the study of *Making a*
  Bible with its commentators. It could be an introduction to *beginning*
Mishnah, or study of practical, daily halakhah. Above all, one
must spend some time learning at least the rudiments of
Hebrew. It is also advisable not to study alone, but whenever
possible to join a group, or find a teacher, or study with a
friend. And remember this: in study of Torah, it is the effort that
is crucial, not only the results. We are not required to know the
entire Torah, but we are required to make an effort to do so.

D: Wish me luck.

R: You'll have much more than mere luck on your side,
  because by its very nature Torah study brings you closer to
God. He will clearly be with you, and with each additional
moment of learning and exposure to the Torah you will be
drawing Him that much closer to you and yourself to Him.
With such a guarantee, who needs luck?

holiness – the jew sanctifies the physical

Rabbi: Would you like to talk about something really deep
today?

David: Are you trying to frighten me?

R: No, just challenge you to do a little thinking about a
subject few people ever discuss.

D: Sounds intriguing. Go ahead.

R: Let me begin with a long question. Many cultures, civilizations and religions have their own primary term — one
idea which, more than any other, defines their essence. For

example, among the Greeks it was the term *kalos*, "beauty." Among religions, Christianity likes to thinks of "love" as its key idea. My question is: what is the one overarching concept in Judaism, one from which everything else seems to flow?

D: That's a tough one. But I have heard it said that Judaism is the religion of strict justice. You know: "An eye for an eye, a tooth for a tooth" — what people call "Old Testament justice."

R: Not quite. The common division of Judaism and Christianity into categories of justice versus love is a cliché that does not hold up under examination. The commandment to "love thy neighbor" comes right out of *Leviticus* 19, and the idea of a loving God is found throughout the Torah. That concept of "an eye for an eye and a tooth for a tooth" in *Exodus* 21:24 was never intended to be read literally. From the very beginning it has meant the monetary value of an eye as compensation for the blinding of an eye, the value of a tooth for a tooth, and so forth. This is the source of the universal concept of paying damages to anyone we injure.

The Torah speaks in its own shorthand, a kind of code which we do not fully comprehend without the guidance of the *Torah She-b'al-peh*, or Oral Torah — which, as we said last time we met, elucidates and clarifies the Written Torah, and applies its principles to new situations. Try again: what is the key idea which defines Judaism?

D: Terms like faith, love, and religious stubbornness come to mind.

R: Those are all accurate descriptions of certain facets of Judaism. We are definitely a people of faith and of love, and we have been stubborn about maintaining our Torah — but there is one term that, more than any other, contains in it the essence of Judaism. That is the Hebrew word *kedushah*, translated as "holiness" or "sanctity," from which many other *kadosh* terms derive. The word has many significant additional connotations, such as "separate," "apart," "unique," "different," "prepared," but primarily it connotes the idea of separation from the merely physical.

When the Torah and the Prophets describe God as *kadosh*, they are saying that God is separate, apart, unique, different.

The core of Judaism

And when the Jewish people is described by God, over and over again in the Torah, as an *am kadosh*, a holy people, that means that we are to be a unique people — unique and distinct in our outlook on the world, in our approach to life and to service of God. Every single aspect of Jewish religious life, every single commandment in the Torah, has as its ultimate, underlying motif this concept of *kedushah*.

Variations of Kaddish

D: I've heard of mourners reciting *Kaddish*. Is that connected?

R: Yes, and that is an important point, because *Kaddish* is not a prayer for the dead; it does not mention death at all. In the *Kaddish* we sanctify and glorify God, because we are reaffirming our faith and trust in God at times of tragedy, and because glorifying God is the best way to give merit and honor to the soul of the departed. Not surprisingly, variations of this word are pervasive in Jewish religious life. Here are a few:

— The *Kiddush* prayer on Shabbat and holidays, through which we sanctify the day.

— The *Kedushah* prayer, which is recited during the *Amidah* every day in the synagogue, and which echoes the daily proclamation of the angels that God is holy.

— God's dwelling place on earth is the Holy Temple — in Hebrew, the *Beit Hamikdash* — literally, the "House of Holiness."

— The Holy Land is *kadosh*; certain days of the year, festivals and Shabbat, are holy seasons, times of *kedushah*.

— When a Jew behaves in such a way as to bring glory to the Name of God, that is known as *kiddush Hashem*, "sanctification of the Name."

As I mentioned earlier, underlying this term is the concept of something separated from everything else for a specific purpose. Thus, in *Leviticus* 20:26, God says to Israel: "Thou shalt be holy, *kedoshim*, unto Me . . . and I will separate you from the nations to be Mine," which uses *kadosh* in this sense of separate. Similarly, the betrothal ceremony under the marriage canopy is called *kiddushin*, because it sets the woman apart by forbidding her to all men except her husband. In the same way, the property of the Holy Temple is called *hekdesh*, which means that it is specifically designated for sacred purposes, and is therefore forbidden for profane use. And the prayer book describes God as *mekadesh Yisrael v'hazemanim,* "He Who sanctifies Israel and the seasons," which also connotes setting them apart.

There is, as you see, holy space and holy time. But above all else, the overriding purpose of Torah and its commandments is to create a holy human being. In fact, there is an explicit commandment in *Leviticus* 19 which covers it all: "Thou shalt be holy because I, the Lord, am holy." *Holy space, holy time*

D: Let me try to understand that last commandment: to be holy "because I, the Lord, am holy." I don't quite get it — because God is holy, therefore I am also supposed to be holy? God is God, and I am just a person. I cannot possibly be holy like God is. He is in an entirely different realm, He does things that no human can do. He creates, I do not create; He is the source of all things, I am here today and gone tomorrow. What sort of reason is that — "because I, the Lord, am holy"?

R: What you say is true enough, but being holy like God is an ideal which we strive to reach within this mundane life — even though in its ideal state it is unreachable for a mortal being. But this is one of the glories of being a human being and a Jew. We strive for the stars, even though we may not be able to reach higher than the treetops.

At the same time, keep in mind that the Torah is not asking us to enter some fairy-land called holiness.

This concept of *kedushah* is part of daily life and can be attained through ordinary, mundane, daily activities. We're not being asked to become angels. The Torah wants us to become Godlike, although obviously we will never become fully like God. But He has certain attributes which we must try to emulate.

For example, the great sage Abba Shaul says in *Shabbat* 123a: "Just as God is merciful, so shall you be merciful; just as He is long-suffering, so shall you be long-suffering." We try to imitate God's qualities. The pinnacle of imitation of God is to strive to be like God, to be holy as He is.

D: That's all well and good, but the term *kadosh* still makes me think of nunneries and monasteries and saints and abstinence and monks and priests with hoods and long, black capes.

Asceticism **R:** Well, you are manifesting the Western bias — which is
and really the Christian way of looking at life — in your
withdrawal upbringing and education, but that is not surprising. From
that perspective, "holy" does imply asceticism, abstinence,
withdrawal from society. Not so in the Jewish sense of the
word. As we've already discussed, *kedushah* does not mean a
repudiation of the physical; it means the utilization of the
physical and the material in the service of God. To be holy
does not mean to go on constant fasts, or to suffer flagellation
or regimens of self-denial. God gave us a physical world and a
physical body not so that we should reject them or turn our
backs on them. Instead, He guides us in utilizing the physical
world in order better to reach out to Him. Paradoxically, there
is only one gate through which the spiritual arrives at its realization: the gate of the material.

D: You are being very abstract. In concrete terms, what is
expected of me if I want to reach for holiness? What does
it mean in my daily life? Am I to go around fasting all the
time?

To **R:** Not at all. But we can learn to view our appetites — for
transform food and other things — in their proper perspective. These
the appetites and hungers are not evil in themselves; after all, God
physical has given them to us. They are perfectly legitimate human
desires, needs and wants. But as a person moves forward on
the road to holiness, he becomes less obsessed by food, for
example, or by physical things of any sort.

The Torah does not demand that we deny ourselves physical pleasures. Instead, it wants us to be in control of the
physical and not vice-versa, as so often happens to our own
detriment. We are to enjoy the physical appetites, we are to
satisfy our legitimate physical needs, but we must be careful
not to let those appetites consume us. And as we learn to control the physical, we gradually transform it into something
spiritual.

D: Again, if you will excuse me, those are only words which
don't mean very much to me. "Attaching oneself to God,"
"mastering and transforming the physical" — these are just
pretty slogans.

R: Let me be more specific. You attach yourself to God by
being constantly aware of His Presence. The Psalmist says
in 16:8: *Shiviti Hashem l'negdi tamid,* "I place God before me
always." "Always" — literally. Whatever a person does, he or
she must strive to realize that it is being done in the Presence
of God.

This is the ideal: to be aware constantly of Him as we go
through the ordinary day. If I may use a rather unholy example, it's like working out for a football team or auditioning for
a part in a play. You are conscious of every motion you make
because you know that coaches or directors are watching you.
Living a life of *kedushah* leads to such awareness. As for
transforming the physical, that's precisely what the mitzvot
help us do, because they enable us to use our minds, our bodies, our possessions and our surroundings for constructive
purposes. That's one of the key elements of *kedushah.*

D: Well, keeping God's Presence constantly before me is *Awareness*
noble theory, but it is rather other-worldly, wouldn't *of His*
you say? *Presence*

R: It doesn't occur overnight, granted, but it is hardly other-
worldly. Prayer, exposure to Torah, acts of kindness, charity — all make their impact upon us, with very practical
possibilities. Imagine how different life would be if people
were to keep this idea of God's Presence before them as they
went through the day. It might have a very positive effect on
the crime rate, for one thing, wouldn't you think?

D: Yes, but it would be very inhibiting to ordinary people.

R: Well, maybe we need to be inhibited about some things.
And in the long pull, we discover that instead of being
inhibited, we are in fact liberated and uplifted. If we really
were convinced that God is beside us, that would give us
strength, confidence, and ultimately a sense of profound
peace.

Nevertheless, I grant you that keeping God's Presence
always before us is not exactly society's major priority. But
this is what separates the truly religious individual from the
non-religious one or from the perfunctorily religious one who
is just going through the motions.

God does not ask for the impossible

D: It all sounds so lofty. Are you saying that this is actually doable?

R: Of course it is. God never asks for the impossible. Obviously, this doesn't just happen by itself. It takes effort, concentration, prayer and ongoing study of Torah. And then the real challenge is simultaneously to be certain that we remain an integral part of this world and the people around us, and not become spiritual hermits. God wants us to function within this world, not out of it, and thereby to help elevate and sanctify it. That's what that very challenging passage in *Exodus* 22 means: *Anshei kodesh tiheyun li*, "Thou shalt be holy people unto Me." That is to say: be people, be human, be a man or a woman, but at the same time be holy; strive to attach your lives to Me.

D: All that is fine, and I know that *kedushah* is the key concept in Judaism. What happens now?

R: What happens now is that with this knowledge you can begin to understand some very important things about Judaism.

D: Such as?

R: Such as how we view life, and our role in the world, and our relationship to God and to other people, and the role of the spiritual and the physical in the Jewish world view. And more.

D: All that is very impressive, but since I will never reach holiness, I am doomed to failure before I begin. What is the point in even trying?

R: Judaism in general, and *kedushah* in particular, are not all or nothing. Any degree of holiness we achieve changes our lives to that degree. Our task is not to arrive at the peak overnight; our first task is just to know that there is a peak. Even a small effort to reach for it so elevates our sights and lifts our horizons that we emerge far better just for having made the effort. If we are serious about moving forward, God has His own ways of helping us.

The Talmud in *Yoma* 39a says, *Adam mekadesh atzmo*

m'at, mekadshin oto harbeh, "When a person sanctifies himself a little, he is sanctified (by God) greatly."

Ultimately, we become that which we really want to become. God does not influence our choices — that would interfere with the freedom of will He gave us — but He does enable us to go the way we truly want to go, good or bad. If, in our heart of hearts, we want to achieve closeness to God, He helps us. And if we choose the opposite path, He makes that possible as well. And, as the sole Judge, He judges us not only by our achievements in reaching *kedushah*, but by the sincerity of our efforts in getting there. Every single step is an achievement.

We become what we want to become

D: This holiness sounds like a fine ideal — but why should I reach for it in the first place? What is really wrong with letting the physical take over? It certainly is much more pleasurable, for one thing.

R: There is nothing "wrong" with the physical *per se*. The problem arises when we allow it, as you say, to "take over." Physical drives are very powerful. They can control us completely, master us totally, and so swallow us up that our personal humanity is at risk. We become a network of nerve endings and appetites that demand immediate gratification. Which is one definition of an animal. You can't convince a dog to delay its gratification, or tell a cat that it should abstain from rummaging through the garbage and instead reach out to something higher, or suggest to a tiger to stop chewing the lamb because there are more sublime things in life than eating lamb's meat.

But we human beings do have the potential for spirituality, and deep down we yearn for it. At the same time, we have the capacity to descend to very low levels and devote our entire lives solely to the gratification of our senses. Despite all of our vast potential — for good, and love, and creativity, and healing, and poetry, and spiritual and intellectual growth — we can still sink lower than a savage.

To pull down or to reach up

D: I don't want to be flip, but you haven't answered my question: what really is wrong with being a beast? If I don't believe in God, if I don't like to put restrictions on myself, if I want to satisfy my desires, then it is perfectly normal to do anything I want whenever I have the urge. Why should that be wrong? I want something — why shouldn't I take it without guilt and all that conscience-stricken stuff? Why should I want to become *kadosh* in the first place if it will not allow me to enjoy what I want, when I want it? Why should I accept a life of restrictions when I can have a life of total freedom and pleasure?

R: That so-called pleasure-filled life you describe is not that pleasurable, or joyous, or free. On the contrary, by any objective measure, it is miserable. Look at the heroes of contemporary culture who live lives of total hedonism, devoid of all morals or ethics. Do you see joy on their faces? Do you think they find satisfaction for their souls, for example, in their sexual excesses? They don't even find satisfaction for their bodies, because if they did, they wouldn't maintain their frenetic, non-stop search for fun and pleasure. Words like content, or serene, or peaceful — do you think these accurately describe such people? The real words are: desperate, haunted, unhappy, alienated. You have to look long and hard at them to find any expressions of joy or celebration of life.

These people are a mirror of significant segments of contemporary society. Take our so-called post-modern music, painting and books, which are the "artistic" embodiments of this culture. They are really celebrations of narcissism, bitterness, nihilism and violence — which are in turn a reflection of lives filled with despair, contempt and hatred. Much of today's "pleasure-now" culture has come to this pass because they are not living natural lives; they are in fact living artificial, pumped-up lives.

The natural and the unnatural

D: How can you say that? They're doing what comes naturally.

R: Yes — what comes naturally to an animal. But they are human beings, not animals, and they are denying themselves something essential to the human soul — that hunger for higher things — and that's why they find no contentment. Any of us can fall prey to this illness. If we don't recognize what is gnawing within us, we try to satiate ourselves in other ways. We constantly buy new gadgets, take exotic trips, look for exciting adventures, amass needless possessions — and then wonder why we are still vaguely discontented. And the sadness is that the longer we go without satisfying this natural hunger of the spirit, the deeper we sink into the morass of searching for something that cannot be: happiness and contentment based on the body and on the physical senses alone.

So I don't accept the thesis that to live without any restraints is to have freedom. These people you describe are not free. They are actually slaves, because they have no freedom within themselves. Instead, they are being controlled. They are the puppets, not the puppeteers. They are slaves to their every glance, their every appetite.

We have had an entire culture permeated, for example, with the so-called joys of free sex — they call it "recreational sex." Our society has been drenched with the ideology that whatever you want is acceptable, that there is no discipline and no restraints of any sort. Contemporary popular music is filled with this message, as are the commercials in the media, as is our literature, as is our entertainment. To call the results disastrous is an understatement. We have a society in America — and the world imitates America — in which it is perfectly common for children to have children, in which family structure has crumbled, in which schools are not permitted to teach "values" concerning sex or stealing or adultery or any other deviant behavior, where there is little or no accountability for almost anything. *The contemporary scene*

We live in the ultimate no-fault society. The prevailing attitude is that no one is at fault for anything he does. There are few norms of behavior, little respect for authority, a dwindling number of ideals or traditions to look up to, no accountability — just self-indulgence and indolence.

Look around you at the results: murder, drugs, crime, disease, violence, illegitimacy, lawlessness, bestiality. Even in the so-called higher strata of society, soaring divorce rates are the norm, as are adultery, greed, selfishness, the "what's-in-it-for-me" mentality. We are in many ways worse than animals. At least they do not consciously destroy their own species.

Really, now, how long do you think any society can go on without some moral underpinning, without some spirituality? You don't have to believe in God to see what is plainly before us. This is the inevitable result of unrestrained — even of restrained — hedonism. Life around us today is a vindication of everything the Torah has been warning about for thousands of years. Tragically, we Jews in this century became victims of the very things we were warned about — when human bestiality reached its nadir and six million Jews were murdered by so-called cultured and civilized people.

Declaring independence   I grant you that holiness is not easy to attain, but it is the real declaration of human independence. The serenity of a Shabbat, the joy of a Succot, the contentment of a Pesach, the spirituality of a Yom Kippur, the majesty of a Rosh Hashanah, the quiet, historical evocations of a Shavuot, the daily contact with God through prayer, the satisfaction of doing kindness to others — these enrich and deepen one's life. But what we see around us today, my friend, is precisely what happens when we abandon even the concept of holiness.

D: I must have touched a sensitive nerve to set you off like that.

R: Well, it's a free discussion. Refute it.

D: I can't. But does that mean I have to go to the other extreme and become holy?

Holiness and normality   **R:** In Judaism, holiness is not an extreme. It involves living a perfectly normal life, but allowing the Torah to be its underpinning. This is open to any Jew.

D: Are you saying that there are no special groups of holy people within Judaism?

R: Every Jew has the same potential access to God. Judaism has no caste or sect which automatically possesses greater holiness than that of other Jews. Yes, we do believe that a person who devotes his entire life to studying the word of God, whose life is a reach for saintliness and piety, may have a greater entree, if you will, to God. And sometimes such people may be asked to keep us in mind in their prayers. But they became exemplary through their own efforts, not through heredity or a vested office. The highest spiritual levels are open to every single Jew or Jewess, no matter what earthly struggles he or she is engaged in.

D: What about the *Kohen?* Is he not born into a holy family, and is he not by nature closer to God?

R: Not automatically. Granted, his special inheritance, which *Access* he receives by virtue of his descent from Aaron, the first *to God's* *Kohen,* entitled his forebears to the privilege of being in *presence* charge of the ancient *Beit Hamikdash* in Jerusalem, to offer the sacrifices, to devote their lives to God's service. But a *Kohen* has no monopoly on the kind of personal holiness we are discussing. Theoretically, it is possible for a non-*Kohen* to achieve a higher level of sanctity than a *Kohen.* In fact, the Talmud says that a Torah scholar of illegitimate birth is more deserving of respect than a High Priest who is an ignoramus. It all depends on how a person — *Kohen* or non-*Kohen* — lives his life and fulfills his specific role in God's universe. When you get down to it, every Jew has the same right of access to God's presence.

D: Well, you've made your point. But I am curious: aren't truly religious people attracted at all by the merely physical? Don't they have temptations and desires like everyone else?

R: Of course. Every human being is tempted by the physical and is drawn to it in some way — even religious people. This is not necessarily evil. The Torah does not ask us to renounce life, to turn our backs on the healthy impulses with which God endowed us.

The fact is that you cannot achieve holiness without the physical. What matters in the long run is how people handle these appetites and desires and impulses. Ideally, the religious person is disciplined enough to realize that not every temptation must be satisfied, not every hunger must be fed. Religious people are not blown over by the fact that they are attracted to physical things. Instead, the religious life — the life of *kedushah* — teaches us how to relate to them.

D: But didn't Moses achieve holiness by climbing up Mount Sinai and staying there alone for all that time? Solitude, being away from people, removing yourself from temptation — isn't that the way he achieved holiness?

R: Moses achieved holiness not by climbing Mount Sinai, but by having already lived a holy life on earth. To live a life of holiness on the top of a mountain, in lonely communion with God, is a wondrous thing. But when the Torah speaks of a holy life, it is referring to life here on Earth, not in a desert away from people, not on top of a mountain removed from all earthly temptations. Granted, in every generation there have been Jews who chose to separate themselves from society in order to seek out God, but unless there are unique circumstances, our tradition frowns on this kind of separation.

This is the key point: true holiness on this earth is achieved by human beings living human lives — with a spouse, with children, with the usual concerns about the future, about health, about earning a living, about all the mundane details of daily life.

Holiness within the world In fact, holiness is most meaningful when it is achieved within the context of daily life, within the marketplace, with all of its anti-holy temptations and opportunities to wound, cheat and lie.

God does not expect us to transform ourselves into angels. An angel cannot become holier — he is holy to start with. God wants you to become holy within this world.

D: Well, I'm relieved to hear that: I wouldn't make a very good angel.

Let me backtrack. You say that even religious people, holy people, are not free from physical temptations, but that they learn how to control them and utilize them properly. But you also claim that the striving for holiness is a natural aspect of every person's make-up. In effect, you are claiming two opposite things: we are tempted by the physical, and at the same time we have a longing for the spiritual. How can this be?

R: Good question. But this is the great glory of being human.

We are pulled simultaneously upward and downward. We have a natural yearning for higher things, and natural urges for earthly things. This is the given fact of life. I grant you that on the surface it appears to be contradictory, but this physical-spiritual dichotomy has confused and agitated mankind from the very beginning of history. The pagans, for example, simply worshiped the physical. They took the easy way out and decided not to fight a physicality so pervasive and so pleasurable, it would be foolish to reject it. So they embraced it totally, identified themselves completely with it, made a deity out of the body and out of the entire physical universe.

Paganism was just that: a worship of the body and an effort to transform the material world into a god — or gods, to be more accurate. Every aspect of the physical universe had its deities. Every manifestation of the physical within man, no matter how base, was also worshiped. Public sexual activity — "orgy" would be the more precise term — was part of the pagan worship cult. Even bodily excretions became part of the worship of certain cults. *Where paganism failed*

D: They sound like sheer madmen.

R: No, don't make the mistake of assuming that the pagans were total fools. They sensed that there was more to the universe than what they saw, and therefore they made these efforts, futile as they were, to reach out to what they thought was beyond. The problem was that they tried to reach beyond this world by making gods out of the most physical things within this physical world and by worshipping them. As a result, they never got beyond idealizing the very physical world they were attempting to transcend. So it is not surprising that the more the pagans satisfied their urges, the less they were truly satisfied — because this higher yearning within man can be met only by addressing itself to things beyond the physical, beyond the here-and-now. If a person is dying of thirst, it is foolish to buy him a new tie. He needs water. If a person is starving, it is futile to give him a new shirt. He must have food. This is where the pagans failed: in their inability to satisfy their inner longings for transcendence.

By the way, contemporary man has the same spiritual needs but is unable to satisfy them because, like the pagans, we ignore the spiritual elements in life. Some things never change.

D: How do you know that this hunger for spirituality is really there? After all, there are millions of people who seem to be having a great time without feeding these so-called spiritual needs.

Disco-joy **R:** You need to differentiate between having some fun —
and   which quickly dissipates — and attaining a truly lasting
God-joy status of joy.

We've already talked about that. I think hedonists are so
desperately in search of fun and pleasure that they lose all
sense of true joy in their lives, because of their frenzied pursuit of it. The faster they pursue it, the faster it eludes them.
"Disco joy" evaporates as soon as you turn off the lights and
sound.

But there is a "God joy," and that kind of joy lasts. Next
time you're in a synagogue where there is really intense prayer
(there are all kinds of synagogues, so make sure
you find one that is serious about its Judaism and is not just
a pretty edifice), look at those praying faces. I'll let you decide
where you find real joy, even on a somber day like Yom
Kippur. Or take the Shabbat: I don't think that you can equal
the sense of tranquility, happiness and serenity which you
find when friends and loved ones sit together around
the Shabbat table. Why? Because their "transcendence" needs
are being met; something else besides their bodies is being
fed.

D: Right along with their chicken.

R: Yes, right along with their chicken. The physical, remember, plays a major role in supporting the spiritual. Shabbat
is certainly a spiritual day — but did you know that, unless it
coincides with Yom Kippur, we are forbidden to fast on
Shabbat?

Yes, right along with the wine and the chicken and the
fish and the soup and the drinks and the dessert — alongside all these, the real main course presides: *simchah, oneg,*
pleasure and delight. And if you still have doubts about
man's need to satisfy his hunger, just look at what happened
in the Soviet Union. After all, here was a very powerful
state, totally preoccupied with its physical existence for
generations, that simply collapsed. There were numerous
reasons for its collapse, many of them purely material. But
one of the factors was that its people were steadily denied
the basic need of any human being: the right to seek
transcendence.

D: Okay, so the ancient pagans, just like some of us moderns, flunked the transcendence test. Then what happened?

R: Along came the Christians. Although originally an offshoot of Judaism, Christianity soon proposed a radically different method of addressing the problem of the physical. For them, the physical was a mortal enemy to be fought zealously, to be defeated, to be completely destroyed. Every manifestation of the desires of the human body was an avenue leading to evil. For the Christians, sex within marriage was a concession to man's baser nature; therefore, truly holy people — like priests, nuns and monks — did not marry. The Christians were the polar opposites of the pagans, perhaps as a reaction to them. All manifestations of the physical were to be shunted aside and uprooted because they were the work of the devil.

Classical Christianity and the body

D: Well, at least they didn't underestimate the spiritual aspect. What was wrong with that?

R: What was wrong was that here again, spirituality cannot exist in a vacuum. As we discussed before, it requires the physical for it to be implemented. This is the great teaching of Judaism: it tries to establish a careful symbiosis between these two major forces in human life. Not a symbiosis where they are both equal, mind you, but where the physical becomes a handmaiden of the spiritual. If you are patient, I will try to explain.

D: I am physically, spiritually and transcendentally patient.

R: Then let me try to slake your spiritual thirst for transcendence. Judaism approaches the issue of the physical in a completely unique way. The physical world, says the Torah, is not inherently evil. In fact, the Sages in *Nedarim* 10a say that it is wrong to renounce it, because the human body, if we deal with it properly, is the avenue towards holiness and service of God.

The physical pathway to God

D: How does one "deal with it properly"? What I don't understand about all this is that if God does not want us to be tempted by the physical or to satisfy our appetites, why does He place these strong appetites and desires and distractions in our paths?

R: I'll try to answer both your questions together. God wants us to make free choices. When a person rejects what is false — even though it is attractive and glittering and desirable and pleasurable — and opts for that which, on the surface, is less glittering but is true, that choice is significant. It means that the person has overcome a challenge. But if falsehood were unattractive in any case, or clearly and obviously harmful, then rejecting it would hardly be a meaningful decision. You might reward a child for not raiding the cookie jar; you won't reward him for staying out of the oven.

Not only in Synagogue God wants wants us to be attracted by the physical things in life, but to harness those things into His service — to live our ordinary, mundane lives in a holy way. He wants us to enjoy our food — but to shun forbidden food; to be happy in our marriage — but to avoid forbidden relationships; to succeed in business — but not at the cost of honesty and ethical dealing; to live comfortably — but to share what we have with holy causes and needy people.

The opportunity to achieve holiness exists not only in the synagogue on Yom Kippur, but on every day and night of the year — in the kitchen, in the bedroom, in the office, in the marketplace, in interpersonal relationships. Every single aspect of life can be elevated into holiness.

Judaism does not deny us the pleasure of satisfying our appetites, but it does want us to know that He put these appetites before us in the first place so that we would elevate them. In other words, the real purpose of physical appetites in this world is that they be overcome and transcended, so that we become their masters and not the other way around — and by so doing we achieve *kedushah*.

D: Let's face it. We are consumed by the physical and its influence. It permeates our every single moment. It surrounds us and suffocates us.

Potential sanctity *R:* Of course we're surrounded by it. That's precisely the point. Think about it: there is not a single material element in the universe which does not have a potentially holy function: the leather in the tefillin, or the wool in the tzitzit, or the grapes in the wine, or the wheat in the matzah, or the water in the mikveh, or the parchment in the mezuzah or Torah scroll, or the *etrog* and the *lulav*. The Jew is given the power by God to transform all these into holiness.

The same is true of us. We are flesh and blood and bones, but we too can become holy. *Kedushah*, in other words, is not something out of this world; it is well inside this world. Our personal sanctuary — literally a place of sanctity — is everything around us: our bodies, our homes, our families, our businesses, our professions, our relationships with others — all together they constitute a structure of potential holiness within life. *Not out of this world*

There is nothing mysterious about it, no voodoo, no chanting, no mantras, no secret rites. Whenever a person resists the temptations to cheat, to lie, to hurt someone, to be an animal — or when a person performs an act of *chesed* and compassion, or senses the Presence of God in a mundane activity, or performs a mitzvah like tefillin or *tzedakah* or mezuzah or Shabbat or mikveh — that person is already within the framework of holiness.

It is not easy, but it is far from futile, and the prize at each stage of the journey — fulfilling God's purpose for us, and thereby adding serenity and meaning to our lives — is eminently worth it. Remember that entering into the *kedushah* framework means we are climbing a spiritual Mt. Everest — and not just because it is there, but because God is there. It is essential to recognize that God is not only at the top; He is there at every step of the way, so that as we move along we not only come closer to Him, but He is always there helping us along the way.

D: Let's get specific. You've been talking about "elevating" and "transforming " the physical. These are vague and abstract words. Tell me: how does one, for example, elevate and transform sex or food?

R: Good question. On its own, sex can be merely an animal act. But under the Torah's guidelines, and by elevating it through marriage, it can give us insights into some deeply spiritual matters. Believe it or not, sexual activity can give us a small inkling of what is involved in the ideal service of God — its all-absorbing nature, its intense pleasure, its total concentration, its expression of love. Therefore, Judaism never *Elevating sex and food* considered sex in marriage as an evil or a weakness, but as a positive good. Every Jew — rabbis, scholars, people engaged in holy things — is encouraged to marry. Not only to procreate, but also to enhance life physically and spiritually.

D: But why can't sex outside of marriage do these same things for us?

R: Outside of marriage, sex enhances our selfishness and is often just self-gratification, a means of satisfying one's appetites, without thought of the other. Marriage transforms the person from a self-oriented individual into an other-oriented one, who is concerned with the needs and desires of others, in this case, his or her mate. The commitments of marriage, the responsibilities within it, the give-and-take of the relationship, the sacrifices and compromises required to make it work and to raise children — all work against the selfish impulse within people. Marriage helps a person become a giver rather than a taker.

As for raising the physical, the act of eating provides a good example. It can be done like an animal — simply to fill an empty stomach or enjoy exotic tastes; or it can be done like a Jew — to gain strength in order to be able to serve God and bring Him into our lives; and in order to increase our sense of joy in being alive in God's universe; and in order to provide an opportunity for us to realize the wonders of God in nature. After all, you plant a tiny seed, and from that seed there emerges fruit, vegetables and grains, which sustain us and give us life. All from a mysterious combination of earth, air, sun, rain — which are supplied free of charge by God.

The kashruth laws are designed to lift us beyond the natural appetite and need for food, and to raise us up to a level higher than that of the beasts. And the fact that we are expected to acknowledge God before and after we eat makes our food different from the animals. Viewed in this way, the ordinary physical act of eating can become like an offering in the Holy Temple — which is why the Sages compare the table to the Altar. And that's real elevation and transformation.

What I am saying is that every single aspect of the physical world can become touched by *kedushah*, with the end result that a person can transform his physical body into a holy place, a living, breathing, Holy Temple. That's what I mean by dealing properly with the physical.

D: How will I know when I've finally achieved the status of holiness?

A holiness diploma

R: You won't know. For one thing, one never fully "achieves" it. The important thing is to enter the process and begin the climb upward. For another thing, the moment you become conscious of your personal holiness, that is the very moment that you are anything but holy.

It's a never-ending process. No one awards you a Certificate of Holiness which entitles the bearer to be called Holy Man or Holy Woman. The Torah's command in *Leviticus* 19, "Thou shalt be holy," is a constant challenge, because every new step adds new holiness to our selves. It is not like the mitzvah of placing a mezuzah on the door, where you perform an objective, circumscribed act, and you know that you have completed the mitzvah properly. The mitzvah to be *kadosh* is a lifelong pursuit, the super-commandment behind all other commandments, and one never fully achieves it, because there is no limit to man's capacity to grow and improve. The United States Declaration of Independence refers to the pursuit of happiness. What the Torah wants is the pursuit of holiness.

D: I thought you said that God does not ask the impossible of us. How can God give us a commandment that we cannot ever possibly fulfill properly?

R: But you do fulfill it — with every new move towards holiness. We fulfill the commandment by engaging in the struggle. God does not demand a final score from us. He wants us only to be involved in the process of coming closer to Him. As Rabbi Tarfon puts it in *Avot* 2:21: "You are not required to complete the task, but you are not free to withdraw from it."

Involvement in the journey

D: And I'm not free to ignore it, either: just to say it isn't there, just to walk away from it.

R: Not so. You have free choice, remember? But it would be foolish to ignore it because you would be denying yourself — your body and your soul — some tremendous satisfactions.

And in a higher sense, by accepting the challenge, you are fulfilling God's wishes for you, living in accordance with His
will. We ought not to forget that this is at the bottom of everything in Judaism.

D: Well, I'm not walking away, but I do want you to know
that I am a little frightened by the prospect of changing my
life — because that's really what you're talking about.

R: If you are adventurous and open to new things, then the
search for *kedushah* in life is a tremendous adventure,
filled with excitement and newness and freshness. The decision is yours. Our conversations, remember, are not designed
to persuade you, but to lay things out before you. That way,
you can make informed, intelligent choices, and not go
through life on automatic pilot — while deep down you keep
wondering if there isn't some better way.

That's one thing the religious life does for us, by the way:
it prevents us from living like robots, doing only that for
which we are programmed and nothing else. We are not animals who can only do what comes naturally. Only a human
being has the capacity to reach higher, to do not what comes
naturally, but what comes *super*naturally.

D: But can people really achieve such heights — to be
constantly aware of the presence of God, to strive to be
close to Him? All this seems so unnatural, so — if I may use
the word — holy.

R: Well, spiritual heights are certainly not commonly found,
but that doesn't mean they are unnatural. Remember: the
mere desire to be close to God is in itself a major step towards
holiness. As I said earlier, our task is not to reach the top of
the mountain, but to begin the climb.

Where to
begin?

D: Well, if I decided to follow this up, how would I begin?

R: Study basic Jewish texts, think, pray, perform mitzvot,
find a good teacher — and do all this with heart and concentration. That's the first step. It's also the middle step and
the last step. Because every single mitzvah in the Torah contains in it a Divine seed which helps us develop into
individuals who are *kadosh*. The third paragraph of the daily

Shema contains the verse from *Numbers* 15:40: . . . *lemaan tizkeru,* "so that you may remember and perform all My commandments and be holy to your God." Note the progression: first there is performance of mitzvot, and only then can there be holiness. In other words, every time we perform a sacred act, every time we study a basic text, or pray with heart and feeling, or do an act of real kindness, we become more *kadosh* within ourselves. That's why the blessing preceding the performance of every mitzvah has the words *asher kid'shanu b'mitzvotav v'tzivanu,* "Who has sanctified us with His mitzvot and has commanded us . . ." The purpose of the mitzvot is to sanctify us.

D: And supposing I begin doing all this. Where do I go from there?

R: You don't go anywhere. You just let things seep into yourself and let them become part of you. Gradually, your life will open up to exciting new possibilities.

D: Is there any turning back?

R: A person can always turn back. But the chances are that once you start out on this path, you won't want to turn back. You are far too intelligent for that.

D: Intelligent or not, I am a bit nervous. But I will admit that I am intrigued, so I will try to absorb this discussion, and then we will see what happens.

R: The worst that could happen is that you will become an even better person. My guess is that you probably will survive. As far as we can determine, no one in all of Jewish history has ever been hurt by a touch of holiness.

mitzvah – the jew directs his deeds

. . . in which is discussed . . . Commandment and Commander / Awe and love / Form and chaos / The function of positive and negative mitzvot / Asking why / Religious and observant Jews / Mechanical mitzvot / Idolatry, adultery, murder / Fear / Pleasure / Blind obedience / The religious personality / Why should God care? / The container of Godliness . . .

David: Today I'd like to ask you about a term we have been using very frequently, but which really needs some clarification. What exactly does the term "mitzvah" mean?

Rabbi: That's an important question, because mitzvah is a basic Jewish term — and also one of the most frequently misused.

Command-
ment
and Com-
mander

First and foremost, mitzvah is a Hebrew word that means "commandment." That implies that there is a Commander — a *Metzaveh* — and someone who is commanded — a *metzuveh*. In effect, each one of us is a *metzuveh* performing a mitzvah given by the *Metzaveh*.

This is not merely a play on words. The key word here is *Metzaveh*, Commander, which means that God Himself is involved with every commandment that we perform, and that each commandment so observed represents a tacit acceptance that we are fulfilling God's will by this particular act, be it tefillin, or charity, or observance of Shabbat or Yom Tov. In other words, there is no mitzvah detached from God.

It also suggests that the performance of a mitzvah subtly affects us and enhances our faith in the *Metzaveh*. That is to say, with each mitzvah we perform, we are making a statement that we believe in God; and with each mitzvah our belief in Him is strengthened. So there's a lot more to that term than meets the eye.

This explains why the first of the Ten Commandments is a statement that God exists and acts in history. Before we begin, says God, you must accept Me as your Creator and your Source. Then I can present to you the guidelines which are the Commandments.

Altogether, including the famous Ten Commandments, the Torah contains a total of 613 commandments: 248 positive — "thou shalt" — commandments, and 365 negative — "thou shalt not" — commandments. This division between positive and negative commandments reflects two ways of serving God.

1) We can serve Him out of *yir'ah* — reverence, awe and fear — and on the higher level of pure *ahavah* — love. The negative commandments, the *mitzvot lo taaseh*, are expressions of fear; we refrain from behaving in ways that are displeasing to Him — we don't cheat in business, or slander others, or eat on Yom Kippur — because we recognize His sovereignty and are afraid to violate it. *Awe and love*

2) The positive commandments, *mitzvot aseh*, are an expression of our love for God. That is, we get up out of our easy chairs or stop whatever we are doing, and perform a specific action — give *tzedakah* (charity), affix a mezuzah, immerse ourselves in the mikveh, wear tefillin, do acts of kindness, observe Shabbat — because we love God and want to come close to Him through the fulfillment of His wishes.

D: But isn't performing the negative commandments also an expression of love for God?

R: Not to the same extent. A "thou-shalt-not" is a prohibition warning us *not* to act, not to do a certain thing; it's not a call to action, but a call to non-action. Therefore, it is not a positive means of drawing closer to Him. When we refrain from stealing, or gossiping, or eating on Yom Kippur, or desecrating the Shabbat, or hurting others, what are we actually doing? Nothing. So refraining from a violation of God's law is not a positive expression of love, because love by its very nature expresses itself in an active reaching out to the other. Rather, when we refrain from doing certain things — even tempting things — we are expressing our awe, fear and reverence for Him: we choose not to go against His wishes, we are fearful of losing our closeness to Him.

Here is an analogy that is not perfect but is instructive. An athlete will practice hard to improve his skills; that is positive. He will also avoid activities that may lead to an injury; that is negative. Avoiding injury is obviously important, but it will not move him forward.

D: Besides being fearful of losing our closeness to Him, isn't there another reason we refrain from certain things? Specifically, are we not also fearful of getting punished?

R: Yes, that too. After all, the concept of *s'char v'onesh* — reward and punishment — is a basic component of our relationship with God.

D: But are we supposed to serve God out of fear?

Fearing fear *R:* We moderns are in fear of the term "fear," but objectively speaking, to fear and be in awe of the Omnipotent Creator of the universe is perfectly in order. It is even necessary, as a means of avoiding transgression. After all, aren't highways much safer when drivers know that the area is well covered by radar?

In general, it's important to understand that there are two kinds of fear of God, as the great R. Moshe Chaim Luzzato points out in Chapter 24 of his *Path of the Just.* The less lofty kind is fear of punishment. The highest kind is *yir'at haromemut*, "fear/awe of God's greatness," which is an awareness of God's transcendence and power.

These two levels of *yir'ah* are almost complete opposites. The first is like the fear one has of disobeying a taskmaster with a billy club or a gun; the second is like willing obedience to a great person we respect and revere.

The ideal service of God is the kind that fulfills His will not because He rewards and punishes — although He surely does — but through a fusion of awe and love: the recognition of His overpowering greatness as contrasted to our vulnerability; the desire to be in His proximity through the means of doing His will; the avoidance of sin so that we not be torn away from His Presence; and the recognition that He loves us and wishes to be close to us.

D: Why must there be so many negative commandments? Are we little children that we have to be constantly told what not to do?

R: Important question, so listen carefully to my response.   *Boundaries*

Just as in the physical world there are limits and boundaries beyond which we may not go, so also in the spiritual world. In the physical world there exist land and ocean, heaven and earth, fire and water, winter and summer. Everything has its limits, borders and designated place. So is it also in our relationship to God and in our personal behavior. There are limits and boundaries beyond which we may not go. This we may eat, this we may not. This person we may marry, this person we may not. This action is permissible, this is forbidden. This is kosher, this is *treifah*.

The very first limitation is found in the Garden of Eden: everything is freely available to Adam and Eve except the fruit of one tree, all of which we discussed in our conversation about kashruth. It is forbidden for many reasons, one of which is that man must know that not everything is within his domain. If everything is permissible to him, he begins to believe that he and no one else is the master of the universe. A second reason is that without restrictions and boundaries there can be no Eden, no joy in life. That is, God wants to teach man that limits, boundaries, "thou-shalt-nots," are the essential components of order and of being human. Life without limits or borders is rapidly reduced to chaos.

Form from chaos
Let's look at that idea of chaos a little more closely. When God creates the world at the opening of the Torah, the world is in a state of *tohu* and *bohu*, which are terms denoting formlessness and chaos. Everything is confused with everything else, all is mixed together, everything invades and impinges on everything else. That is to say, there are no boundaries. All is a formless, amorphous expanse.

God returns to this scene, and He sets boundary lines: earth is here and not there; oceans here and not there; fish here and not there; beasts here and not there; vegetation here and not there. Thus does the earth take shape, and thus does form overcome formlessness and chaos. The six days of Creation are an exercise in establishing structure and balance in God's world, and structure means the setting of limits.

In fact, all of Torah is a struggle against the primeval chaos. The beast in man resists limits and fights structure and order: "I want what I want when I want it." Man apparently has an inherent desire to return to that primeval *tohu* and *bohu*, and the Torah addresses this by setting clear limits on his behavior.

All this is in response to your question of why there are so many negative commandments. The negative thou-shalt-nots set limits on our behavior. The nature of man is such that we have to become unbeastly, de-animalized, before we can reach positively up towards God, and perhaps because of this we require so many order-imposing and chaos-destroying negative commandments.

D: It doesn't seem that God has a great deal of faith in us.

R: On the contrary, He does. If He didn't, He would never have entrusted his Torah to us, in effect making us an active partner in the affairs of His world. But as our Maker, who better than He is aware of our failings and our weaknesses? It's precisely because He knows our potential for greatness that He attempts to raise us up beyond the level of the lower creatures. The mitzvot — negative and positive — are the tools God uses to transform us into beings who, as Psalm 8:6 puts it, are just "a little lower than the angels . . ."

D: Am I really expected to perform 613 commandments, with all the sub-commandments that they engender? It's hopeless; I can never do that.

R: Before you become discouraged, let me repeat the major characteristic of God's relationship to His creatures: He never asks us to do the impossible; whatever He asks of us is eminently doable. Granted, not always easy, but doable. And He, in His own hidden way, helps us along when we want to serve Him in earnest. Because of this, my answer is yes, we are all expected to follow God's law — not only because every Jew is subject to the demands of the Torah, but also because doing so adds a new dimension of pleasure and meaning to life.

Now, this matter of the 613 needs a little attention. Let's *613* first look at them on a basic level, after which we'll delve *mitzvot: a* beneath the surface. In actual practice, a large number of them *summary* — such as the commandments concerning the various sacrifices, or the purity and defilement laws — are not applicable today, since the Temple in Jerusalem does not exist. In addition, many mitzvot, such as the laws of the Sabbatical Year, when the land must lie fallow, do not apply outside the land of Israel.

The fact is that of the 613 total, a little less than half — about 270 — are applicable today. But lest even this smaller number seem overwhelming, bear in mind that, when you really get down to it, they fall under only a few broad categories of mitzvot, in which there are obviously many details: Shabbat; the various practices of each Yom Tov; kashruth, prayer, tefillin, tzitzit, mezuzah, family purity mitzvot such as mikveh — plus, of course, mitzvot such as charity and general *chesed*, or kindness.

In a broader sense, there are two categories of mitzvot. Some deal with interpersonal relationships, such as the laws of charity, lending, lovingkindness, honest dealing, visiting the sick and bereaved. Others concern the relationship between us and God, such as kashruth, or tefillin, or mikveh, or Shabbat, or prayer, or Yom Kippur — plus such inner beliefs as faith in God.

Some mitzvot are relatively easy to perform and are finite

in time, such as placing a mezuzah on the doorpost; some are quite difficult, such as proper honor of parents, or giving appropriate charity, and are ongoing. Six mitzvot listed by some of our law codes (but which will take us too far afield to discuss in detail) are permanent, incumbent upon us at all times, such as the commandment to believe in God — which, according to Maimonides, is based on the first of the Ten Commandments. Some mitzvot must be performed daily, such as the recitation of the major statement of faith, the *Shema Yisrael*, and the obligation to pray to God. By contrast, there are certain mitzvot we can perform only once a year, such as dwelling in the succah, or eating the Pesach matzah, or hearing the shofar on Rosh Hashanah. And there are some that rarely come our way, such as the mitzvah of sending away the mother bird from the nest before we take the fledgling or the egg — which is called *shiluach haken* (*Deuteronomy* 22:6) — or the commandment to bury the dead.

Some of the 613, such as the mitzvah to help the poor, are readily understood, while others are not, such as the prohibition against wearing linen and wool mixed in the same garment — known as *shatnez* — outlined in *Leviticus* 19:19, or the mysterious laws of the Red Cow of *Numbers* 19. The mitzvot that we understand — or think we understand — are called *mishpatim*, or "judgments," and those we don't clearly understand are *chukim*, or "decrees."

There is also a category of mitzvot called *edot*, "testimonies," which remind us either of key events in Jewish history or of basic religious truths. Examples of these are the various festivals, and commandments such as tefillin. But no matter how we categorize them, the mitzvot are not separate and discrete commandments; they are all part of one entity, one organism with 613 parts.

D: My grandmother used to say, "Get me a glass of water, you'll have a mitzvah."

R: In the broad sense she was right; since you were doing a kindness, that would be a mitzvah — but your *bobbe* was not using the word in its most accurate sense. The best working definition is this: mitzvah is a Torah commandment. But it is such a widely used term that it tends to get stretched out of its pristine meaning.

D: Those *chukim*, the mitzvot we don't understand — am I expected to perform something that makes no sense? *Not understanding*

R: Correction: they make no sense *to you*, but they do make sense on another, deeper plane, even if it is a plane that can be understood only by the Divine Intelligence. Think about it: if you are only going to do that which makes sense to you and ignore the commandments you do not understand, you are in effect saying that the final arbiter and judge of what you do as a Jew is not God and Torah, but you yourself. If it appeals to your reason, you will do it; if it doesn't, you will not. But when you try to justify God's laws by human reason, you are in effect judging the Infinite by the standards of the finite, and subordinating the Divine command to the mortal mind.

I realize that in our skeptical day and age, what I'm saying is a form of heresy, but there is an Authority which stands higher than that which appeals to our minds or hearts or appetites or egos. When we deal with Torah, we are dealing with God's will, which is beyond our comprehension. A person who trusts in God dedicates himself to following Him no matter what.

And remember what we have already discussed: in Judaism, the physical is not condemned or denied, but uplifted. Celibacy is not required of us, nor is mortification of the flesh. Torah makes serious demands, yes, but they are demands from a loving, understanding Creator, so they are all doable — and they are collectively designed to enhance our lives on this earth.

D: But are we never allowed to ask why?

R: Not only allowed, but encouraged. There is an entire literature called *taamei hamitzvot*, "reasons for the mitzvot." And the Talmud itself probes relentlessly into the sources, if not the reasons, of every single mitzvah, analyzing them and subjecting them to the deepest scrutiny. To ask why is perfectly legitimate. We are encouraged to ask and think and analyze and question. That's what Torah study is all about.

The bottom line, however, is that even if the reasons we discover do not appeal to us, even if we still do not understand, we are nevertheless bound to observe the commandments — because ultimately they are God's will and contain Divine secrets which are beyond human comprehension. The truth is that it may be more important to ask *what* than to ask *why*. That is, it is a full-time task to know what the Torah says; we ought not to allow the why's to distract us too much.

I'll let you in on a religious secret: even those mitzvot which we claim to understand are in reality also beyond our understanding. Can you and I really be certain that we know everything that was in God's mind when He told us to love our neighbor? Do we really think that we understand all the profound considerations that lie behind "thou shalt not steal"? My advice would be to observe the *chukim* as if they were *mishpatim* — and the *mishpatim* as if they were *chukim*. It is not really up to us to make the distinction.

D: May I interject something at this point? One of the things emerging from all of our discussions — especially this matter of understanding and not understanding mitzvot — is my growing realization that the Western orientation to life is quite different from that of the Torah. In the West, the mind and the body are primary. The "me" has to be satisfied. Everything revolves around what makes me feel good, or gives me pleasure, or appeals to my logic. I am the final authority. But the Torah scheme of things requires a much more profound sense of humility. There is a definite emphasis on the mind, but hovering over everything is God, and that alone does tend to make one a bit humble — which is new and strange to my generation. The point you make about doing mitzvot in the "I-do-not-understand" mode is fascinating.

R: And what you are saying is just as fascinating, because one of the primary purposes of Judaism is to help us understand that we are not the masters of the universe, but the servants of the King of Kings. This sounds very medieval and benighted to contemporary ears, but it is precisely what the Torah wants of us: to crown God finally and conclusively as our King, and to adhere to His will as His subjects. Each mitzvah is a physical manifestation both of God's cosmic Will and of a spiritual aspect of His essence that He shares with us. Through the mitzvot, God allows us, so to speak, to "touch" a part of Him, to sense Him in ways that go beyond the merely physical. Whenever we perform a mitzvah, we are in fact in contact with holiness.

D: I have often wondered: once a person observes all the mitzvot, does that make him a religious Jew? *Religious and observant*

R: That's a most interesting question. I would say that observing all the mitzvot and practicing the normative halachic regimen makes one an *observant* Jew, and quite possibly, but not necessarily, a fully religious Jew.

What I mean is that one can be observant and not yet be religious. Becoming observant is step one on the ladder which leads to becoming truly religious. But one has to work at becoming religious; it does not come automatically.

D: You are talking in riddles. What is your definition of "religious"? I'm not observant of all the mitzvot, but I definitely feel I'm religious. Why should I have to do the mitzvot if I am already feeling religious?

R: "Feeling religious"? That's a pretty generality, but it really doesn't translate into very much. Let me ask you some questions. In what sense do you feel that you are religious? *Feeling religious*

D: Well, I believe in God, and I try to be a good person.

R: Do you believe that this God in Whom you believe cares about you?

D: Yes.

R: Do you believe that He listens to you?

D: Yes.

R: Do you pray to Him or talk to Him in any way?

D: Yes, in my own way.

R: How often are you in touch with Him?

D: Not too often, I admit.

R: When was the last time you prayed to Him?

D: I admit it — a long time ago.

R: Are you ever in touch with Him when you do not need anything from Him, when you don't need His help for something?

D: Probably not.

Don't *R:* Well, with all due respect, what kind of contact do you
call me have with this God of yours? It seems to be more like a "don't-call-me-I'll-call-you" relationship.

Since you raised this issue, let me ask you some further questions. This God in whom you believe, is He righteous by nature, or evil?

D: Certainly He is righteous.

R: If so, and if He created us, does it not follow that He would not simply place us on this earth without some guidelines for living? And since you are nodding your head in agreement, does it not make eminent good sense that the guidelines this good God wants us to follow are embodied in the Torah that He revealed to us at Sinai? Because if these are not His guidelines, what are His guidelines?

D: Maybe He communicates with each person individually, with each in his own way.

R: If that's the only way it is done, we would have total chaos in our relationship to God, because each individual would say, God told me to do it this way, God says it's permissible to steal, or to commit adultery, or to kill, or to choose this code of conduct over others. It seems much more reasonable to acknowledge the basic Jewish belief that God makes His will known to us through His Torah.

D: I suppose I'll have to grant you that.

R: This idea goes further. If you believe in a God Who created us, Who cares for us and Who therefore gives us directions by which to live; and if you believe in a God Who listens to us, does it not follow that first, it would be most natural to reach out to Him and be in contact with Him in some way; and second, that we should take seriously His directions, which we call the Torah?

D: Yes, I suppose so.

R: And since this God is all-powerful and all-knowing, which *Does God* we are not, does it not also make sense that we might not *make* fully comprehend everything He demands of us, and that *demands?* some of His guidelines might initially make us uncomfortable — even though the good and righteous God designed them for our benefit?

D: Yes.

R: Has your God ever asked you to do anything that requires discipline? Has He ever made demands of you that make you uncomfortable?

D: I'm beginning to get your point.

R: Which is that if you have a God Who never makes any demands of you, Who never asks that you say no to yourself, Who permits you to do everything you want when you want it, it seems to me that you don't have a God at all, and that what you are calling "God" is actually your own little self telling you to do what you want, take what you want, enjoy what you want. That may give you some short-term pleasure — very short-term — but you can't call that "God," and you can't call that religion — because a religion that demands nothing and costs nothing is worth nothing.

D: You have really put me into a corner.

R: I apologize for any discomfort, but I'm only trying to show you that your position — which is the position of many people today — is not consistent or logical. Instead of this God of yours lifting you up to a higher level, just the reverse is happening. In other words, to put it bluntly, you are doing as you please, calling it religious, and saying that this God of yours approves of everything you do.

D: But you never explained how you define "religious" as opposed to "observant."

The religious personality *R:* An observant person performs the commandments, even punctiliously, but that is merely the first step towards becoming truly religious — because becoming truly religious is the work of a lifetime. Religious individuals observe all the mitzvot because they represent God's will. They fulfill them not by rote, but with love and joy. For them, observance is not a task to be carried out, a chore to get over with, or a job that has to be done so that they can get on with their daily activities. For such people, every mitzvah is an opportunity to express their love for God, and every manifestation of beauty or power or majesty in the universe — down to the proverbial blade of grass — is a reminder of God's existence. Their every moment is suffused with gratitude for the life God gives them and their loved ones, and for God's sustenance of the world. They are aware of the dangers of serving God only from habit.

They bring heart and love and emotion to every daily task, whether it is a mitzvah or not — and certainly if it is a specific mitzvah — because even the most mundane and ordinary daily task, if it is done in accordance with God's will, can be made sacred. They try to learn as much as they possibly can about God and Torah and the mitzvot.

They try to behave in ways that will be pleasing to God, and to do nothing that might reflect negatively on God's good Name among people. They live their religion with dignity and with humility. They are unselfish and share what they have — their resources and their time — not only with God but also with others. They are kind and considerate and sensitive to others. They give charity generously and quietly.

They view every waking moment as an opportunity to serve God. They see God's hand in everything that occurs, even though they readily acknowledge that they do not understand everything. They accept all that occurs in life with love and with faith. They not only believe that God is the Creator of everything, but trust in Him completely. They are joyous and confident and serene as they go through life.

That is an adumbration of the religious personality. And it all begins — but does not end — with the observance of mitzvot.

D: That's all very beautiful but, if you will forgive me, it sounds like an idyllic, fairy-tale description. Do such people actually exist?

R: Of course they exist. They are not commonly found, but there are such wondrous people — living, vital men and women who live their lives — whether as professionals or business people or students or what-have-you — in precisely this way. I did not exaggerate one iota. And they are the products of the mitzvah system.

    The very fact that there are people who have achieved this ideal makes it possible for others to reach that level. Being religious does not mean living in a never-never land. It is a flesh-and-blood enterprise, and it is definitely attainable.

D: I am troubled by something: we are required to perform such a huge panoply of mitzvot — I wonder how it can ever be possible to avoid doing them perfunctorily. Don't they tend to become stale after a while? Isn't there a danger that they will be performed simply automatically, without thought or feeling, and without any awareness of God or His Will, or all the nice things you mentioned before?

R: You have touched on a very crucial issue: the problem of rote behavior in religion. The only comfort is that the problem is not a new one. The Prophets of old already railed against service of God that is automatic, external, superficial, and lacks heart and feeling. *Isaiah 29:13* minces no words:

Robotic religion

> *This people draws near to Me with their mouth, and with their lips they honor Me, but their heart they have removed from Me; their reverence for Me is but the acquired precept of man — mitzvat anashim melumadah.*

    Human nature has not changed; we have the identical problems today, perhaps even more so.

    The truth is that this is a lurking danger throughout the gamut of the mitzvah system, because it is perfectly natural that repeated performance of the same act can lead to dullness, boredom and thoughtless, mechanical behavior. It requires some effort and concentration to retain the sense of freshness that service of God requires. That's why many prayer books contain a preliminary paragraph that is recited prior to the beginning of prayer, or the donning of the tefillin, or the eating of matzah on Pesach, or the taking of the *lulav* and *etrog* on Succot — the purpose of which is to remind us that we are about to perform a mitzvah. We have less problems with, say, Yom Kippur, because that comes only once a year — but that, too, can be desanctified by undue emphasis on the superficial aspect of fasting, and insufficient emphasis on the purpose of the fast. Pesach, too, can fall into a routine of frantic spring cleaning or complaints about matzah's effect on the digestive system — unless one bears in mind what Pesach is truly all about. And obviously, the daily blessings over food are the most susceptible to mindless mumbling of words.

We really need to pause for a moment and think prior to and during the performance of any mitzvah or blessing: Why am I doing this? Who commanded me to do this? To Whom am I at this moment directing my full intentions? All this is known as *kavannah*.

Relative value of mitzvot

D: I've often wondered: Are certain mitzvot more important than others?

R: You raise an interesting point. As far as we are concerned, every single mitzvah carries the same weight. We are under the same obligation to perform an apparently "easy" mitzvah — such as, say, to place a mezuzah on the doorpost — as to perform a difficult one — such as to close down our work on the busiest day of the week, or to lay down our lives on behalf of God, which is the ultimate sanctification of God's Name: *kiddush Hashem*. In the eternal scheme of things, that which seems easy and simple to us — perhaps a smile and a good morning to an unfortunate person — may carry greater weight in God's eyes than that which seems very difficult and complicated. So we should not fall into the trap of placing relative value on various mitzvot. As the Sages put it in *Avot* 2:1: "Be as scrupulous in performing a 'minor' mitzvah as a 'major' one, for you do not know the reward given for the respective mitzvot."

Obviously, certain prohibitions are capital offenses, others are more like felonies, while still others can be compared to misdemeanors — but we are not competent to determine which are more or less important in God's scheme of things.

Having said all this, however, it is important to note that there are three commandments for which we are obligated to give up life itself rather than violate them. These are the prohibitions against idolatry, murder and immorality (adultery, incest and homosexuality). If we are ordered to murder someone on pain of death, we must by Jewish law give up our own lives. The same holds true for the other two cardinal sins; we may never violate them, even on the pain of death. These are known as *yehareg v'al yaavor* mitzvot — literally, "let one be killed and not violate." This is not true of the other mitzvot, all of which take second place to human life. That is, if it is a matter of life and death, we must eat on Yom Kippur, or violate the Shabbat, or eat any forbidden food. In that sense, these three major prohibitions can perhaps be said to be more significant than the other commandments. *Three cardinal sins*

D: But what is so special about these three commandments?

There are a number of other mitzvot that seem just as significant, and for which we are not required to give our lives.

R: These three may differ because underlying each of them is a profound fact of our religious life which we mentioned earlier: the essence of Judaism is to accept God as our Sovereign and to make ourselves subservient to Him and His will. That is to say, God is King and not we. Each of these three transgressions represents a direct assault on this key concept — on God Himself, on God's qualities that reside in others, and on God's qualities which reside within our own selves.

By engaging in idolatry, a person is saying in effect that God is not Sovereign of the universe, that there is something other than God to which he is subservient. Therefore, we must first surrender our own lives rather than rebel directly against God by engaging in idolatry. Jewish history is sadly — and proudly — filled with numerous such incidents, where entire communities martyred themselves for this principle.

Murder is the destruction of the image of God that resides in others, and is in effect an assault on God Himself. This, too, requires one to give up his own life first. As the Talmud expresses it in *Pesachim* 25b, what makes you think that your blood is redder than the other person's? He is created in God's image just as you are.

Adultery, incest, and homosexuality are a rebellion against the creative power that God shares with us, which is the human sexual drive. Through it, we help preserve the continuity of humanity, and we become, quite literally, God's partners in creation. But this creative power may not be permitted to run wild and to be used at our whim without discipline. When this Divine creativity is used in a way which perverts this power, it is a perversion of the Godliness within ourselves.

To sum up the concept of surrendering life for murder, idolatry and sexual deviation: these three cardinal sins are a separate unit of their own because they represent rebellion against a) God Himself; b) God's image in others; and c) God's creative powers within our own selves. By surrendering our lives for them, we affirm the three great manifestations of Godliness in the world.

D: Do any of the positive commandments carry special weight?

R: In the thou-shalt category, we have already seen the crucial importance of Torah study. There is one particular mitzvah so crucial that it needs to be fulfilled constantly: the commandment to believe in God, which is the very first of the Ten Commandments: *Anochi . . . I am the Lord your God Who took you out of the land of Egypt . . .* Although this is an intellectual rather than a performance mitzvah, it is nevertheless a crucial one.

D: And if someone tries to prevent me from studying Torah on pain of death, am I supposed to give up my life for that mitzvah?

R: The answer is no, but that is a fascinating question. One is required to give up his life only in order to avoid doing something evil, but not in order to be able to do something good. To avoid the enormity of a crime we surrender life, but not to be able to perform a positive deed, even one as central as Torah study.

D: The more we talk, the more I wonder about this mitzvah system; it seems so total, so all-encompassing. Isn't it overly restrictive? It seems that at every moment of the day a person has to worry if he is doing something right or wrong. *Mitzvot as restrictive*

R: Exactly.

D: Do you actually think that it's a good thing never to be free, for any moment of the day or night, to do as we please, but always to feel like we're under critical scrutiny? Is it good always to have to worry about whether or not we're doing the right thing, or doing the right thing in the right way? Are you telling me that God wants us to live in a constant state of tension and worry, that this is the way to joy and happiness?

R: Yes, it is good to feel that we are being watched, especially when the One watching is our loving God, Who not only watches us but watches over us. After all, God is not a tyrant out to punish us and cause us suffering. He is a loving Father Who wants us only to share His goodness and to attain true joy in this world.

Yes, it is good to try always to do the right thing and to do it in the right way. It is good to serve God through prayer and observance of His commandments, and it is good to serve others — which is also service of God — by giving, by sharing, by lovingkindness, by charity.

But no, God does not want us to live in a state of anxiety and tension, and that is not at all what the mitzvah system does. On the contrary, those who live by it find it, in fact, a source of deep peace and contentment.

D: You mean they don't worry about what might happen to them if they fail to perform a commandment in just the right way? Are they not worried about the punishments for wrongdoing that are found all over the Bible?

R: Obviously, a believing Jew makes every effort to perform the commandments, and to perform them in just the right way. But fear of punishment is not uppermost in his mind. In practice, what is uppermost is the desire to fulfill the will of God as expressed in the Torah.

God: intimacy and distance
The greatest reward is the closeness to God which is attained by the performance of a mitzvah, and the greatest punishment is the distance that is created between us when we violate His laws. But on an ordinary level, reward and punishment are an almost automatic cause and effect. They are built into every commandment and into every violation. The fulfillment of God's will implements the built-in reward that is an integral part of the commandment; the violation of God's will implements the punishment which is an integral part of that violation. They are a law of spiritual nature, no different from, say, the natural law of gravity: when you step out of a window, you will surely fall downward, and when you violate Yom Kippur, you cut yourself off from your people. The awareness of this law of spiritual nature does not affect the joy and serenity of the practicing Jew, any more than walking by an open window affects his physical well-being.

D: Nevertheless, I must say that for me all those do's and don't's seem to take all the joy out of life. Can there ever be true pleasure or real joy under such a system?

Heightened joy
R: Paradoxically, only under such a system can there be true joy and pleasure. Look at it objectively, and you will see that in Judaism no physical pleasures are removed from us. We are encouraged to marry, to raise children. Eating and drinking are not proscribed. Social contact is encouraged and in fact enhanced. Nothing is withheld from us. Granted, we are not permitted unbridled, undisciplined pleasure. Everything has its place and its time. Further, Judaism introduces us to a realm of spiritual pleasure that would otherwise be unknown. The end result of it all is not ephemeral or diminished pleasure, but intensely heightened pleasure. In a certain sense, the Torah is actually the Book which guides us through these pleasures, because God, in fact, created the world for our benefit.

D: I'll take your word for it that it brings joy to people who live by it, but I must say in all honesty that to me, all that rigor and "do this" and "don't do that" seems rather stultifying. I mean, doesn't that reduce our sense of freedom and turn us into automatons, when at every moment we are under some kind of discipline and at every turn we have to do something in a precise, exact, predetermined way? Everywhere we turn, we have some duty to perform: we have to recite a blessing before we eat, we have to recite a blessing after we eat; when we get up in the morning, we have to pray, when we go to sleep at night, we have to pray, in the middle of the day we have to pray; when we are hungry, we have to worry if the food we want is permissible or forbidden, when we walk into our house, we have to make certain there is a mezuzah on the door—

R: —and when we go into our business, we have to worry about giving honest weights and measurements, and in all of our dealings we have to be honest, and when we speak to anyone, we have to be sure we do not lie, or gossip, or insult, or wound with our words, and we have to worry not to steal, or cheat, or commit adultery.

D: Well, the things you mention don't create any burdens, they're natural.

R: But doesn't such a fine person feel "stultified" by maintaining such standards? Doesn't it cramp his style and destroy his freedom if he constantly has to be concerned about living ethically and morally, and he can't lie or cheat when he feels it is necessary?

D: You are comparing apples and oranges. Ethical and moral behavior are accepted universally.

R: Surely you realize that this natural bent of yours towards ethical behavior is not just a spontaneous thing that happened to occur in your life and in the lives of millions of others. Although we do have an ingrained sense of right and justice within us, the *yetzer tov,* the inclination to do evil — the *yetzer hara* — is far more powerful. People are not born naturally unselfish or ethical or caring or moral. As the *Book of Job* says in 11:12, "Man is born as a wild ass . . ." Did you ever hear of a baby not crying at night out of consideration for its mother? All the ethical and moral values that we cherish

Ethical norms and Judaism

have to be carefully taught and nurtured — by parents, teachers, friends, society at large. The very fact that every civilized society puts value on these qualities is a tribute to the influence of the Torah's ideals — at least in this regard — on all of mankind. It is certainly more natural to steal than to refrain from it, more natural to take and grab than to give and share. When you look at it objectively, it is clear that the Torah tries to do just the reverse: to make it natural for us to think of God at all times, to make it second nature not to cheat or steal or be selfish.

It's really a tribute to the Torah that its ethical system is so pervasive that it is the foundation stone for living, as you put it, a civilized life. For a good part of the world, this has become so ingrained that it has become second nature. Even though they don't always follow it in practice, at least in theory they acknowledge its importance.

A different dimension   On a different level, the same is true of the observant Jew. In addition to being ethical and moral, he lives in a separate dimension as well. He, too, wouldn't think of getting up in the morning and not praying, or of not acknowledging God before and after food. The only difference is that in one set of instances — the ones that are important to you — you are used to them and they are already part of your nature — and, I might add, they don't single you out as being different from the rest of society. But the other set of instances is totally strange to you — plus they would tend to mark you as different from everyone else.

D: Perhaps so, but the fact is that an observant Jew can't even leave the bathroom without reciting a blessing, for heaven's sake.

R: Exactly — for heaven's sake. That's precisely my point.
Even in the minutest detail of life, even when one performs natural bodily functions, one acknowledges God as His Creator and Protector and Friend and Miracle-worker.

When you have a chance, by the way, take a look at the words of that prayer you are ridiculing. It thanks God for the miracle of the human body, for the wondrous system of channels and tubes and orifices that He installed within us. The human body is the most intricate "machine" in the universe, and the prayer thanking God for it happens to be one of the most magnificent of all our magnificent prayers. And it keeps us from defining ourselves as mere animals.

Similarly, when I eat, should I not acknowledge God's bounty? When I enter my home, is it not wonderful to find Him symbolically present through the mezuzah on the doorpost, and to remember that it contains the eternal credo of the Jew, *Shema Yisrael*, attesting that God is unique and singular? Is that a burden or a privilege? And when I arise after a night's sleep, should I not acknowledge His Presence and pray for a good day? And when I retire at night, is it so constricting to acknowledge His Kingship and to pray for a good night? This is hardly robotic behavior or a loss of one's personal freedom. On the contrary, it seems the most normal thing in the world to do.

D: But aren't you advocating blind obedience?

R: Probably the highest rung of service to God occurs pre- *The* cisely at the point when we so believe in Him and have so *servant* much faith in Him that we are ready to follow His directions *of faith* even though we do not fully comprehend them. Imagine a newly inducted army recruit who finds himself on a terrifying battlefield. He is ready to follow his lieutenant's orders even though he doesn't comprehend what is happening, because he knows and trusts him, and he knows that the lieutenant is concerned with the safety and welfare of his troops. You might call that blind obedience. I would call that the kind of loyalty, training and discipline that wins battles.

And, by the way, what you call blind obedience has some literally miraculous results. For example, it often happens that God's will and our own will do not coincide; we would like to do certain things that are perfectly natural, but God's law says that we may not. So we put aside our desires in favor of God's. In effect, we are setting aside our own inclinations, what we would like to do, in favor of God's law. Now, that is more than a fine and religious thing to do, because when we overcome these natural inclinations, we in effect enter a supernatural mode, the realm of God Himself. And when we enter God's realm, we become somewhat like Him — not subject to the ordinary, natural rules of history, or logic, or nature. This is what we mean quite literally when we say that God is super-natural. For putting aside our natural wishes, God rewards us by introducing us into His supernatural realm, where we are not subject to the same historical logic and forces that govern other nations and peoples. That might explain something which cannot be explained in any rational way: the miraculous longevity and dynamism of the Jewish people.

In the service of God, the highest form of service is to perform a mitzvah simply for one reason: God wants me to do this. Period.

D: I don't see how I can be expected to do something whose reasons I don't understand.

But I don't understand why

R: There are countless things in life whose functions we don't at all comprehend. Take the human eye. Science knows a great deal about the structure and the function of the eye, the chemistry of individual optic nerve cells, and the ways we decide what to look at and how to process the vast number of confusing and vague messages we receive from the outside world. But even with this mass of knowledge, science has no real idea of how the visual system within us creates order out of the billions of tiny pieces of separate data that bombard it every second. But certainly no one says that he will not open his eyes unless he first learns how it works.

Another example: contemporary physics has taught us that we do not understand how atoms behave, or what goes on within them. Quantum mechanics underscores the mystery of the universe, which, from the limited human perspective, seems to be one of physical uncertainty and probability. The components of matter in the physical world — neutrons, protons, electrons — cannot be precisely measured or described. Contemporary science realizes that there are limits to knowledge. The universe, it turns out, is very secretive, not subject to our reason — even in the laboratory of the scientist. On a less abstract level, what is the reason you shake someone's hand to say hello, or to seal a deal? What is the reason you wear a tie? What is the reason you wear a handkerchief in your lapel pocket? Why do you have a lapel in the first place? Come now, David, your entire life is filled with acts and gestures and symbols whose real meaning and origin you know nothing about — and those are only mundane, secular things with no connection to God or Torah or religion.

Does it make sense that we, with our ephemeral, mortal *The mortal* human brain which understands nothing about the mysteries *brain* of life and death, whose minds haven't even come up with a cure for the common cold, who still cower before thunder and lightning, who are helpless and powerless in the face of crisis and sickness and tragedy — should insist on sitting back in our lounge chairs and knowing the reasons for every mitzvah before we deign to perform them?

The truth is that anything you think you understand immediately, at first hearing, is probably not worth understanding. The obverse side of this is that if you already know something, God doesn't have to tell you.

There is something else to keep in mind as well. When the Jews stand at Sinai and God offers them the Torah, their response, in *Exodus* 24:7, is *Naaseh venishma*, "We will do and we will understand." This response is not in logical order; first one understands, then one does. But the Israelites are expressing a profound truth: in the realm of serving God, it is precisely this reverse logic that makes sense. Very often, we understand the profound reasons that undergird a mitzvah only after we have lived that mitzvah and performed it with sincerity and devotion for a long time, and gradually the super-rational reasons penetrate our hearts, and we begin to understand on a level that transcends the merely logical or rational.

Not everything in the world is subject to rational explanation, and not everything has to be transparent to our reason. There is a realm of understanding and comprehension that transcends the mind. Sometimes the heart senses and actually knows that something is real, or true, or significant — and it does not require any intellectual or logical support. I think it was Blaise Pascal who said that the heart has its reasons that reason does not know.

In other words, we should use our minds to the fullest extent possible, stretch them to the limits — but all the time serve God like a child, on pure trust.

D: Which you have always said is the best way to serve God anyway.

R: Yes, but don't make the mistake of thinking that it is simple-minded to serve God in this childlike manner. It comes as a reward after years of study and diligent learning and prayer. And remember: for non-believers, all the reasons in the world do not suffice; and for believers, even a single reason is unnecessary.

Why should God care?

D: Let me ask you something : do you really think the Creator of this vast universe actually cares about the details of my life? Does what I eat matter to Him? Surely He has more significant cosmic matters to worry about than how my chicken was slaughtered! And is He going to feel insulted if we poor mortals don't say thank you after we eat? Why should it matter to Him if we observe Yom Kippur, or eat matzot on Pesach, or sit in a succah on Succot? Do you think it really matters in the eternal scheme of things if I observe the 613 commandments or not?

R: I can't speak for God, but all the evidence of the Torah is that every little detail of our lives matters to Him: how we live, how we relate to others, how we relate to Him, how we relate to ourselves. I dare say it matters to Him, because it is only through the mitzvot that a Jew can find his way clearly through the underbrush of this world. More: it is only through the mitzvot that one can transform the underbrush into a beautiful path through life.

As to why God would care to do this — it is because God is essentially the embodiment of all good in the universe, the essence of goodness — which by definition must share itself with others. The goodness that God shares with us includes serenity, contentment, peace within our own beings and with other people around us. God Himself promises us that His Torah and its mitzvot are for our own benefit. This is found throughout the Torah, and especially in *Deuteronomy* 6 and 10, where length of days, and serenity, and *tov* — good — are all by-products of observing the Torah.

So the answer is yes, it matters a great deal to God. He is the Creator of the vast cosmos, but at the same time He is concerned with our welfare here on earth. For example, the daily *Amidah* begins by praising the "great and glorious God, wondrous, mighty, Most High sovereign," and the very next phrase is: "Who bestows goodness and kindness." If you read that carefully, it states that being the Most High does not preclude His bestowing kindness. God is our King, *Malkenu*, but He is also our Father, *Avinu*. And every daily blessing begins with *Baruch Atah*, "Blessed art Thou," in the second person, and ends by referring to God in the third person — He is near and intimate, yet distant and apart. That is, He is simultaneously immanent — close by — and transcendent — far above us in every way. Thus, He is not too busy with cosmic matters to listen to us when we call on Him. We are, in fact, His cosmic matters.

I cannot explain to you the full reasons behind any of the mitzvot, or why certain mitzvot are to be done in certain ways. The point is that it is not God who benefits from these mitzvot, but we. He does not gain anything when we eat matzah — God is perfect, He lacks nothing, so nothing we do fills His needs. It is not God's needs that are filled, but our own.

We, not God, benefit

Beyond all this is the idea expressed by the Sages in *Bereshit Rabbah* 44:1 that God gave us the mitzvot *letzaref bahen et haberiot*, "to purify His creatures through them." That is to say, the performance of mitzvot makes us better human beings. They make us conscious of others, they make us less selfish and self-centered, they help us focus on ultimate things, they help us distinguish between things that really matter and things that don't, they give purpose and meaning to life, they lift us above the animals and civilize us and make us aware of God's existence. And the end result is that they transform us into holier and ultimately happier and more serene people. But I can't say it better than King David did in Psalm 19:

> *The Torah of God is perfect, restoring the soul; the testimony of God is trustworthy, making the simple one wise; the orders of God are upright, gladdening the heart; the mitzvah of God is clear, enlightening the eyes.*

D: Well, I wouldn't want to argue with King David. It's apparent that there's more to that little word "mitzvah" than meets the eye.

R: That's true of every aspect of Torah and Judaism. But let's unravel one further layer here. A mitzvah is the physical embodiment of a spiritual and Divine force, encased in the physical act we perform. Tefillin, for example, are not only square, black boxes containing the *Shema Yisrael* and three other Torah sections. Tefillin represent a very crucial aspect of God's own Being, which God wants to share with us. Its shape represents something spiritual, as does its color, as do its contents. If we had the ability to place a Divine X-ray on the tefillin, we would see right through them into the Godly force that they contain.

Thus, when I perform a mitzvah, I am not just fulfilling God's command — which is significant in itself. Beyond this, I am attaching my soul and body to Him. Man and God become unified through the mitzvah. We become sanctified, Godlike, and we can thus bring elements and aspects of His essence into our very beings. With tefillin, a man actually sanctifies his arm and head and fingers, and makes them vehicles for God's blessing; with mikveh, a woman sanctifies her entire physical self in the same way, as we all do when we enter a succah; when I give *tzedakah* to the poor, my outreaching hand is sanctified once again, as are my possessions; when I speak words of Torah or prayer, my entire apparatus of thought and physical speech becomes ennobled and sanctified. The mitzvah is the medium through which the emanations of God's holiness are transmitted to our material world.

This is what the Sages mean when they say that the 248 positive mitzvot match the 248 organs of the human body. They are saying that through the positive mitzvot, each part of the human body is elevated and made holy and brought closer to its Creator because it has been utilized in the service of the Holy One Himself. As for the 365 — in physiological terms they parallel the muscles and ligaments that control bodily motion. They also represent the idea that we should not sully the days of our years — embodied in the solar year of 365 —

by violating God's will and thus distancing ourselves from Him.

D: Well, we have come a long way in our discussion of mitzvah. I think at least I have a sense now of some of the ideas that lie beneath the surface of that word. Next time my grandmother asks me to do a mitzvah and bring her a glass of water, I'll ask her if she is aware that when I perform that mitzvah, I am actually elevating my hands and fingers, sanctifying them, bringing them closer to God.

R: Excellent. But remember that Judaism is a religion of action, not just theory. So while you're philosophizing with her, don't forget to bring her the water.

shabbat – the jew
discovers
serenity

. . . in which is discussed . . . Witness of Creation / Shabbat,
a day of don't's? / A space for
God to enter / Shabbat as return / Completing all our labor /
Sanctuaries in space and in time / Restrictions that liberate /
Definition of work / The thirty-nine steps / The desert
Tabernacle / An extra soul / This world and the next world /
Acts of trust / Building by not building / Queen or bride? . . .

David: The problem with discussing Judaism is that once
you begin to learn about some of these things, you must go on
to learn about other ones. They are all so intertwined.

Rabbi: Why is that a problem?

D: It's a problem when you're as lax as I am.

R: Well, Judaism is the best antidote for that. A halachically
    oriented Jew, for example, can never sleep until noon —
because Jewish law requires him to recite the *Shema* before
three hours of the day have elapsed, and to pray the morning
service before the end of the fourth hour. In general, ours is an

intellectually and physically rigorous way of life. So if you want to cure laziness, try Judaism.

D: Who wants to cure it?

R: Well, at least if you know you're lazy, that's a beginning. What would you like to discuss — energetically — today?

D: I need to talk about Shabbat. In religious circles that seems to be the key issue. I see that Shabbat observance is a kind of measuring rod by which a person's Jewishness is gauged. For example, I've been told that if a person is not a Sabbath observer, he cannot be a legal witness at a traditional Jewish wedding, so I need to know more about it.

All I do know is that it's a day of don't's. Don't drive your car, don't handle money, don't answer the telephone, don't do business, don't listen to the radio or TV, don't turn on the lights, don't do anything. It seems so forbidding. But what puzzles me is that those who observe it fully seem to love it and look forward to it, and behave as if they couldn't live without it — literally. Something is wrong either with my perception of the day, or with these people. And the fact is, they all do seem quite normal.

A day of don't's

R: And so do you. Let's begin from the beginning. For one thing, Shabbat is mentioned at least fifteen times in the Torah. But even before it became part of the Torah, Shabbat was in God's plan prior to Creation. That is to say, Shabbat is part of the original blueprint of the world, according to the thirteenth chapter of *Pirke d'R. Eliezer.* In the *Lecha Dodi* poem which we sing on Friday nights, there is a significant statement about Shabbat: *Sof ma'aseh bemachashavah techilah* — "Last in deed, but first in thought."

Thus, Shabbat is not just an afterthought. Chronologically, it was the last act of Creation, but it was in fact uppermost in God's mind when He began the Creation. The period of holiness that we call Shabbat is in fact the cornerstone of Judaism. Without it, there is no Judaism.

D: That's a broad statement. How is that?

R: The idea is that just as He ceased creating on the seventh day, so do we. By not engaging in creative work on this day, we are not only fulfilling the fourth of the Ten Commandments, but we are underscoring our belief in the reason stated in that commandment: that God created the world in six days and rested on the seventh.

Witness to Creation   Thus, Sabbath observance is our way of bearing witness that God is the Creator of the universe.

D: I don't understand: because God rested on the seventh day, therefore I, too, have to rest on the seventh day? I am not God, and I didn't create the world. What does His decision to rest have to do with me?

R: We have discussed this issue before, but it bears repetition: remember that one of the cardinal purposes of the religious life is to teach us how to emulate God. Although we are surely not God, we are asked by God to use Him as a model for our lives — and in fact He invites us to be partners with Him in the continuing creation and existence of the world. We are required to emulate His qualities of kindness, compassion, patience, and so forth. He also shares with us some of His creative powers — such as the ability to procreate or to help things grow. In a way, when we cease working on the seventh day, we are emulating His ways. As we will see later, He doesn't need the rest, but certain good things happen to us when we imitate His rest on the Shabbat. And God wants good things to happen to us.

D: Such as?

R: Such as giving us a sense of spiritual purpose, and allowing us to explore our higher selves — besides giving us a day of physical and spiritual rejuvenation.

Bear in mind also that by observing Shabbat, a Jew is in effect restating that there is only one Master in the universe. This may not seem to be a very significant statement, but the fact is that without it, man does tend to see himself as the dominating force in the world.

Shabbat is the antidote to this, because on Shabbat man releases everything that has been under his control. He removes his fingers from the buttons, lets go of the controls, releases the steering wheel. He is no longer the master. God alone is the Master. On Shabbat we say to God: "I am not omnipotent. You are. I hereby restore the world to You, its rightful Owner."

There is a further point: when we end our labors on Shabbat, we are in fact declaring that we believe that God created us all; thus, by observing the Shabbat, the Jew affirms the existence of God. That's why the Torah in *Exodus* 31:17 describes Shabbat as an *ot*; that is, a sign or a symbol of the special relationship between God and the Children of Israel, a kind of private understanding between us, a unifying banner around which the Jewish people gather and through which they bear living witness to God's Presence.

Now, before we go on, you should understand that by underscoring the belief that there is a God Who creates, Shabbat suggests a parallel concept; namely, the existence of a creating God means that the world has purpose and reason, that life is not a result of mere chance or coincidence. Because if the world came into existence only as a result of a freak occurrence and there is no purposeful Creator, that would mean that all is still chaos. And if all is chaos and there is no purpose to the world and all of life is a matter of random chance, the natural result is that we end up living without any framework or discipline — in our own chaos — merely reverting to our instincts, appetites and urges. That, my friend, has throughout history signaled the beginning of the end for any civilization. The idea of a purposeful, creating God has major implications for our view of the world and of ourselves.

Purpose and purpose-lessness

D: Your description of a purposeless world sounds very much like life as we know it today.

R: Exactly. With the results that we see all around us — all of which stem from the unwillingness to believe that there is Someone out there Who created everything for a reason, Who wants us to live in a certain way, and Who observes how well we do so.

If you don't subscribe to this concept, the natural thing to do is to have as much pleasure as possible while you're on this earth — to "eat and drink, for tomorrow we die," as Isaiah in 22:13 puts it in describing his own society (times have not really changed, have they?). By observing the Shabbat, we countervail this temptation to ignore God's Presence, and so every seventh day we remind ourselves Who really is in charge.

D: I'll have to digest some of that, but first let me ask you about this "resting" that God does on the seventh day. It's difficult to understand what this is supposed to mean, since obviously the Creator doesn't get tired.

R: Right you are. One of the purposes of God's so-called "rest" — the Hebrew word is *shabbat* — is to establish a paradigm for us mortals, as we said before. We are to engage in work and labor all week long, and utilize the materials of the universe that God presents to us; but we have to call a halt on day number seven, just as He did.

Space for Him to enter

It is obviously ludicrous to assume that God requires rest in order to recoup His strength so that He can continue His work. In fact, even on Shabbat God is not really inactive, since He continuously gives life to the universe — otherwise it would cease to exist. God's "rest" on the seventh day is designed to be a model for our human Shabbat rest. The reason we refrain from work is not because human beings must relax in order to work more effectively the next week.

D: What, then, is the reason?

R: Obviously, no one can say for certain what is in God's mind — that is far beyond our capacity to know. But a major achievement of Shabbat is that it allows us to pull back from the world and from the immediate business of ordinary life in order to contemplate things from a different perspective. For one thing, Shabbat admits God into our lives, allowing Him to penetrate our souls. By withdrawing from ordinary things, we open ourselves to new dimensions, to spiritual influences which cannot easily infiltrate our lives during the week. On Shabbat those influences have a chance to break through and be felt.

Remember, the Ten Commandments do not tell us merely to rest on the seventh day. The actual words are that the seventh day shall be a Shabbat "unto your God." The real purpose of Shabbat is to create a space for God to enter our lives, in the countless ways that He can do this.

D: That's a pretty phrase — "God entering our lives." What does it mean?

R: Surprising things happen when we let go of the physical things which control us during the week, and when we allow our souls to rise to the surface. It's as if a window is thrown open within us, allowing fresh air to enter.

In this case, the fresh air is God, Who has been waiting patiently outside for a chance to come into our lives. When you "do" Shabbat in the way it's supposed to be done, He comes in — through prayer, which has a different impact on us and on Him on Shabbat; through Torah study, which chips away at the barnacles which encrust our spirits; through a renewed awareness of the world around us and of the people around us; and even through the special wine and food and songs of the day. We rest, as do members of our family, as does our servant, as does our beast of burden. (And as does the beast of burden within us.) When this happens, we achieve a sense of internal peace, of harmony and oneness with the world, and with people, and with nature. Discord, anger, resentment, strife are all set aside. It actually happens when you give it a chance.

Maybe that's what the Talmud in *Beitzah* 16a has in mind when it tells us that God said to Moses: "I have a great gift in My treasure house; Shabbat is its name, and I want to give it to Israel. Go and so inform them . . ." Once you allow Shabbat to become part of your life, you really comprehend why God calls it a great gift.

Shabbat also offers us another gift: it enables us to put a *Shabbat* new perspective on the week. It allows us to turn our attention *as return* to our non-material needs and to make certain that we do not neglect them, as we often do during the work week. It's a time when we can turn towards God and thereby return to our personal and religious roots. As a matter of fact, the word Shabbat means not only "rest," but also "return." Just as God stands back after His Creation and contemplates it, so do we withdraw from our creative activity upon the earth — we unplug ourselves from the apparatus of ordinary life — and return to our original selves.

That's why the Ten Commandments say that during the

six days of the week "Thou shalt do all thy work . . ." —
which is a strange statement, because no one can complete all
his labor in six days, or in six years or six decades. Only God
can complete all His labor. But we mortals are supposed to try
to emulate God. So when the Torah says that we are to complete all our labor during the weekdays, it means that we are
to behave on Shabbat *as if* we have done all our labor.
Nothing ordinary should be permitted to interfere with the
spirituality of Shabbat. And that's what helps us "return," to
come back to our true, inner selves.

D: But a person can't really control what's going on in his
head.

R: I grant you that it is not easy, but it can be done.
   Admittedly, it takes effort, but the idea is to discipline
yourself so that when you enter the doorway of Shabbat you
are able to deposit all thoughts of the week behind you, as if
they simply do not exist.
   That deal that you are in the middle of; that project that
has you tossing at night; that trip whose planning occupies
your spare time — they are to be treated as if they were
complete. On Shabbat these things have no life, because you
are entering another realm entirely — just as a world-class
surgeon or athlete leaves everything behind when he enters
the operating theater or the playing field and concentrates
only on the task at hand. If during the Shabbat day a person
is thinking constantly of his business, his essential Shabbat
is disturbed. If he is thinking of the things he did not complete during the week, or the things he still has to do after
Shabbat, he is carrying excess baggage that diminishes the
harmony of Shabbat. He will not enjoy the complete sanctity of the day, nor benefit from its total emotional and
spiritual rest. Completing "all your work" means that you
forget about the past week. It is a closed book. It is done.
And you forget about the coming week. Do not plan ahead
for anything.

The purpose of the week   In fact, Jewish law forbids us to utilize Shabbat to prepare for the weekdays. For example, if I am leaving for a
trip on Sunday, I may not pack my luggage on Shabbat.
When I utilize the holy day to prepare for the weekday

act, Shabbat becomes subservient to the weekday; the holy day becomes secondary and the weekday primary, instead of the other way around. Shabbat is the purpose of the week, the climax of the week, the pinnacle towards which the other days lead. Shabbat is an island in time, independent of and not connected with any other kind of time. Or, to stretch the image a bit, an island of calm in the raging ocean of life.

The point is that a totally different and unique attitude envelops us on Shabbat. A new world, a new universe. Everything else grinds to a halt. Shabbat is not just a comma, not just a semicolon, not even a period.

D: How about a new chapter?

R: Not even a new chapter. Shabbat is a totally different *A different* book. Let me revise that island image. Shabbat is not only *planet* an island in the raging seas. Shabbat is a different planet entirely, in which we are not even aware that there are such things as raging seas lapping at the edges. Ideally, the Jew becomes a new person on Shabbat, his attitudes are new and fresh, his outlook new and fresh, his relationship to God and to family and to other people, new and fresh — because he has entered a new and fresh world, completely different from the world in which he lives the rest of the week.

D: Do you mean that the rest of the week doesn't count?

R: Not at all. The work week is extremely important and worthwhile. The Torah does not negate it at all; in fact, it commands us, "Six days shalt thou labor." Those mundane six days are important; that's why we have only one Shabbat out of every seven days, but that seventh day makes the other six days worthwhile and gives them focus and meaning. By withdrawing from activity within the physical realm, we are better able to enter the spiritual realm and begin to see life from a fresh perspective. We realize that far from owning the world, we actually "borrow" the world from God during the week, and on Shabbat we return the loan — which is another facet of "return."

In a way, this is the blessing that God gives to this day: that we are prevented from becoming mere beasts of burden.

Otherwise, there is the great danger of becoming slaves to what we are doing, without any regard for our higher selves.

Creative rest

D: And all these good things happen just because I'm not working on Shabbat?

Not just a pause

R: Not at all. The idea of Shabbat rest is not simply cessation of work, or simply being idle. Theoretically, a person could crawl into his bed on Friday evening and stay there until Saturday night, and he will not have violated any Shabbat laws. But he will not really have observed the Shabbat. Shabbat rest is a dynamic, positive thing. Like weekday labor, Shabbat rest has to be creative and purposeful. It is the mirror image, the photographic negative, of *melachah*, work. It is a rest which moves us to a higher spiritual level, to one of majesty and renewal, offering a new perspective on the affairs of the week, on our own labor, on our relationship with society, with other people, with our families, with ourselves, with God.

Yes, it is also a physical cessation from work, but it is not just lounging around, reading the newspapers, drinking beer, and catching up on social obligations. It is a disciplined, purposeful, creative rest. This kind of rest is facilitated by the negative guidelines of Shabbat and is enhanced by its positive guidelines.

Shabbat, in other words, is not just a twenty-four-hour interruption between the work of one week and the work of the next week. In fact, the concept of Oneg Shabbat, the "delight of Shabbat" — which is based on a passage in *Isaiah* 58:13 — reminds us that the purpose of all Creation and the purpose of all Torah, including the laws of Shabbat, is to give us pleasure, joy and delight. This is what God wants for us, and this is why He shares His Torah and mitzvot with us. Nothing gives God greater joy than to share His goodness and His serenity and His harmony with His creatures. That's why He is called *Hatov Vehameitiv* — "the Good and the Beneficent One."

D: I dare say that God's idea of delight and pleasure is no doubt somewhat different from ours.

R: No doubt. And a lot more lasting, too. Because Shabbat is designed to be a foretaste of the World to Come, an introduction to a new kind of delight and pleasure. Those who observe Shabbat sense this — though it is not easy to describe. They experience a taste of life in Paradise. Although mortals can experience only a glimmer of it, even the glimmer is quite magnificent.

This idea is found between the lines of the Bible. On each of the six days of Creation, it is written: "And it was evening and it was morning," followed by the day of the week. But for the seventh day, this evening-morning formula is absent. Why?

Because Shabbat is not just another day. Ordinary days of the natural universe are framed by the limitations of night and day, evenings and mornings — but Shabbat represents another realm, the realm of primal perfection which was the Creation, a realm we call eternity. It has no physical boundaries or limitations, and thus there is no "and it was evening and it was morning . . ." *Restrictions that liberate*

What emerges is that, on a very profound level, the very prohibitions of Shabbat, which on the surface seem to be so restrictive, are actually the vehicles which usher us into a completely new dimension. That which appears to be physically restrictive turns out to be spiritually liberating. The don't's are actually the strategies which make certain that the special, unique harmony of the day will not be interrupted.

D: But it doesn't make sense — restrictions creating liberation!

R: Look at it from another perspective. The restrictions are like the barriers at the side of a bridge. They force us to stay on the path and prevent us from falling over the side. The so-called barriers of Shabbat are designed to keep us on the path of a spiritual day.

Look at what has happened, for example, to the Christian Sunday. It has lost much of its religious meaning, and is in fact a shambles. It's a day when killing and maiming on the highways is at its peak. Saturday night is a time of drunkenness and madness, when the emergency rooms are filled with victims of shootings and stabbings. Shopping malls are mobbed, sports stadiums are packed. Sunday has degenerated from what was supposed to be a spiritual day into a day of brutality at worst, and of sheer materialism at best. This could never happen to the Jewish Shabbat if it is kept properly. That, of course, is a big "if" — but I am comforted by the fact that more and more Jews are dipping into Shabbat.

D: I guess it does require a plunge of sorts. But it frightens me.

R: It may seem frightening at first, but soon enough the waters become very comfortable. In any case, this is how those seemingly forbidding do's and don't's create a special kind of day for us. At the very least, if I cannot watch TV, then I pick up a book. If I cannot ride somewhere, I stay in the neighborhood or at home, and so visiting with friends becomes natural. Talking with one's own family has become almost a rarity in modern society, except for those who observe Shabbat. Or I may read something Jewish, or just think, which we rarely have time to do during the week. I might even consider visiting the neighborhood synagogue. And if there is a study group there, I might join in it Friday night or Shabbat afternoon. And so forth. And before you know it, the day is transformed from a day of ordinary activity into something quite spiritual and constructive.

Besides which, Shabbat is not only a series of thou-shalt's. There are many thou-shalt not's, many do's. That's why the set of Commandments in *Exodus* speaks of "remembering" (*zachor*) the Shabbat day, and the set in *Deuteronomy* speaks of "observing" or "protecting" (*shamor*) the Shabbat day.

"Remember" and "protect"

D: Aren't these basically the same words? Why do we need two different terms?

R: Because they are similar only on the surface. The difference between the two verbs is this: *zachor* refers to the positive aspects of Shabbat, the things we are required to do. *Shamor* refers to the negative aspects, the acts we are to refrain from doing; that is, to protect the Shabbat from profane things. One set gives us thou-shalt's; the other gives us thou-shalt-not's — two sides of the same coin. In any case, the Shabbat is a combination of do's and don't's. To stress the don't's and forget the do's is a distortion of the meaning of the day.

In point of fact, Shabbat represents the classic model of *Holy and* the separation of the holy from the profane. Remember that *profane* the Hebrew word for holy — *kadosh* — bears the connotation of something apart and separate. When God "sanctified" the Shabbat day, He not only made it holy; He made it special and different from all the other days, a day that helps us realize our higher yearnings. One should dress and eat better on Shabbat, for example. It is a time of joy, not of total withdrawal from the physical world. It is a day of pleasure, delight, *oneg* — different from all the others. A person comes home from synagogue on Friday evening to a table specially set, candles glowing, family gathered around. They sing a song of welcome to the Sabbath Queen; they chant *Proverbs* 31 — the hymn of praise to the "accomplished woman," known in Hebrew as *Eishet Chayil*; the Shabbat *Kiddush* prayer is recited over wine, as is the blessing over the special Shabbat challah-bread. The meal is unhurried, there are often guests at the table, the week's Torah portion is discussed, table songs are sung. Husband is king, wife is queen. It is a radiant moment.

D: This doesn't sound very restrictive or forbidding to me. It sounds like a very good time.

R: Yes, literally: a time that is good — and not just because we enjoy the Friday night wine and fish and soup and chicken. The complex don't's and do's are designed to help us focus on the issues and things that really matter in life, so that Shabbat can become a day of majesty, when man and God meet and touch one another.

Certainly we are required to live in this world, to earn a *This world* living, take part in society — but one day a week we are *and the* helped to ascend to a plateau high above the ordinary world *next* and look beyond the here-and-now. That's one reason Shabbat is referred to as *me'ein olam haba*, a "semblance of the World to Come," a kind of taste of Paradise, as I mentioned earlier. That is to say, if you want to have an idea of the eternal rest and joy and delight and tranquility and bliss and exultation and spiritual fulfillment (I'm running out of words, but you get the idea) that are present in the World to Come — some preview and precursor of all this — it is to be found in the observance of Shabbat.

Another reason for this term is that just as we prepare in this world for life in the World to Come, so do we prepare during the weekdays for life on Shabbat. The weekdays represent this world, and the Shabbat represents the next world. It's not just a pretty phrase when the Talmud, in *Tamid* 7:4, refers to the World to Come as *yom she-kulo Shabbat*, "a day which is a complete and eternal Shabbat." During the days of the week — which is akin to life in this world — the Jew is in a state of "becoming." On Shabbat — which represents the World to Come — he enters the state of pure "being."

D: You say we don't really know the underlying Divine purpose of Shabbat. But doesn't the Torah say something about the Egyptian slavery?

R: In the Ten Commandments in *Exodus* 19, we find this: "For in six days God created the heavens and the earth." But in the repetition of the Commandments, in *Deuteronomy* 5, we find what you are citing: "You were slaves in Egypt, and God redeemed you from slavery."

Two rationales   *D:* Why do we need two different rationales for Shabbat? Especially when the two don't seem to have any connection with each other.

R: We need two because these are in fact the two major elements of Shabbat. The first rationale reminds us that there is only one Creator, as we just discussed. The second turns our attention to those aspects of daily life that hobble our independence. Slavery does not mean only chains and whips and demanding overseers. It can also mean the oppressive realization that we cannot survive without the gadgets and conveniences our grandparents never even imagined.

By relinquishing our ongoing conquest of the natural universe, by pausing in our manipulation of things, by not relying on machines for one day, we become truly free and independent. On Shabbat we find suddenly that they are quite dispensable. That car which we depend upon so much all week — which in many ways enslaves us — we are liberated from it. That electricity without which we cannot function — one day a week we learn to function without creating it. (We are allowed to enjoy it on Shabbat as long as we don't initiate it or bring it into being on Shabbat.) So Shabbat represents a freedom from all types of slavery — the reason given in the second set of Commandments. The two rationales really complement one another.

D: Nice theory, but let's be practical. How can we turn our backs on the activities that make up our very existence?

R: No one asks that we turn our backs on anything. What is asked is that we look at our mundane lives from a fresh perspective. This results not in a rejection of our activities, but in an ability to place them in their proper niche — where they don't control us, but we control them. People who are subjugated to their businesses, bosses or schoolwork for 168 hours a week cannot imagine the exquisite joy of being free for over twenty-four hours each week. This gives us an opportunity to pay some attention to our own higher selves. The results are ironic. By acknowledging God as the Master, we become masters of our own lives. *A fresh perspective*

D: Is a person actually required to shut everything down once a week?

R: His business and profession, yes. Literally shut down.

Let's face it: over and above all else, Shabbat observance is really a great act of faith. When the merchant closes his place of business late Friday afternoon, even though there may be customers at the door and even though closing may cost him money, that is a statement of faith and trust in God. That fellow is saying: "Yes, I need to earn a living, but I also realize that ultimately my livelihood is given me by God, and I want to recognize that there is something in my life that is higher and more compelling than making money. God has enjoined me from doing business on Shabbat, and that's that."

The turn of the key in the lock of that office or business as Shabbat approaches may seem like a prosaic act, but it is noble and majestic, a statement of faith as eloquent in its own ordinary way as is the *Shema Yisrael* prayer. This person in effect is saying, "Logically, it makes no sense for me to close up shop when my main consideration in going into this profession or business was to make a decent living — and now I'm actually turning down money; but I believe that if I follow *The turn of the key* the Torah I will not only not lose, but I will gain. Even if I lose some income, I will still gain other more important things, because there are things in this world more valuable than money, even if they are beyond my understanding."

(By the way, the same kind of thing happened in the wilderness after the Israelites left Egypt. Do you remember how they were fed? Through the miraculous *manna* that fell from heaven. Check the sixteenth chapter of *Exodus*, where God tells them that on Shabbat there will be no *manna* and that they will collect double portions on Friday. This, too, was a test of their faith and trust in God.)

In any case, the fellow who closes on Friday afternoon may not think of it as an act of faith, but that's what it is. And imagine the impact of this weekly turn of the key on his children and family, and on the community around him. As time goes on, this person's faith in God continues to grow and deepen. Faith has that characteristic: it grows on us, and within us. And it affects a wide circle of people beyond ourselves.

All this explains why Shabbat is so central to Judaism that a knowledgeable Jew who wantonly desecrates Shabbat is regarded as if he had denied the existence of God. It's not just another commandment; it contains the essence of the Torah's message about the interaction between God, man and the universe.

Incidentally, that term "central" is not just a figure of speech. Even though chronologically Shabbat is day number seven, it is in another sense the mid-point of the week. That is, the last three days of the week anticipate the coming of Shabbat, from which they receive their sanctity, and the first three days of the week are still aglow from the previous Shabbat. If you can imagine a curve, Shabbat is at the top of the curve, with the previous three days of the week leading up to it and the succeeding three days of the week leading down from it.

And it's also significant, from another perspective, that in Judaism the days of the week have no names of their own. Sunday is "the first day of Shabbat," Monday is "the second day of Shabbat," and so forth. Every day is connected to the Shabbat.

In sum, Shabbat contains these concepts: God as Creator and active Force within our world; God Who sets us free; Shabbat as a precursor of the World to Come; Shabbat as an act of faith. These are powerful ideas.

D: I guess the corollary of all this is that once you are able to observe Shabbat, the rest of the Torah is not that difficult. The negative laws of Shabbat, the don't's, are beginning to intrigue me — especially the way they seem to weave a kind of pattern of sanctity and keep us from wandering off the path of spirituality. But I am curious: these don't's — where do they come from? And how is it that certain simple acts, such as flicking on the light switch, are forbidden on Shabbat?

R: We really ought to be using the original Hebrew term, *Defining* because it would be less confusing. What we call "labor" *"work"* is *melachah* in Hebrew, but it does not really mean "work" or "labor" in the sense of muscular exertion. Rather, *melachah* is a special legal term which denotes productive activity or creative labor, an act which produces something in its wake. The Torah does not say, "Thou shalt do no work on Shabbat"; it says, "Thou shalt do no *melachah* on Shabbat." It's true that flicking the light switch is an easy, simple act, but it transforms energy into light — and therefore it's as much a productive activity as the rubbing together of stones to create sparks that could be nurtured into a flame.

There are all kinds of *melachah* activity which represent specific categories of creative labor on Shabbat. Sowing seeds is *melachah*; so is weaving, and baking, and trapping, and building, and writing, and sewing. That means that we don't write or type a letter on Shabbat, or bake a cake, or pick flowers, or cut the grass or water it, or sew on a button, or fertilize the ground, or create fire in any way — such as by driving a car or smoking a cigarette.

All told, there are thirty-nine principal categories of *melachah* on Shabbat. And each of these categories is divided into sub-categories, so that a huge range of activities is covered by the Shabbat laws — and they are either permissible or impermissible on Shabbat. The ones that are forbidden represent a type of creative labor which distracts us from the ultimate purpose, which is—

D: —to remember that God ceased creating, and to remember that the purpose of Shabbat is to make us free again.

R: Excellent.

D: Could we be having this type of discussion on a Shabbat?

R: Why not?

D: Well, it's creative and it is intellectual labor of sorts. Thinking is never easy.

R: Nothing that is in the realm of intellect is forbidden *per se* on Shabbat. One is permitted to work all of Shabbat day on a difficult passage in the Talmud or the Torah — that's not only permissible, but is considered a mitzvah. The thirty-nine categories of Shabbat *melachah* include only physical activities, not cerebral labor. Of course, in ideal terms, our intellects should focus particularly on Jewish matters on Shabbat.

D: Where do these categories come from?

The desert **R:** Now that's the most fascinating point of all. The source of
Tabernacle   the *melachah* restrictions is found in the construction of
and   the desert Tabernacle — called the Mishkan. *Exodus* 25-27
Shabbat   presents a detailed architect's blueprint for how to construct the Mishkan. This Mishkan, after all, was the resting place for God's Presence on earth, and as such it was an extremely significant structure. The Torah itself, in *Exodus* 35, refers to the task of constructing it as *avodat hakodesh,* "sacred service."

And yet, as crucial as it was, the work of building the Mishkan had to be suspended on Shabbat. That is to say, the sanctity of the Shabbat overrode the importance of the Mishkan. That principle still applies, by the way; thus, Shabbat labor does not become permissible for the sake of attending or conducting synagogue services.

A crucial   From this — and from the fact that the Torah in *Exodus* 35
concept   connects the construction of the Mishkan with the laws of the Shabbat — Jewish law derives the concept that the type of *melachah* that went into its construction is the type of *melachah* which is forbidden on Shabbat. This is the crucial

point to remember: whatever needed to be done to build the Mishkan is by definition a *melachah*. Therefore, the type of labor that is forbidden on Shabbat is precisely the type of labor that went into the construction of the Mishkan.

Those thirty-nine categories and their derivatives, it goes without saying, comprise some of the most complex material of the Talmud. In addition, the single longest section of the *Shulchan Aruch*, the Jewish Code of Law, deals with Shabbat.

The thirty-nine categories themselves fall into three primary divisions. Some of the *melachot* are agricultural, such as sowing seeds; some have to do with food preparation, such as baking; and some deal with craftsmanship, such as writing or drawing. Carrying from one domain to another is also forbidden, not because it is creative labor *per se*, but because the act of moving things from a public domain to a private domain, or vice versa, symbolizes the world at work: commerce, trading, bartering, buying, selling, lending, taking, giving, moving, transferring. All the interaction of society, all the commercial interconnectedness of people at work, is symbolized by the act of carrying from domain to domain, or within the public domain.

D: I don't quite get the connection between the Mishkan and Shabbat. Surely there were other acts of labor in the Bible which could have served as a model for Shabbat non-labor. Maybe that way we wouldn't have had so many complex categories.

R: Your question is a good one, and our mystical tradition provides a fascinating answer. It suggests that the thirty-nine creative actions required to construct the Mishkan actually mirror the thirty-nine creative actions with which God created the world. The Mishkan itself is a microcosm of the universe and parallels the world which God created.

The Mishkan: a microcosm

What emerges now is that when we desist from the thirty-nine types of creative labor on Shabbat, we imitate God, Who also desisted from His thirty-nine labors on Shabbat — which are mirrored in the construction of the Mishkan.

An exciting idea emerges from all this; namely, that by our "work stoppage" on the seventh day, by refraining from certain activities and performing other activities because they are

God's will, we, like God, are building a totally new structure which is called Shabbat.

Thus, it emerges that throughout life, a person engages in two kinds of construction: a) the six-day-a-week physical construction of things and objects and energy; and b) the seventh-day-of-the-week spiritual construction. This second kind of construction is in the abstract, non-tangible realm. When we constructed the Mishkan, we built a sanctuary in space; but when we construct the Shabbat, we build a sanctuary in time. Space is physical, and you need physical things to construct anything within space. But time is an intangible.

Building in time   **D:** But how do you "build" in the realm of time? How do you "build" a spiritual structure?

R: The building blocks are the do's and the don't's of Shabbat. Through careful attention to their details, we gradually construct the spiritual temple of Shabbat. The first thing we do is discard and eliminate precisely those elements which go into the construction of physical and material things. When we put these aside, we can concentrate on the spiritual construction. And the thirty-nine categories of *melachah* are precisely those physical building materials we put aside as we build the sanctuary in time.

A significant by-product of all this is that Shabbat sanctifies the passage of time. It helps us realize the holiness and the value of time itself, and it helps us transform the common and the humdrum into something special and uncommon.

D: Why isn't it enough just to refrain from exerting myself on Shabbat?

R: Remember that *melachah* does not simply mean physical exertion, and Shabbat rest — which is called *menuchah* — does not simply mean physical rest. In *melachah*, the criterion of work is not the amount of effort or exertion; the end result, the creativity and the productivity, is the criterion. That's why striking a match, which takes minimal effort, is *melachah* — because it creates something that was not present before: the flame. God did not have to exert any effort to create the world: He spoke and it became. In understanding the laws of

Shabbat, the result of a particular action is crucial and not the
the amount of effort or energy we put into the action.

But I am getting away from myself. I started to say that *The extra*
Shabbat creates a twenty-four-hour sanctuary in time. By fol- *dimension*
lowing the design outlined in the Torah's blueprint, we can
succeed in building for ourselves a new structure called
menuchah. In fact, there is an ancient Talmudic tradition
recorded in *Beitzah* 16a that on Shabbat the Jew is presented
with the gift of a *neshamah yeteirah*, an additional soul, an
extra spiritual dimension specifically created for the Shabbat.

That's not just a pretty concept, this idea of sacredness of
time. In our festival prayers, we refer to God as the One Who
sanctifies Israel and the seasons — literally, "times" —
mekadesh Yisrael vehazemanim. Which, by the way, teaches
us to take time seriously, to use it wisely, not to expend it care-
lessly — just as we would treat anything that is precious.

We physically enter this spiritual sanctuary on Friday night
with the *Kiddush* prayer, and throughout Shabbat we dwell in
its various chambers — chambers of prayer, study, contemplation, song, food, pleasures, physical rest — and then we leave
the sanctuary Saturday night through the door we call
Havdalah, the exit prayer which separates Shabbat from the
mundane, work-a-day week.

D: What you're saying is that by refraining from building in a
physical sense, we are in fact building in a spiritual sense.
That is certainly provocative, but I'm not quite sure I grasp it
fully.

R: Let's put it this way: in a painting, the blank spaces help
set off the filled spaces. In music, the stops and pauses are
an integral part of the music. Without the pauses, there is no
rhythm or beat. The same is true of speech and of writing.
Imagine reading a text that has no space between the words.
Canyoumakethissentenceout? The pauses of Shabbat — the
cessation of activity, the "not-doing" — create a kind of magical symphony of pauses and stops that allow us to be still, to
call a halt, to be alone with ourselves.

During the week, every creative act builds; on Shabbat,
the cessation of creative activity constitutes the necessary
pauses, and the positive spiritual things we do on Shabbat

build the day into something sacred. That's the difference between building in the realm of space — the earthly Mishkan — and building in the realm of time — which is the Shabbat. In the realm of the spirit, refraining from physical creation is the beginning of spiritual creation.

Let me point out some strange language in *Genesis* 2:2: "And God completed on the seventh day all the work that He had done." He completed His work on the seventh day? Did not God complete His work in six days and rest on the seventh?

The answer is that even though He completed the material universe in six days, the world was not yet complete. The essential component of *menuchah* was missing from the whole, the component of the spirit. Without Shabbat, it was like creating a person with a body but no soul. By resting on the Shabbat, by calling a halt to the physical act of creation, the world was completed. Not creating became the final act of creating.

D: So God invites man to build the Shabbat, just as He invited man to build the Mishkan.

R: Now you've grasped it! Plus this: when the Torah says, in the very next verse, "For on the seventh day God rested from all His labor which He had done," the text uses an extra word which at first glance seems to make no sense. That word is *la'asot*, "to do." The phrase seems to hang there — "which He had done to do"?

D: What does it mean?

God and the Jew shape the Shabbat

R: It means that God and man together "do" the Shabbat. *La'asot* means that God has given man the concept, the time period and the tools with which to build this wondrous day.

It's curious that later on, the Torah has this same unusual usage of *la'asot* in connection with Shabbat. In *Exodus* 31:16, the verse states, *Veshamru benei Yisrael et haShabbat*, "The Children of Israel shall observe the Shabbat" — and then it continues, *la'asot et haShabbat*, "to make the Shabbat for their generations as an everlasting covenant" — which is quite unclear. But here, too, it makes sense when you translate it as the Jewish people "doing" or "making" or "building" this day with the tools given us by God. The same is true of that strange word at the end of Friday night *Kiddush*: *asher bara Elohim la'asot*, "which God created to do." What does *la'asot*, "to do," mean here? As we just said, the Jew "does" Shabbat, creates it, together with God.

D: What you're saying, in other words, is that without the Jew there is no Shabbat.

R: Exactly. In fact, there's a magnificent tradition that under-   *Shabbat's*
scores the idea that the Jew and Shabbat are natural part-   *partner*
ners. The Shabbat complained to God that every day of the week has a partner except the Shabbat. The first day has the fourth, when God "completed" what He created on day one by illuminating the earth on day four. On day five, He "completed" His creation of day two — the division of the lower waters of earth from those of heaven — by placing fish in the waters and winged creatures in the skies; on day six He completed what He created on day three — revealing the dry land and creating vegetation — by creating the beasts to walk on dry land, and of course by creating Adam and Eve. Only the Shabbat is without a partner. God, says *Bereshit Rabba* 11:9, acknowledged the complaint and said to the Shabbat: "Be assured that you will have a partner. The Jewish people will be your partner."

Which is more than just a pretty tale. What it really is saying is that the Jewish people complete the Shabbat by living it and observing it. And it also means that Shabbat is alone and unique and different, and the Jewish people are also alone and unique and different. They are a natural pair, as you suggest, and Shabbat depends on the Children of Israel to bring its purpose to fruition.

D: If it's so important to withdraw from the ordinary world and build this great moment in time, why not do it more frequently? If once a week is so significant, maybe twice a week would be even better.

R: Believe me, it would be quite sufficient if everyone were to keep just the one day a week. If God stipulates that the seventh of each week is what we need, we are not required —

or even permitted — to improve upon His blueprint. We believe God's law to be perfect. We may not tack on minus signs or plus signs. The Torah explicitly warns us against adding to the commandments or subtracting from them, even if we have the noblest and most pious motives. We are not permitted to add, say, a fifth paragraph to the four which are already prescribed for tefillin; or to add additional verses to the mezuzah parchments. And certainly we may not reduce the number. *Lo tosifu . . . velo tigra-u*, says *Deuteronomy* 4:2, repeating it in 13:1: "You may not add, nor may you diminish" from the mitzvot.

Repairing
the world
I want to make another point concerning the relationship of Shabbat to the work of the week. Our withdrawal on Shabbat is not meant to diminish the great value the Torah places upon labor. Work is a positive and a good thing, and God does not want us to be idle. Judaism in general does not believe in withdrawing from society. God truly wants us to be engaged in building up the world in a thousand different ways.

This is called *tikkun ha-olam*, productively repairing and developing the world. In Judaism, there are no monks or monasteries. We are to be part of the world. We are to marry, bear children, raise them, take part in the ongoing struggles of the marketplace and the professions. At the same time, however, our productive labor must have limits. We are to be the masters of our work, and not the reverse. God does not want our work to consume us, devour us, possess us — as it can easily do. He gave us the Shabbat so that we will strike a balance; He wants us to fuse the physical and the spiritual together, to have them complement one another. We may not work seven days a week — nor may we have Shabbat seven days a week. This fusion of the holy and the mundane, of heaven and earth, is typical of the Torah. It assigns a proper place and balance to each.

D: All of this is intellectually exciting and even emotionally moving, but I am afraid of it.

R: Afraid of what?

D: Afraid of all the requirements, afraid of all the beautiful do's and all the beautiful don't's. Even with all the good and profound reasons that undergird them, I am frightened of taking the plunge.

R: Who says you have to plunge? Try sticking in a little toe.

D: What do you mean?

R: I mean that you don't have to jump in all at once. You can *A step at* take it one step at a time. For example, if it is too much at *a time* the beginning to refrain totally from, say, the use of electricity, then set aside just Friday night for that. If observing all of Shabbat is intimidating, then observe a part of Shabbat. See that the candles are lit for Friday evening, dress differently, have a special meal, recite *Kiddush.* You are, after all, starting fresh, and it may be too much to expect you to observe this complex day all in one fell swoop. So choose a few hours during the day, or one or two hours on Friday night. That way you'll get a taste of it, and you can add to the menu as time goes by. Nobody is pushing you on this. You can go at your own speed. Set aside a corner of the twenty-four hours of Saturday for Shabbat. The corner can be the entire twenty-four hours, or it can be one hour. The point is not to stop at theorizing, but to go on and actually live it — even on a minimal level. From there, you will be able to build up to more.

D: But isn't that hypocrisy? Wouldn't it be more honest if I either observed it all or observed nothing?

R: That's like saying that if I can't make a million dollars immediately, I won't try to make a living at all. A hypocrite is one who pretends to be that which he is not, who puts on a performance for others in order to impress them. But if you are unable to observe all the mitzvot — or if you are unable to observe a single mitzvah fully — and you decide that you will try to observe what you can at this stage in your life, that is hardly hypocritical — because you're not trying to impress anyone; you are simply doing as much as you can. And surely you won't object if you find yourself wanting to do more and more as time goes on.

Besides which, there are some good empirical reasons for you not to be afraid. First, you can take it step by step. In addition, you can get help and support along the way from many others who have taken the dip into the waters and have found it refreshing. You have the encouragement of knowing that the Jewish people historically has had a love affair with the Shabbat — certainly not the kind of relationship one would have with a forbidding, severe and frightening day. For the Jews, the Shabbat is a queen — *Shabbat ha-malkah* — and the Talmud in *Bava Kama* 32b refers to it as a bride, a *kallah*.

Queen and bride

D: Well, which is it, queen or bride?

R: Good question — because the images used in our tradition are not frivolous. There is a difference between a queen and a bride. A queen dominates, gives instructions, rules, guides, endows with gifts and accepts the homage of her subjects. A bride, though equally regal, does not dominate. She is a partner and is unified with us. A queen is external, outside us; a bride is internal, part of us. That's how Shabbat is: she exists in God's realm, independent of us, but she is also dependent on us, on how we sanctify her. So Shabbat is both queen and bride.

The amazing thing is that this seemingly rigorous day has engendered thousands of poems and songs about her. Shabbat observers look forward to it each week, save the best food and clothing for it — which, incidentally, is another method of fulfilling the commandment to "remember the Shabbat day": we remember it all week long. *Bava Kama* 119b speaks about setting aside special things for Shabbat, as befits a queen and bride.

D: You make it sound so inviting and appealing. How come more people don't keep it? Are they all impenetrable?

R: No, just uninformed. They may not have had the type of discussion you and I just had . . .

yom tov – the jew celebrates holy days

. . . in which is discussed . . . The difference between Yom Tov and Shabbat / Between Yom Kippur and Shabbat / Pilgrimage and non-pilgrimage festivals / Heaven penetrates earth / Slavery / Reliving events / The dateless festival / Transcending clock and calendar / Diaspora's extra day / Spring, the keystone season / Lunar leap years / Legislating joy / Change and accountability . . .

Rabbi: In our last meeting, we discussed Shabbat. I thought that today we might look at the festivals, the general concept of *chag*, or, as it is more widely known, Yom Tov.

David: But aren't Yom Tov and Shabbat basically the same? I know, for example, that observant Jews don't drive their cars either on Yom Tov or Shabbat. Don't the restrictions of Shabbat also apply to Yom Tov?

Shabbat and Yom Tov — similar but not identical

R: Well, yes and no. They do share many of the same restrictions, but the laws of Yom Tov observance are less strict than Shabbat. They are similar in many ways, but certainly not identical — not only in the way we practice them, but in the concepts and ideas which undergird them.

First, though, let's set up our definitions. What do we mean when we say "Yom Tov"? Purim and Chanukah, for example, are very significant days in the Jewish calendar but they are not Yom Tov. A Yom Tov is a festival whose observance is commanded in the Torah, in the Five Books. Purim is in the Bible, in the Book of Esther, but since it is not in the Five Books, it does not attain the sanctity of a Yom Tov.

D: In practical terms, what does that mean? Aren't we just as obligated to observe Purim and Chanukah as we are, say, Pesach?

R: Of course. But the holiness of a Biblically ordained Yom Tov is much greater than is a post-Biblical celebration. That is to say, the manner of observance, and the restrictions and the penalties for non-observance, are completely different. On Purim and Chanukah — on non-Biblical festivals — there are no labor restrictions. We may sew, plant, build, write — any of the acts of creative labor which are prohibited on the Biblical festivals. In practical terms, we may work on Purim and Chanukah, or engage in commerce, or handle money, or drive a car — activities which are prohibited on a Biblical Yom Tov.

Further, Yom Tov prayer in the synagogue is similar to that of Shabbat. In addition, we recite *Kiddush* at home to usher in the festival, and in the synagogue we pray not only *shacharit*, but *musaf* as well, and there is a full Torah reading, plus recitation of additional Psalms. The atmosphere, and most of the prayers themselves, are very much like Shabbat.

Now, while we make efforts to sanctify Chanukah and Purim, the very fact that labor is permitted on those days mitigates against their being as holy a time as Shabbat or Yom Tov. Chanukah and Purim do have special Torah readings in the synagogue, but these are very brief, and only three people are called to the Torah instead of the six on Yom Tov and the eight on Shabbat. Nor do Chanukah and Purim require the *musaf* service, or the recitation of *Kiddush.*

D: Are you saying that we can measure the degree of holiness of a day by its restrictions?

R: Precisely. Shabbat and Yom Kippur have the most restrictions, and they happen to be our holiest days. Yom Tov has a few less restrictions, and is somewhat less holy. Purim and Chanukah have practically no restrictions, and they bear even less sanctity as compared to Shabbat.

D: I never thought of thou-shalt-nots as a gauge of sanctity.

R: That's why we're having these discussions: to explore the things one never thinks of. Remember that the Biblical thou-shalt-nots are not merely negative commandments. They are the means by which something is made less earthly, mundane, physical, and material. Restrictions help us realize that it is on a different level. By refraining from doing something, we refrain from making it ordinary. The sacred is by definition somewhat off limits, unfamiliar, less visible. In the Temple, the Holy of Holies was entered only once a year, and then only by the High Priest. God represents the ultimate sanctity within the universe, and of course, God is completely unseen, the most removed from our gaze and understanding. So, the answer is, Yes: the more sacred something is, the more untouchable it is and the more restrictions are attached to it.

Incidentally, a good rule of thumb for determining the gravity or sanctity of any commandment — and not just holy days — is to look at the penalty for its violation. The penalty for committing adultery, for example, or violating Yom Kippur, is much more severe than the penalty for eating forbidden foods.

To return to Yom Tov: now we know that not every "Jewish holiday" is a Biblically ordained Yom Tov. But even in this category, there are differences. Three of the Biblical festivals — all except Rosh Hashanah and Yom Kippur — are specifically pilgrimage festivals, during which the Israelites were commanded to go up and bring offerings to the *Beit Hamikdash*, the Holy Temple in Jerusalem. These are Pesach, Shavuot, and Succot. This is quite specific in *Exodus* 23:14 and in *Deuteronomy* 16:16. Note that the Torah refers to the pilgrimage festivals as *regalim* — literally, "foot" holidays —

in the sense that we walk up to Jerusalem on those days. More significantly, the Jew goes up to Jerusalem "to see" and "to be seen."

D: Like some fashionable synagogues today.

R: Not at all. To see the spirit of God as embodied in the Temple and the sacrificial service uplifts the participant and fills him with a sense of awe and wonder. And to be seen by God means to be observed, examined and scrutinized by the Creator.

The Torah also refers to Yom Tov as *chag*, meaning "festival" or "celebration," and as *mo'ed*, "appointed season" which suggests a sacred meeting with God at a specific time.

D: But isn't Shabbat also a sacred meeting time?

R: Technically, yes, and the Torah also describes Shabbat as a *mo'ed* — as in *Leviticus* 23:1-2. But Shabbat and Yom Tov are not identical. On an elementary level, some things which are forbidden on Shabbat are permitted on Yom Tov — such as using fire for cooking. On a deeper level, the date for Yom Tov is not automatic. It could not be observed on the date set by the Torah until the religious court officially declared the advent of the new moon — as we will discuss later. This means that the time for celebrating Yom Tov, while Divinely ordained, is in fact given over to the Jew himself, through the instrument of his court.

D: And Shabbat? Doesn't the Jewish court have anything to do with that?

The courts and Shabbat *R:* No. Shabbat occurs automatically every seventh day because Shabbat is not a day in the lunar month which requires determination by the court. Ever since Creation, Shabbat has occurred every seventh day and requires no human intercession. It is literally God's own day.

There's another fascinating difference between Shabbat and Yom Tov. Shabbat essentially celebrates God's Creation of the world. We rest on Shabbat because God ceased creating and rested on the seventh day, and we emulate Him. But on Yom Tov we mark events that occur to us, events orchestrated by God, in which God performs things for us. The pilgrimage festivals center on the Egyptian and wilderness experiences. Rosh Hashanah and Yom Kippur mark a time when God invites us to return to Him spiritually, when He historically forgave us — and still forgives us — for our sins. On Shabbat, we reach up to God; on Yom Tov, God reaches down to us.

Perhaps that's why Yom Tov contains the strong element of *simchah* — God coming into our arena, the King paying us a personal visit. On Shabbat, however, the key term is not *simchah*/joy, but *oneg*, a spiritual delight — because we enter God's realm on Shabbat.

That's why Shabbat is *me'ein olam haba* — a "foretaste of the World to Come," and that's why Shabbat is a less public time than Yom Tov. Yom Tov, which saw thousands of pilgrims coming up to Jerusalem, contains an element of the public in it, of interaction between people. Where Yom Tov represents a reaching out to others, Shabbat is more contemplative, reaching inward. In addition, it might be said that Yom Tov represents the sanctification of the body, while Shabbat represents the sanctification of the soul.

Shabbat differs from Yom Tov

D: Now that I'm beginning to see the difference between Shabbat and Yom Tov, let me get one thing clear about the other holy days. You keep referring to Pesach, Shavuot and Succot. What about Rosh Hashanah and Yom Kippur? Aren't they mentioned in the Torah as festivals?

R: They are, of course, sacred days, and they are referred to in *Leviticus* 23:32 and in *Numbers* 29:1-11. But these are not pilgrimage festivals — the Jews are not required to be physically present in Jerusalem — although special offerings are brought at the Holy Temple/ *Beit Hamikdash*. And of these two, Yom Kippur is more like Shabbat than a Yom Tov, as we'll see later on.

In any case, now we know what is meant by Yom Tov: one of these five seasons: Pesach, Shavuot, Succot — the three pilgrimage festivals — or Rosh Hashanah or Yom Kippur. And we know that though there are similarities, they are different from Shabbat. These festivals may have different names in the Torah — for example, Passover is called *Chag Hamatzot*, and Rosh Hashanah is *Yom Teruah*, and Shavuot is *Yom*

Habikkurim, "the Festival of First Offerings" and Succot is *Chag Ha'asif*, the "Festival of Ingathering." But we'll use their popular names for our purposes. Chanukah and Purim are holy days, but since they are not mentioned in the Five Books — having historically occurred later — they are not technically Yom Tov. And there is a major post-Biblical day of mourning and fasting: the Ninth of Av, Tishah B'Av, plus several "minor" fast days — all of which commemorate and mourn the destruction of Jerusalem and the Holy Temple.

Heaven **D:** Now that we know our definitions, and the differences
visits earth between Shabbat and Yom Tov, where do we go from here?

R: From here we go, I hope, to a better understanding of the major practical and philosophic aspects of each Yom Tov — which will in turn give us a deeper insight and perspective on God, Torah, the Jewish people, and God's role in these matters.

D: A pretty tall order for the Jewish holidays.

R: That's precisely the point. These are more than just holidays, more than a vacation from work, more than a chance to dress and eat better — though resting from labor, and eating and dressing well are in fact integral aspects of Shabbat and Yom Tov. In the Torah's scheme of things, every Yom Tov represents certain Divine concepts and ideas, which, through the various observances and practices of the day, become newly absorbed and imprinted into our hearts, souls and minds.

In an earlier discussion, for example, we saw that Shabbat is not just a day of rest, but that, among other things, it contains in it the idea of God as Creator. Similarly, each individual Yom Tov represents a major idea. Pesach is not just a festival of freedom from slavery. It is not merely a commemoration of a historical event that took place once upon a time — the way the Fourth of July commemorates the Declaration of Independence which took place in 1776. Pesach is the time when, every single year, the same historical event takes place once again on a spiritual level and we free ourselves from slavery once again. Bear this in mind: On our holy days, we don't simply remember events. We relive them.

D: But we're no longer in slavery.

Slavery today

R: Yes we are — but slavery in a different form. When we feel
obligated to behave in ways that are designed to please
society but not necessarily God, and when we are hooked to
our own passions and cannot control our various appetites, we
are in fact slaves. There are all kinds of oppressors, all kinds of
slave masters, and all kinds of slavery. And Pesach presents the
opportunity to free ourselves once again from whatever personal or communal slavery is currently oppressing us.

Pesach is in fact the time when it is least difficult to make
ourselves free. This was the season of the year when the element of pure freedom in its pristine sense was introduced into
the world. And once it enters the world, it can be appropriated
by us, particularly at the time of the year when it first
appeared. This is the "window of opportunity."

But there's much more to Pesach. In Egypt, it marks the
time of rebellion by the Jews against the idolatry and spiritual
defilement of the Egyptians. When we were ordered, in one of
the very first commandments given to us as a people, to
slaughter the lamb (*Exodus* 12:21), we were in fact being commanded to slaughter an Egyptian idol — for they used to
worship the lamb. This was an act of profound faith on the
part of the Jewish people — imagine slaves doing this to the
gods of their masters! — and also a permanent act of defiance
against the influences of idolatry and immorality of all kinds.
This was the spiritual freedom which Pesach represents.

This freedom from idolatry, this act of defiance against it,
is what reenters the world each year at this season. At Pesach
time we not only remember these events, but we also receive
once again the spiritual forces, impulses, and emanations
which made these events possible in the first place.

Revisiting freedom

D: And I will resist the temptation to object that we are no
longer idolaters today.

R: Because you know that's not true — idolatry still surrounds us today, and it takes a great deal of faith and
courage to defy it. After all, idolatry is anything, other than
the One God, for which we are prepared to offer up our lives
and our most cherished possessions. Idolatry comes in many

forms, in a variety of masks and guises and faces. If we are ready to offer up everything we have, including our faith in God and His Torah, in exchange for money, power, prestige — that is idolatry in modern dress.

During the Pesach season, we are reminded of this, as well as the elements of courage, faith and defiance which initially entered the world on that first Pesach. All these become manifest again, and are once again available to us. This is not to say that we cannot defy idolatry at other times in the year, but only that at this time of the year — the "window" — it is much easier to do so.

And, of course, there are the more general ideas of Pesach. It is the season when God intervened openly in history, for there was no doubt about Who was doing the redeeming and the freeing. And Pesach is the time of great miracles, the corollary of which is, once again, that God is still present, and though His miracles are less visible and less obvious today, He still is the Master of Miracles. He still — shall I say, Thank God? — intervenes in human history, and He still helps redeem us from all kinds of slavery and idolatry.

"A remembrance of Egypt"

D: All this is something to contemplate as I eat the matzot.

R: Definitely. And there's more. Because what happened on that first Pesach was not merely that a people escaped to freedom in a miraculous way, and that the Sea split open for them, and that the military might of the Egyptians was entirely destroyed in the miracle of the Red Sea. Pesach and the Exodus from Egypt are so central in Judaism — practically everything we do is *zecher litziat Mitzrayim*, "a remembrance of the Exodus from Egypt," and we are required to remember this miracle at the Sea every single day of our lives — not simply because it was a great triumph for the Israelites, but for more profound reasons. For one thing, Pesach shows the possibility of throwing off all kinds of yokes. Not merely the external yoke of Pharaoh's slavery and cruelty, but also the internal yoke of self-inflicted slavery: *chametz* symbolizes the yoke placed upon us by our capitulation to earthly desires, by our not mastering them — therefore even a tiny drop of *chametz* is forbidden, because even a tiny bit of arrogance makes us un-free.

Incidentally, there are two other motifs which underlie the pervasiveness of *zecher litziat Mitzrayim*. One, which we have discussed at another session, is the concept of *hakarat hatov*, "acknowledging the good" which God did for us by redeeming us from abject slavery — and, by extension, the need to exercise this quality in our ongoing relationships with God and with other people. This is the antithesis of today's "what-have-you-done-for-me-lately" philosophy. The second motif is that the Exodus underscored that there was a universal God Who controls the destiny of all nations and individuals, and not, as Egypt claimed, that her Pharaoh was god.

Acknow-ledging the good

In addition to all this, Passover is also called *zeman cheruteinu*, "the season of our freedom," which refers to freedom from all kinds of enslavement. In Egypt it was not merely a freedom from physical slavery; it was also a freedom and an escape from the spiritual enslavement represented by the alluring and enticing Egyptian society, a society which was steeped in immorality of all kinds and in physicality and defilement of every kind. It was this environment which threatened to pull Israel down into the depths of degradation, and it was from this that we were redeemed as much as from physical enslavement. Therefore, Pesach represents a *zeman cheruteinu* that is more than a Jewish Independence Day. What happens on every subsequent Pesach is that the potential of freeing oneself from the defilement of one's environment reenters the world once again, and enables us to experience what was experienced once before.

One more point: the mitzvot of every Yom Tov, whether they be matzot, or etrog, or shofar, are actually the vehicles which enable the ideas, concepts and inner meaning of the Yom Tov to take root in our souls. The matzot, for example, are symbols of this freedom from spiritual slavery and from idolatry — because they represent, among other things, the simple, basic, pure ingredients of service of God. As "poor-man's bread," and as the "bread of affliction" — *lechem oni* — they are symbols of humility. They do not rise or become inflated with their own self-importance. They represent the basic essentials of a person who has been purified from dross. It's the *chametz*, the bread, the risen dough, that we eliminate

Physical abstractions

from our lives during Pesach, because leavening represents arrogance and conceit and pride — all of which are major barriers against true service of God. When you're puffed up with your own self, it's difficult for God to find space to enter.

D: And all of this reappears on Pesach each year?

R: Yes. That's really what we mean when we refer to Passover as *zeman cheruteinu*, "the season of our freedom." Not just then, but now as well.

D: If *chametz* represents arrogance, why not refrain from it all year round?

R: Good point. As we will see when we discuss the idea of holiness, every aspect of our selves — both the physical and the spiritual — can be utilized in God's service. Even pride and arrogance can be used for sacred ends. Nevertheless, you make a good point, but let's leave that discussion for later.

D: This concept of the reappearance of certain heavenly impulses every festival fascinates me. Does this hold true for days like Tishah B'Av when we mourn the destruction of Jerusalem? If on Pesach, as you said, the element of real freedom re-enters our world, shall I assume that on a day of sadness the element of true mourning reenters our world?

R: An excellent question, but the answer is No. The sad event does not reoccur even spiritually. Rather, the days of mourning and fasting are designed to engender within us a sense of *teshuvah*, to remind us that we have lost our past glory as a people and were exiled because of our sins and the distancing from God that resulted. Maimonides in his Laws of Fasting discusses this explicitly. The only events and impulses that reoccur in the spiritual realm and which we reexperience each year are the Biblical holidays — and though they are all serious, they are not at all sad but joyous.

D: It's a kindness from above that sadness does not reenter the world on days of mourning. We already have enough. Let's move to the other festivals. What ideas do they represent?

R: Let's take the next in line: Shavuot. Technically, since it commemorates the giving of the Torah to Israel at Sinai, it's a separate Yom Tov from Pesach, but on a higher level it is the climactic event of Pesach. In fact, it's the only Yom Tov in the Torah without its own date. The Torah simply tells us in *Leviticus* 23:15-22 and in *Numbers* 28:26 that on the "fiftieth day" after Passover, we celebrate a *mikra kodesh,* a "holy convocation." In this sense, one might even call Shavuot the last day of Pesach, because there is in fact a seven-week bridge which connects the two festivals. That is the period we call *Sefirat HaOmer,* the Counting of the *Omer,* wherein we actually make a daily count of the forty-nine days from the second day of Passover to Shavuot, in accordance with the Torah's commandment in *Leviticus* 23:15-22, "and thou shalt count seven full weeks. . . ." In fact, Shavuot literally means "weeks." *Shavuot, climax of Passover*

But, once again, Shavuot is not merely a day when we recall a historical event. On Shavuot our souls stand at Sinai again, we experience the giving of the Torah, and we once again accept the privileges and obligations of the Torah — which means that Shavuot embodies a key element of Judaism: God's Revelation to Israel.

This is the core of our faith — that God reveals His will to us, presents to us His guide for living, and tells us how to come close to Him, how to unite with Him, how to live a full and satisfying life, and achieve joy and bliss through the Torah.

D: That's all well and good. But how does one go about accepting the Torah all over again? Just by thinking it, or by saying so?

R: More than that. We reaccept the Torah by a renewed attempt to comprehend it through study and learning. That's one of the reasons for the widespread practice of the all-night Torah study vigil on Shavuot, because it is through study that we recommit ourselves to that which the Torah represents. And, of course, you recall that we spent an entire session discussing why Torah study is considered the most important of all the mitzvot.

It's interesting that the Talmudic Sages say that the soul of every Jew who ever lived, or will ever live, was present at Mt.

Sinai when the Torah was given. This is a suggestive idea, and among its many layers of meaning is the concept that, once having done so, it is easier for us to accept it again. They — that is, you and I — were elevated spiritually to great heights when we accepted the Torah, which means that we have the potential of being elevated to similar heights on every subsequent Shavuot.

D: You mean that we today can achieve the same experience as those who stood at Mount Sinai? You can't be serious!

R: I don't claim that we will actually be able to relive that once-in-history moment of God's Revelation, but we can achieve a very high level of receptivity to Torah on Shavuot. Besides, there is nothing wrong with aiming for the heights.

Dateless festival   *D:* What specifically do Jews do to observe Shavuot? I've never heard of a special Shavuot practice, but then again I've never heard of a lot of things. Are there special mitzvot, like the Pesach matzah, or the succah booths?

R: In this case, your "never having heard" turns out to be accurate. Strangely enough, there is no specific mitzvah that we must perform in order to celebrate Shavuot: no lulav, no etrog, no obligatory food like matzah (though it is a non-obligatory custom among some Jews to eat at least one dairy meal on Shavuot), no shofar as on Rosh Hashanah, and, of course, no fasting. (Fasting, by the way, is forbidden on a Yom Tov — and also on Shabbat when it coincides with, say, the Ninth of Av day of mourning. However, when Yom Kippur falls on a Shabbat we do fast, because Yom Kippur is a unique, Divinely ordained time for fasting — which is for repentance purposes and not because of any mourning.)

There were, of course, special offerings in the Temple on Shavuot. In addition to the element of Revelation at Sinai, the Torah's name for Shavuot is *Yom Habikkurim,* "the Day of First Offerings," during which time there was a Temple offering of the first wheat crop. Today, to our sorrow, we have no Temple and therefore no offerings, and as a result there is no single distinctive Shavuot mitzvah *per se.*

D: That itself makes Shavuot distinctive: it has no special mitzvah, and has no actual date of its own. Why do you think that is?

R: Perhaps it's meant to convey the idea that the message of Shavuot — the Revelation of God at Sinai and all the vast and resonant emanations of that event — cannot be encapsulated in any physical mitzvah. Or perhaps it has something to do with its integral connection with Pesach, as we said earlier, so that, conceptually speaking, it's as if it were the last day of Pesach. In this regard it would be similar to Shemini Atzeret — literally, "the Eighth Day of Assembly" — which immediately follows the last day of Succot, but is a fully separate Yom Tov in its own right — on which we don't have the mitzvah of dwelling in the succah, or of the lulav and etrog or any other Succot practices. In fact, the Sages in the Mishnah and Talmud have a special name for Shavuot. They call it *Atzeret,* which means "Ingathering" or "Time of Closing" — which is redolent of Shemini Atzeret.

Or perhaps in celebration of His Revelation to us, God just wants us to spend a special, sacred day with Him without any special duties other than to interact with one another and celebrate a festival together.

As for its having no date of its own in the Written Torah, this underscores the importance of the Oral Tradition. It turns out that the only way the date of the anniversary of the Revelation at Sinai can be determined is to refer to the Oral Tradition. This means that Shavuot celebrates not only the Torah received by those physically present at Sinai, but also the accompanying Oral Torah — the *Torah sheb'al peh* — which began at Sinai and has continued ever since. We have already discussed the Oral Torah at one of our earlier meetings.

We might also consider the idea that the datelessness of this Yom Tov underscores the idea that the Torah is eternal and timeless, transcending the limitations of clock and calendar.

D: If Shavuot has no special commandments or practices, how then do we mark it?

R: Don't misunderstand. It's a Yom Tov like every other major Yom Tov. There are special prayers and special

Torah readings in the synagogue, we recite the Hallel Psalms, we partake of the festive Yom Tov meals, and the day is suffused with *simchah* just like the other pilgrimage festivals of Pesach and Succot. Yes, it is the shortest of the pilgrimage festivals: Pesach and Succot are each a week long — with one day added in the Diaspora — and Shavuot is only one day in Israel and two in the Diaspora. But it is certainly not an orphan Yom Tov, if that's what you mean. It has the same sanctity and the same religious status, the same joy, and the same restrictions, as the two other pilgrimage festivals, and for that matter, as Rosh Hashanah.

D: Nevertheless, isn't it curious that Shavuot is only a one day festival in the Torah?

R: As we just mentioned, Shavuot is conceptually the closing day of Pesach, and as such is similar to the one-day Shemini Atzeret which is the closing day of Succot. These one-day holidays are designed to allow Israel and God to spend additional time together before they separate one from the other.

And a further thought: the brief duration of Shavuot may be connected to the fact that its dominant theme — reaffirmation of the centrality of Torah and rededication to its study — is a year-round constant of Jewish life, and does not require a full week to reinforce it. By contrast, the dominant theme of Pesach — the introduction of true freedom into the world — and the dominant theme of Succot — which, as we will see, is to remind us of our transient status in this world — do not receive year-round emphasis and therefore require a full week during which their Divine sparks and impulses can penetrate our souls.

Diaspora's extra day   *D:* On this matter of the length of festivals, why is it that we observe an extra day of Yom Tov outside of the Holy Land? It seems so strange, and at times it's rather confusing.

R: You raise an important point. Remember that in Biblical and post-Biblical times there were no fixed calendars *per se*. In order to celebrate Succot on the prescribed fifteenth of the month, they would simply count fifteen days from the appearance of the new moon.

D: But that could be chaotic. Different communities might see the new moon at different times and thus begin the month on different days.

R: Good point. Remember, though, that at most there could only be a one-day error — since a lunar month contains either twenty-nine days or thirty days. But the Torah obviates this problem by giving the Sanhedrin the exclusive power of officially declaring the beginning of the new moon. As soon as the courts, based on the visual evidence of witnesses, determined that the new crescent moon had in fact risen, they would formally declare that day as the beginning of the new month, and would immediately dispatch runners and send signals to the outlying districts of the land in order to inform everyone.

In this way, every Jewish community would celebrate the new moon together. It was a kind of semi-holiday involving the offering of special sacrifices and the recitation of special prayers. More importantly, they would celebrate say, Succot, on the same fifteenth day of the month, without confusion.

But what was a community to do if it were geographically far removed from the Holy Land, and it took a long time for the new-moon declaration to reach them? In order to prevent such potential chaos, the Sages established the practice that such distant communities, in order to be certain that they were celebrating Yom Tov on the proper day, must add one day to their Yom Tov observance. This became a universally accepted practice for Diaspora communities. And even after the Sages issued their perpetual calendar that revealed the precise time of the appearance of the new moon, the Diaspora communities still maintained the practice of the double observance.

D: But why? The reason for the practice no longer existed!

R: Even though the technical reason — the doubt about the new moon — no longer existed, the second day was maintained as an obvious symbol and reminder of the fact that they were living in exile and not on their ancestral land.

Beyond this reason, there is another factor suggested by our mystical sages, and that is that the sacred influences and

Divine emanations that descend upon us on each holy day have their greatest impact on those Jews who are in the land of holiness, that is, Israel. But when Jews are not in the Holy Land, the impact of these emanations takes a bit longer to take effect. It's as if the heavens were covered with clouds, and the sun cannot break through. Therefore a second day is needed, over and above the technical reason for it.

The Jewish **D:** There's a related matter which confuses me, and that is
leap year the subject of the Jewish leap year. In the solar year, we simply add one day every four years. But the Jewish leap year is much more irregular, and when it does occur, it's not just one day but an entire month which is added. Can you clarify this for me?

R: I'll try. Let's have a brief astronomy lesson. As we've already discussed, the Jewish year consists of twelve moon months of either twenty-nine or thirty days, which means that a lunar year contains about 354 days. The sun year, as we know, has 365 days. This means that every twelve months the moon lags about eleven days behind the sun — so that in three years, it is more than thirty-three days behind the sun, and in just six years, the moon has drifted some two months behind the sun.

The month To which you might say, "Who cares and so what?"
of spring which is a legitimate reaction, if things were ordinary. However, the problem for the religious calendar is that Pesach must by Biblical law occur only and exclusively in the spring of the year. The Torah refers several times to the Pesach month, Nissan, as *chodesh ha'aviv*, "the month of spring" (*Exodus* 13:4; 23:15; 34:18; *Deuteronomy* 16:1). Spring and the rest of the seasons are controlled by the sun, not the moon. If Nissan is allowed to behave according to its own devices and without any adjustment, it will gradually begin to slide into different seasons, with the result that Pesach will before very long be celebrated in the winter, fall, and summer, thus obviating the Torah's intention that it be celebrated exclusively in the spring. In fact, the Mohammadan calendar, which is consistently lunar, finds itself commemorating its important Ramadan festival in different seasons of the year.

The Sanhedrin solved this problem by proclaiming a thirteenth month every few years in order to prevent Nissan and Pesach from drifting out of the spring season. When the Jews went into exile and communication was difficult, the Sages in the fourth century C.E. worked out a perpetual calendar which gives us a leap month seven times every nineteen years. This perpetual calendar is the one we Jews follow until this very day.

But let us return to Yom Tov. The historical progression is logical. First, Exodus from Egypt and the theme of freedom, which is followed by the giving of the Torah and its theme of Revelation. God redeems us in order to give us the Commandments.

Less obvious is the sub-theme: be sure that you understand the true essence of freedom. You are only really free when you are subservient to God. That is to say, on Pesach we become free, and on Shavuot we discover that freedom does not mean free of restraints. Quite the contrary.

D: Those are pretty weighty ideas.

R: And we haven't even discussed the third pilgrimage festival, which is Succot. And after that, we need to touch on Rosh Hashanah and Yom Kippur in some depth. So there are more weighty ideas approaching.

D: All I know about Succot is that we are supposed to build a booth and eat in it for about a week.

Succot: booths and much more

R: That's correct as far as it goes. But there's much more.

D: There always is, isn't there?

R: Thank God there is, otherwise our religion would be completely reduced to platitudes and empty theories — to which it has already been reduced in the minds of far too many Jews. But let's get back to the real meaning of Succot.

Why these booths, these succot? First of all, the Torah explicitly commands us: "Thou shalt dwell in succot for seven days . . ." (*Leviticus* 23:42). The succah is a dwelling whose key element is the roof — which must be temporary. If the roof is permanent, the succah is invalid. This is the entire point of this Yom Tov: that we move out of our permanent homes and enter a temporary abode whose roof is such that if it should rain, the rain can seep inside.

On one level, this recalls the temporary dwellings of our forefathers in their desert sojourn. But on a deeper level, it symbolizes a profound religious and moral truth: that we live in this world only as temporary guests, for a finite period of time. Every guest has a reservation, but no guest knows how long his reservation lasts. For some it may run for seventy, eighty, ninety years — for others, less. No one ever knows when precisely his reservation runs out.

D: That's rather sobering. Doesn't that put a damper on what is supposed to be a happy time?

R: Not at all. First of all, an awareness of our transitory status can do wonders to concentrate the mind on eternal things that really matter. And when a person is able to achieve this state — concerning himself less with silliness and more with significant matters — he has gone a long way towards personal satisfaction and inner happiness and contentment.

Defying imper- manence Secondly, Succot is a time of joy because the succah represents something beyond the impermanence of life on this earth. It symbolizes living under a different set of rules which defy the impermanence and evanescence of this world and infuse a touch of eternity into our temporariness. Once a person recognizes that this world is finite and that, although the physical and the material have their specific roles to play, they are not to be in control of us but we of them — once a person recognizes this, that person is infinitely happier, because he is not hitching his wagon to goals that possess much surface glitter but are false, that make great promises but cannot deliver.

Living in the temporary succah is a kind of release from the bondage of living in thrall of things that in fact enslave us. And that release is a cause of great joy and delight.

By the way, joy and delight — the term *simchah* — is used three times in the Torah in reference to Succot. While by extension the element of *simchah* applies to Pesach and Shavuot as well, the fact is that there is no Biblical reference to *simchah* in connection with Pesach, and only one in connection with Shavuot (*Deuteronomy* 16:11). The Torah says of

Succot, "*Vesamachta bechagecha* — Thou shalt be joyous in your festivals — *vehayita ach sameach* — thou wilt be exceedingly happy" (*Deuteronomy* 16:14-15). And in *Leviticus* 23:40 there is the commandment, "Thou shalt rejoice before God for seven days."

D: Whether we like it or not.

R: I realize that you cannot legislate joy, but the fact that it is a commandment underscores that we have to make special efforts to achieve joy, and we try not to engage in activities or even conversations that might sadden us. For example, there are no formal mourning requirements on Yom Tov: people do not sit *shiv'ah* and do not practice the public mourning rites. In fact, if a Yom Tov occurs at any time after formal mourning has begun, Yom Tov cancels the *shiv'ah* entirely. In addition, on Yom Tov we are required to dress and eat better to give us a feeling of contentment and satisfaction, and to enable us to demonstrate physically our celebration of the day. The Torah even permits us to cook and bake on Yom Tov so that we will be made even more content by the ability to eat warm, freshly prepared food.

Legislating joy?

But the Torah's statement, "thou wilt be happy," is more than a commandment. It's a promise: if you live Yom Tov in the way prescribed by the Torah, you will surely be happy, and you cannot help but be filled with joy and delight and *simchah*. This is a spiritual law of nature.

And there's one other point about Succot: it has more mitzvot than any other Yom Tov. Besides the succah itself, there are the *lulav*/palm-branch, *etrog*/citron, *hadassim*/myrtle twigs, and *aravot*/willow branches — all of which are held together in our hands while we recite a special blessing over them each day. These contain profound symbolic meanings, one of which is that these four species represent the ultimate unity of all peoples under the dominion of the Almighty.

The symbols of Succot

The succah booth itself is a symbol of union with God, because it symbolizes God's private chamber into which we are invited as His guests, in order to come closer to Him and be united with Him. The succah, in fact, is referred to by Jewish tradition as the *tzila dimehemnuta* — "the altar of faith," that is, dwelling in it symbolizes our faith in God: we leave our permanent home and enter the flimsy dwelling. This act of faith is another reason for the Succot emphasis on joy, because this is what full faith in God engenders: deep, inner joy.

Walking into a mitzvah   Perhaps this is why the idea of *simchah* is repeated in connection with Succot, because true *simchah* means connecting with God through mitzvot — of which Succot has an abundance. This connection becomes manifest on Succot, where we actually walk into the mitzvah physically. Succot is the climactic end of the High Holiday season — the Days of Awe. By then we are cleansed spiritually, and what greater *simchah* and pure joy can there be than this? So the abundance of mitzvot and the concepts they represent adds to the intense joy of this festival.

D: Which makes it the direct opposite of Shavuot, at least in terms of the practices. One contains the least mitzvot, and one contains the most.

R: Interesting point, but we'll have to leave it for now, because I want to get back to what the succah represents according to the Oral Tradition.

The Talmud in *Succah* 11b records two viewpoints about this. According to one opinion, it represents the actual booths in which the Israelites dwelled while they were in the wilderness. A second sage holds that it is a symbol of the clouds of glory which protected Israel from her enemies during the desert sojourn. What emerges is that, over and above its symbolism as a temporary dwelling, the succah is a reenactment of the wandering in the wilderness.

Thus you have Pesach as the reliving of the actual Exodus itself; Shavuot as the reenactment of the giving of the Torah which is the purpose of the Exodus and the climax of Pesach; and Succot as the revisiting of our desert experience during the forty years prior to the entry into the Promised Land.

On another level, Succot is the culmination of the three pilgrimage festivals — the expression of joy and *simchah* which is a result of the freedom of Pesach and the acceptance of the discipline of the Torah which we received on Shavuot. In addition, it represents the joyous reunion of God and Israel after the spiritual stock-taking of Rosh Hashanah and Yom Kippur earlier in the same month.

D: By the time Succot ends, people must be in a state of spiritual exhaustion.

R: Exhilaration would be a more accurate term.

D: I guess at a certain level of spirituality that would be so, but I have a long way to go until I reach that level.

R: We all do, believe me. But let's proceed. We have emphasized the three pilgrimage festivals, but haven't we left out something?

D: Of course, the High Holidays. Whatever happened to them?

R: They're still there. We call them the *Yamim Noraim*, the "Awesome Days." Just fifteen days before Succot, and right at the beginning of Tishrei, we have Rosh Hashanah, followed ten days later by Yom Kippur.

D: Followed five days later by Succot, which lasts a week. No wonder I find it exhausting.

R: No wonder some day you will find it uplifting. But let's look at Rosh Hashanah and Yom Kippur a little more closely. Rosh Hashanah, although it is not a pilgrimage festival, is a Yom Tov like all others. We call it Rosh Hashanah, but the Torah calls it *Yom Teruah*, the Day of the Sounding (of the shofar). In *Leviticus* 23:24, the Torah tells us that "on the first day of the seventh month, there shall be a rest day for you (*Shabbaton*), a remembrance with shofar blasts, a holy convocation."

D: What's this about the seventh month? I thought Rosh Hashanah was our New Year's Day.

R: It is. But remember that the Torah reckons its months from Nissan, the month of the Exodus when we first became a people. Tishrei, the month of Rosh Hashanah, comes six months after Nissan.

Rosh Hashanah celebrates a different kind of beginning. *Birthday of* According to our tradition it marks the anniversary of the *Creation* Creation of the world. Nissan, the first month of the calendar, marks the creation, the first month, of the Jewish people.

Tishrei, the month of Rosh Hashanah, is the first month of the universe, and just as, when God completed His Creation He contemplated and evaluated it, so does He do every Rosh Hashanah — which means that Rosh Hashanah is actually the Day of Judgment for the universe and for mankind collectively and individually.

That explains why, more than any other Yom Tov, Rosh Hashanah's liturgy is not limited to Jewish themes exclusively, but contains so many universal themes as well. On no other occasion, for example, is God referred to as "King over all the earth," and at no other time is God's Holy Temple called a "house of prayer for all the nations." This is all a reflection of the universal judgment of this day.

God evaluates us collectively, just as a shepherd looks over his flock with one glance. And individually, He also judges us like a shepherd who looks at each single sheep as it files through a narrow opening in the gate. So Rosh Hashanah and Yom Kippur — the *Yamim Noraim* — are more than just a Jewish version of New Year's Day. It's a time of great intro-spection, of *teshuvah*/repentance, of stock-taking. According to an ancient Jewish tradition, it marks the creation of Adam and Eve — who were created, who sinned, and who were judged all on the same day.

All of these traditions underscore the idea that Rosh Hashanah is the time of beginnings. For example, the Talmud in *Rosh Hashanah* 10b-11a states that a number of other events took place on Rosh Hashanah: Abraham and Jacob were born on Rosh Hashanah; the three barren women — Sarah, Rachel, and Hannah; the mother of the prophet Samuel — were all remembered by God on Rosh Hashanah, when He decreed that they will give birth. On Rosh Hashanah Joseph was freed from the Egyptian prison and became viceroy of Egypt. And on Rosh Hashanah slavery ended for the Jews in Egypt and they waited for the ten plagues to be completed so that they could go out to freedom.

To recreate ourselves Thus, Rosh Hashanah is a time for significant initiatives. As such, it is an opportunity for us to recreate ourselves, to return to a relationship with God, to strengthen our ties to our faith. And since it's also a time of judgment, a time when Adam and Eve, and by extension all of their descendants are judged, Rosh Hashanah is also a time when the dormant Jewish soul begins to wake up, when the latent spirituality within us begins to stir. According to Maimonides, the shofar is a kind of spiritual alarm clock designed to awaken us from our spiritual torpor.

D: Why can't we awaken our souls all year round?

R: As a matter of fact, we can. But on Rosh Hashanah and Yom Kippur the opportunity is greatest, because that is when God approaches us and beckons us to return to Him. Obviously, there is always the possibility of approaching God, but at certain seasons of the year it is easier to do so. The Awesome Days, the *Yamim Noraim*, are that kind of time.

D: If it's a Yom Tov like any other, then I'm supposed to be happy and be in a state of *simchah.* How is this possible — to be joyous and be filled with awe at the same time?

R: Very good question. On the one hand, Rosh Hashanah is an extremely solemn day, the most solemn of the year after Yom Kippur. Because Rosh Hashanah begins the Ten Days of Repentance, we stand at the bar of judgment on those days. It's as if we were in a courtroom pleading for our very lives.

Our tradition gives us a vivid image: "The Books of the Living and the Books of the Dead are open before Him," which means many things — but one of the things it means is that we pray that our names be inscribed by our loving and understanding God in the one book and not in the other.

The books are opened

Our tradition also tells us that beginning with Rosh Hashanah a Jew has the opportunity to return to God, to perform *teshuvah* — which, as we discussed at our first meeting, literally means to turn around, to return, to start all over again. Rosh Hashanah and its companion, Yom Kippur, are Divine gifts in which we are given the opportunity to reopen our relationship with God, when we have the chance to wipe away the past as if it did not exist, and to start over again with a clean slate.

D: Just like that?

R: No, not just like that. The slate is not wiped clean automatically. The process has to begin with us, with a sense
of true regret, with contrition for past misdeeds, and with a
serious resolution not to repeat them. The opportunity is
given to sincere returners, not to *pro forma* ones who are just
going through the motions. But once the process is properly
done, once the catharsis of Rosh Hashanah and Yom Kippur
make their impact on us, what could be more joyous than
that? So, yes, it's solemnity filled with awe, and also filled
with spiritual joy.

Remember that in the religious context joy is deeply
inward, and is not necessarily manifested by laughter and
smiles. As such, religious joy and religious awe are not contradictions. In fact, they go hand in hand. When you get a
chance, look up the second Psalm, where David says, "Serve
the Lord with fear, and rejoice with trembling."

D: All I remember about Rosh Hashanah and Yom Kippur is
that there was always an interminably long sermon and
interminably long prayers in general. On Rosh Hashanah we
used to begin about 8:00 A.M. and not leave until after about
1:00 P.M. How can people pray that long?

R: Your comment saddens me in a way, because the liturgy of
Rosh Hashanah, especially the *musaf*, is the most magnificent prayer the world has ever seen. It's like a symphony,
perfectly balanced, divided into three separate movements,
devoted to the themes of: a) making God our sovereign and
acknowledging Him as our King; b) remembering His intervention in our history, and underscoring our belief in Divine
Providence — the idea that He listens and cares for us; and c)
recalling the numerous Biblical events where the shofar her-
alds God's presence and protection, and longing for the time
when the shofar will herald the redemption of all mankind
and the coming of the Messiah. Once you grow to understand
prayer in general, and take the time to study the Rosh
Hashanah prayers in particular, you'll surely feel differently.
You may find that five hours are really not enough time at all.

*Shofar,
ram,
alarm
clock*

D: This may sound foolish, because everyone is supposed
to know about the shofar, but what are some of the

underlying aspects of the shofar that make it the major commandment of Rosh Hashanah?

R: First, as you know, a shofar is the horn of a ram —
which immediately reminds us of the ram which appears on the scene just as Abraham is about to fulfill God's command to sacrifice his only son, Isaac. Instead, God stays Abraham's hand — satisfied that Abraham has demonstrated his supreme loyalty and devotion to Him — and the ram is sacrificed instead.

Since the episode itself took place on what was later to be Rosh Hashanah, we read that Torah portion as part of the service, and we listen to the sound of the ram's horn — which is a piercing, elemental sound emanating from the depths of the natural universe, and is designed to penetrate the depths of the human heart. It's a kind of wake-up call for our souls, a reminder of the real purpose of our lives. Remember, the shofar sounded when God gave the Commandments to the Jewish people, and it will sound again to herald the coming of the Messiah.

D: If all this takes place on Rosh Hashanah, what's left for
Yom Kippur?

R: Rosh Hashanah ushers in the *Aseret Yemei Teshuvah*, the
Ten Days of Repentance, which climax on Yom Kippur. It's a period of great introspection, self-analysis, sober stock-taking, intensified prayer and study, more generous charity, increased acts of kindness, and specific resolutions and undertakings for the future.

D: This is serious business, being a Jew.

R: Well, if our conversations have caused you to realize only
that, I am happy.

D: Does Yom Kippur have any special mitzvot?

R: There is the mitzvah of *teshuvah,* repentance, and, of *Becoming*
course, there is the prohibition against eating and other *angels*
physical pleasures. Yom Kippur has the same restrictions as Shabbat — plus the restrictions about "afflicting" oneself — which means that we abstain not only from food and drink,

but also from marital relations, from wearing leather shoes (a symbol of great ease and comfort), from bathing, perfuming and anointing oneself. These are based on *Leviticus* 23:26-27: "On the tenth day of this month is the Day of Atonement. It is a holy convocation, and you shall afflict yourselves . . . and do no work on that day. For it is a day of atonement, to provide you atonement before your God." And in *Leviticus* 16:30 we read that "For on this day he (the High Priest) shall provide atonement to cleanse you; you shall be cleansed of all your sins before God." According to many rabbinic authorities, when we atone for past sins we are actually fulfilling a Biblical commandment.

By the way, based on this passage from *Leviticus* 16, in which it is stressed that we will be cleansed of all our sins before God, the Sages derive the clear implication that Yom Kippur atones only for sins before God, but does not atone for sins between people. If I have insulted you, for example, I cannot ask God to forgive me. Instead, I have to ask you to forgive me first. This is discussed at the end of Tractate *Yoma* in the Talmud. That's the origin of the practice whereby Jews ask each other for forgiveness prior to Yom Kippur, to wipe the slate clean between ourselves and our fellow human beings, before we ask God for forgiveness.

Yom Kippur and Shabbat

D: It might be easier to ask God for forgiveness than to ask another person. One thing puzzles me. Other than the pleasure restrictions, Yom Kippur is just like Shabbat. But you once told me that on Shabbat we refrain from work because we imitate God, Who also ceased His creative labor on the seventh day, and that thereby we reaffirm our belief in God as the Creator of the universe. If Yom Kippur has the same restrictions as Shabbat, does that mean that Yom Kippur is somehow connected with the creation of the world? In fact, you just mentioned that the Torah itself calls it "Shabbat."

R: You raise an interesting point. There is in fact a conceptual connection. Yom Kippur is referred to as "rest" because we do in fact rest, on this one day, from our physical appetites. But there is really no connection between Creation and the reasons for the withdrawal from labor. On Yom Kippur, we refrain from creative labor in order to declare symbolically that, at least for this one day, we are like angels and we leave the physical world behind us. This is integrally connected with the abstentions of Yom Kippur: we refrain from any physical pleasures on this day, and we refrain from utilizing in any way the physical aspects of the world. The restrictions, except for the abstentions, are identical with Shabbat — no fire, no cooking, and so forth — but for a different reason entirely.

But let's remember the key element of Yom Kippur — because when you really thing about it, it is an amazing day. *God invites us back* God asks us to return to Him. He reaches out to us and invites us back, no matter how far we have strayed. He wants us to be close to Him.

D: Why? Does He need us?

R: He does not need us. But His essential goodness invites us back because this is the only way we humans can achieve true joy and bliss on this earth.

D: Joy and bliss and abstentions and fasting? A strange mixture, I would say.

R: But remember, on Yom Kippur we fast not because of any sadness, but in order to become spiritual creatures, as much as is humanly possible, on this one day. It is a day of great cleansing, where the past can be literally washed away.

One of the high points of Yom Kippur is the public confession, where everyone confesses to being a sinner. It is quite a powerful moment — the sight of hundreds of people simultaneously declaring before God that they have sinned, and all asking Him for forgiveness. In addition, of course, there is an opportunity for private confession, in which one simply whispers to God from the depths of the heart.

D: We know what happened on Pesach, Shavuot, and Succot: they're all connected in some way with the Exodus from Egypt, the Divine Revelation, and God's protective care of us. And on Rosh Hashanah, the world was created. Does Yom Kippur have any historical associations?

R: Not in the Bible, but there is a fascinating tradition about a major historical event associated with Yom Kippur. After the sin of the Golden Calf Moses goes up to Mt. Sinai to receive the second set of Commandments. When he comes down from the mountain holding the Tablets, the people Israel meet him, and God grants them forgiveness for their heinous sin. The day that Moses returns is the tenth of Tishrei. This is the day that God chooses to be the day of Yom Kippur when God would forgive Israel — each year on the tenth of Tishrei — for their sins if they truly repent.

Change and account-ability Bear this in mind: the overarching theme of Rosh Hashanah and Yom Kippur is change: to change from what we were before and to become new individuals. The motif behind it all is accountability. We are responsible for our actions. We do not live in a vacuum. What we do or say has an impact and a resonance in the world. Yom Kippur represents the potential for a human being to change and return: we are not eternally condemned to follow a certain habitual path; we do have the ability, if we so choose, to change our ways.

It is amazing: in *Nedarim* 39b the Sages tell us that *teshuvah*, repentance, was created before the world was created. We discussed this at our very first meeeting. That is to say, the idea of repentance, of a person changing himself and changing his course, is an integral part of Creation — and the world could not exist without it.

This is not to imply that *teshuvah* is an easy matter. Changing the course of one's life is never easy. What this means, specifically, is that a change of direction is possible with the help of God. Yom Kippur is also a day which gives us this type of assistance. The idea that a person can change himself is an extremely important element in Creation — and in life.

D: Well, we have taken a great deal of time with the major holidays. What about the more "popular" ones like Chanukah and Purim?

Chanukah and Purim sub-surface **R:** Chanukah and Purim, as we noted earlier, are not mentioned in the Five Books, because they occurred after the giving of the Torah. But they are nevertheless very significant days. Let's take a look at them. Without going into the familiar story of Chanukah, let me simply say that, among other things, it represents the idea that what seems impossible and unnatural is not necessarily so. In the Chanukah prayers, we thank God for having delivered *rabim b'yad m'atim,* "the many into the hands of the few." If we keep trying, we get help from above. When they rekindled the oil they knew it could burn only one day, and they had no thought or promise of a miracle.

I'm suggesting that Chanukah tells us that if we have the faith to do our part, God will do His part. But we must take the first step, and make a beginning. There is obviously much more to Chanukah than this, but these ideas are fundamental to the understanding of the holiday.

D: Would you say the same thing about Purim? Chanukah and Purim do seem to be so similar.

R: They are similar on the surface, but nevertheless quite different. For example, Chanukah celebrates an obvious and open miracle, whereas Purim celebrates a hidden miracle, one that was not that obvious.

Purim is like life today. We are unable to see the moving finger writing, the hidden hand of God. After all, most people don't realize that the story recounted in *Megillat Esther* takes place over a period of nine years — from the third year of the reign of Achashverosh until the twelfth year. Were we living at that time, we would hardly have realized that what was happening was all part of a Divine pattern. Reading it in the Megillah, we see the developing pattern, the delicately unfolding flower of redemption. But living through it, one would have had to be as spiritually attuned as were Esther and Mordechai to see it.

Open and hidden miracles

Purim is thus a reemphasis on the hiddenness of God's providence. And on Purim it is easier for us to reimpress this aspect of service of God, this aspect of faith, into our souls — especially if we bear in mind the Talmudic tradition that on Purim the Jews reaffirmed their determination to return to God, accept the Torah, and perform its commandments, as discussed in Tractate *Shabbat* 88a.

D: All of today's discussion comes as a shock to someone who was always certain that Chanukah is the holiday of religious freedom, and Purim the time when we didn't get annihilated, and Pesach celebrates our escape from oppression, and

Yom Kippur is a time when we are deprived of things to eat, and Succot when we enjoy the lovely booth they build outside the synagogue.

A sliver of knowledge

R: None of your early impressions is entirely false. But they are only a tiny sliver of the truth.

D: And I suspect that there is so much to all of this, that even our own discussions are only a tiny sliver of all there is to know.

R: You are beginning to understand important things: no matter how much we learn, discuss, probe, inquire, and study, what we are dealing with is so profound that even the greatest Biblical and Talmudic scholars have touched only the tip of the iceberg. What's more, the more they learn, the more they realize how tiny is their grasp and understanding of the vastness and the depth of the Torah.

D: I'm ready to settle for such a tiny understanding.

kashRuth – the jew enjoys god's bounty

David: Rabbi, the term "kosher" has become an interna-
tional word. I am interested in knowing more about it,
maybe even trying to observe it myself. Tell me something about it. First of all, is it really so very crucial within
Judaism?

Rabbi: Let's start with a definition. *Kasher* is a Hebrew word
meaning "prepared" or "made ready." Thus, it con-
notes that which is fit or proper; in the context of food, it
means that which is fit for a Jew to eat. Its opposite is another
Hebrew word, *treifah*, which literally means "torn." As used
in Scripture, it refers to an animal that was attacked and killed
in the field, but in common usage it denotes any animal not

permitted for eating. In general, anything *treifah*, whether it is meat or not, is non-kosher, or unfit.

You ask if it is a crucial practice. As a Biblical commandment, it is a mitzvah like all other mitzvot — no less and no more important than, say, placing a mezuzah on the door, or giving charity, or fasting on Yom Kippur, or observing Passover, or loving your neighbor. They are all part of the Torah, and they all carry the same weight. In other words, we do not ascribe relative value or significance to the commandments.

To be sure, the violation of certain mitzvot involves greater penalties than others, and some mitzvot may seem less significant to us than others, but in God's scheme of things each mitzvah is an indispensable element in His blueprint for the world. The kashruth regulations, which are found in *Leviticus* 11, are part of His grand design, which is the Torah. In God's Divine plan, food is more than fuel for the body or a source of pleasure. It represents something much more profound.

Does God really care about our food?

D: How did food become so important a part of God's cosmic scheme of things? It hardly seems worthy of sanctification, since it's so obviously animal activity. I can't believe God really cares one way or the other what we chew, swallow or digest.

R: You would be surprised at the little details with which God is concerned. We will touch on that later. But as to why God should be concerned with the food we eat: food *per se* is not the issue. What is important is how its ingestion can affect us.

D: Of course food affects us. Bad food makes us sick, and healthful food is good for us — obviously.

R: Hear me out. By now you know I'm not referring to a physical diet. Observance of the Torah may be incidentally very healthful, but the Torah is not a book of hygiene. Certainly it is concerned with our total well-being, including the physical, but its ultimate purpose is to help transform us into full human beings — not only physically, but emotionally, intellectually and spiritually; and what we eat and the way we eat are key means of doing this. By full human beings I mean people who are aware of God's existence and sovereignty and are eager to serve Him in joy; who are aware of their fellow human beings and are compassionate and helpful and charitable to them; people who are in control of their own selves, who are complete and whole, and who are constantly developing and growing in every possible way.

In addition, kashruth reminds us about a number of significant things, such as our relationship to the animal world and our right to do with the earth as we please. It also suggests the idea of the table being an altar and not just a place for eating, and about eating as a way of worshiping God.

D: All that derives just from the food I eat?

R: Let me explain. An odd thing happens at the beginning of the world. You remember your Bible: God creates Adam and Eve and places them in the Garden of Eden. In the Garden are all kinds of attractive, delicious and tempting foods, and Adam and Eve are given the task of caring for this delightful paradise. God makes only one demand of them: while they may taste everything in the Garden, they must not eat from one particular tree, and if they do, they will die. You know the rest of the story.

Note something strange: what are the very first words which God utters to his newly minted creatures? One would expect something about duties and responsibilities as the first human beings, about morality or ethics or charity or worship, or kindness, or responsibility to God and other creatures, or relationship to the physical universe. *God's first words to man*

But there's not a word about these. Instead, God's first speech to them is concerned exclusively with do's and don't's about food. On the face of it, nothing cosmic at all, nothing which would strike you as eternal or immortal words. Just — this you may eat, this you must avoid. How come?

D: I had never thought of that. How come, indeed?

R: What we have here is a paradigm of the entire Torah. All the thou-shalts and thou-shalt-nots are encompassed in this very first directive. In it, God speaks to man and tells man how to stay close to Him. He gives directions, guidelines, sets limits and ground rules, the do's and don't's.

The clear implication is that when we follow God's command not to eat from the Tree of Knowledge, we are able to eat from the Tree of Life, meaning that we achieve a relationship with God so intimate that it enriches our entire life. But when, like the first creatures, we follow our own desires, we are banished from the Garden and we lose this priceless opportunity. Think about it. This brief commandment had implications so cosmic that its transgression changed human destiny for the rest of time. We should try to understand it in all of its profundity. In brief, this demand contains in it the kernel of the entire Torah.

Perhaps that's why the normative kashruth laws are among the very first pieces of legislation given to the Jews as a people.

D: But I ask the same question: what was so cosmic about what we may or may not eat — be it in the Garden of Eden, the wilderness or now?

R: Look at it this way: the desire and yearning and need for food is a basic drive, a fundamental instinct shared by all of God's living creatures. It is a symbol of every other human appetite and desire. Therefore, it makes sense that the first words to Adam should deal with food — because while food is a natural desire, natural desires can run amok and become destructive, and so there is a need to place restrictions and boundaries on them. God therefore acts immediately to put brakes on this potential danger.

The food laws, by the way, are not limited to kashruth. Did it ever occur to you that there are a number of other major practices centering around food? At the Passover Seder, we must eat a certain bread called matzah, and for the entire week we are forbidden all leavened bread; on Succot, we may eat any kosher food we want, but it must be eaten within the succah booth for the entire week; on Yom Kippur we may not eat or drink anything; and wine and bread are essential ingredients in the ushering in and sanctification of holy days. There
Even is much more to food than meets the eye — or stomach.
Paradise To return to the Garden: first and foremost, Adam and Eve
has must understand that even a paradise has boundary lines that
boundaries may not be crossed. In life, some things are kosher, some are

not. All the trees in the Garden were kosher — that is, permissible. One tree was not kosher, forbidden. Even in a Garden of Eden there have to be no's. And if we want our world to be a Garden of Eden, and if we want to have the joy of coming close to God, we must learn discipline and self-control — which means being able to say no to the impulse to take a bite out of the appealing, delightful, tempting — but forbidden — fruit. The message is: all appetites, instincts, desires, hungers — though they are natural in origin —require self-control. So it's not just eating that God is talking about.

In all this, an additional lesson is taught to Adam and Eve: they are not, and never will be, God. They are not the masters of this world, though they may be tempted to think so. There is only one God, and He is the only Master Who can do as He pleases. Adam and Eve are subject to this Master. There are limits to what they may or may not do: there is a "thou-shalt-not."

All this, is stated right at the beginning of the Torah, right at the beginning of the world, because this teaching is prologue to everything: there is a God; you are imbued with His spirit and His breath, but you are not the Master; there are boundary lines in life which you cross only at your own peril.

D: Is God so jealous of His sovereignty that He needs to guard it right at the outset?

R: On the contrary. Whatever God commands is for our benefit. God stresses His sovereignty in order to enrich our lives and to enhance our delight and joy. The realization of limits, the acceptance of discipline and self-control, the awareness of God, are the first steps towards true meaning and purpose and pleasure in life. God is filled with love — and He wants us to have a microcosm of Paradise on earth. Paradise begins with the ability to say no to the self. A world without "no" is a world out of control, a hell. Self-control is the power station which harnesses our natural instincts and impulses, and places them in the service of God. Unfortunately, Adam and Eve failed the test.

D: Too bad they were evicted.

R: Yes, but our task is to attempt to return to the Garden of Eden. And our journey of return is powered by the struggle to refine ourselves.

D: So the act of eating is not so simple after all.

R: Well, eating is a necessity of life. It is something we live with, and live from, day and night. How we treat it, what we do with it, how we handle it, can make a major difference in our lives. The kosher food laws take this all-pervasive element of material existence and transform it into a religious act, because our avoidance of certain foods is a constant reminder of the limits that God sets. The ordinariness of eating is thus elevated to a higher level.

This, by the way, is what Torah does with all aspects of physical life, as we keep pointing out. It takes the physical and sublimates it, so that it can be transmogrified into something spiritual. There is nothing evil *pe se* about the body or about physical desires. But God wants us to enhance them so that they not remain merely physical, but are used in the service of God — for our own betterment and the betterment of the world. So, yes, the simple act of eating has many ramifications to it.

This, by the way, should not be surprising. Eating has profound effects, both physically and spiritually. Used correctly, it can keep us alive and sustain us; or it can make us sick and miserable, and shorten our lives. The spiritual impact of food is less obvious, but no less profound. To partake of the Shabbat meals, for example, consists of more than the physical act of sating our stomachs; the food becomes part of the act of sanctifying the day, an integral and necessary aspect of worshiping God. Wine is more than just a liquor when we drink it to usher in the Shabbat. When these are utilized for sacred purposes, food and drink themselves become sanctified and elevated to another realm.

The same holds true for ordinary weekday food, when it is preceded by an acknowledgment of God through a blessing before and after the food. Eating is never just a simple act, neither for the body nor for the soul.

D: That certainly puts a new perspective on food. It's not just there for us to enjoy as we please. It's a means of serving God.

R: Exactly. And there's more.

D: More? This is enough for me to absorb at one sitting.

R: Well, you have my permission to overindulge here. One item is significant right now. It's not only what food discipline does for the individual Jew; it's also what it does for the Jewish people as a whole. The kosher laws are one small part of an entire system of law that has, as one of its functions, the preservation and the separation of the Jewish people from the rest of the world.

D: Really? I thought God wants His world to be one, united — but you're saying just the reverse.

R: An excellent point, and we'll elaborate on it when we deal with the relationship of the Jew to the non-Jewish world. But for now, let me say that God does ultimately want total unity under Him; this is part of the Biblical idea of the End of Days, the Messianic time that the prophets envision, when all of mankind will come to accept the Oneness of God.

But until that time, the people Israel has been appointed *Jewish* to be the living model of sanctity and the teacher of God's *distinc-* ways to the world. If it does not remain separate and apart, *tiveness* but instead assimilates and ultimately disappears, then God has lost His messenger. That is why, when you get right down to it, the Torah contains many laws that inevitably maintain Jewish distinctiveness. This is deliberate. Just as a *Kohen* has special requirements that preserve his sanctity and separate him from the non-*Kohen*, so this entire nation — which the Torah calls a Kingdom of Priests/*Kohanim* — is given special regulations to maintain its sanctity and religious integrity. If this sets Israel apart from others, so be it; it may not seem equitable, but God needs one nation on earth to maintain the ideas of holiness as a model for the rest of the world to emulate.

And remember what we discussed when we talked about the idea of sanctity: one of the important sub-meanings of *kadosh* — holy — is precisely this: separate, distinctive, removed. It is significant that the Torah refers to holiness specifically at the end of these kosher laws in *Leviticus* 11, and just prior to and following the summation of these laws in *Deuteronomy* 14:3-21. It may be a paradox but, as we have already seen, the way we treat physical food can make us holy — not only in the sense of self-discipline but in the literal sense of *kadosh* as separate. We don't know the reasons behind the Torah's laws, but one certain result of the observance of kashruth is that it marks the Jew as distinctive and different.

True, being different is not what most people strive for. They would like to be like everyone else and fade into the background. But although God loves all His creatures equally, He wants us to preserve our distinctiveness as a people.

D: Your comment about God loving His creatures equally makes me think: why are certain animals forbidden and others permitted? Did not God create all animals? Why should some be favored over others?

Cows **R:** Which ones do you consider favored?

and pigs **D:** Apparently God likes cows more than He does pigs, because cows are kosher.

R: You raise an interesting point. Firstly, one could argue the reverse: that by forbidding pigs, God favors them, since they will not be slaughtered and eaten by Jews. Obviously, then, the terms "favored" or "not favored" are inappropriate here. God does love all His creatures equally. In fact, there are laws against causing pain to any animal, there are requirements to feed them properly — even before we feed ourselves — and we are forbidden to hunt them for sport. A special area of Jewish law — called *tzaar baalei chaim* — deals with proper treatment of animals. They must be treated kindly; we may not cause pain to pigs, dogs, cats or horses, which are non-kosher, or to cows or sheep, which are kosher.

As to why the cow and sheep are permitted — given proper slaughter and preparation — and the pig is forbidden: there are reasons, but as is true of much of Torah, the reasons are hidden from us. We mortals are not privy to the mystery; we cannot enter into the immortal mind of

God, but we will talk about some tentative reasons in a moment.

In any case, there is nothing intrinsically "evil" about the pig, but for some inscrutable reason it is considered an unfit food for the Jew. That the pig may be a dirty animal, that it wallows in filth, is a very attractive rationale, but that is beside the point. The nearest we come to a reason is the Torah's statement that the regimen of kashruth is given to us so that we shall be holy, as God is holy.

D: If God didn't want us to eat the pig, why did He create it in the first place?

R: Firstly, there are millions of people for whom the pig is permissible food. But let's broaden your question: why did God create the temptation, say, to steal if He doesn't want us to steal? Why did He place so many impulses within us if He does not want us to satisfy them? Wouldn't it have been easier if we didn't have to struggle against these natural instincts? *The role of temptation*

The answer is fairly obvious: we are not automatons, we were given freedom of choice. We can choose to wound our friend or steal from him; or we can choose to lend a helping hand or give charity. We are forced to do neither. The more tempting or desirable a forbidden act is, the more it means when we turn away from it and choose God's way. When we do this, we become both servant and master: servant of God, and master of ourselves. What I'm saying is that in order for our service of God to be significant, it must be possible not to serve Him. Without forbidden foods in the world, kosher loses its meaning.

D: So we should thank God for creating the pig?

R: In a way, yes.

D: But throughout history many religions and cultures have forbidden certain animals. Even today the Hindus have sacred animals that may not be eaten. Isn't Judaism simply doing the same thing?

R: You just answered your own question: In those societies where animals were forbidden, they were forbidden because the animals were objects of worship and therefore considered holy: the sacred cow. The Torah forbids certain animals because man and not the animal is sacred.

D: So we are back to holiness again. That word keeps popping up everywhere.

R: That's because if you take away the idea of holiness, you have no Judaism. We have already discussed the idea that holiness begins with the physical, not in a never-never land. And kashruth is a paradigm of all of holiness in that it takes a purely physical act and teaches us to hallow it, to elevate it to a higher, Godly plateau, in order to make us better Jews and human beings. That's why it's the first thing God talks about to Adam and Eve.

Kashruth and character

D: You make it sound as if a person's character is affected by kashruth.

R: Quite so. That is true not only of kashruth, but of all the mitzvot. They are an effort on the part of God to make each Jew a better person. The person who lives by Torah is learning to overcome his desires in favor of God's desires. Not "What do I want?," but "What does God want?" The person who can set aside his own wishes in favor of God's will also be able to set aside his wishes in favor of the needs of others, and thus he will ultimately become a better human being — less selfish and less greedy.

D: Do you feel that greed is a real problem today?

R: It always has been — but today it has become accepted, a sign of vitality and toughness. The idea that the world is here to serve the self is ingrained in contemporary life. We have to "enjoy" prayer, otherwise we refuse to pray. If being a Jew isn't "fun," then we simply abandon it. "What's in it for me?" is the current national anthem. The role of God is to serve me, and not vice versa. The very idea that we are supposed to serve God whether or not we benefit from it is foreign to us. We don't realize that what distinguishes humans from animals is the human ability to say no to the self, to deny the self in favor of higher things — and to recognize God as sovereign.

I recall a five-year-old boy approaching me one Shabbat at the synagogue. He had a chocolate bar in his hand. It was fresh, glistening, appetizing, unopened. "Is this kosher, rabbi?" he asked. I looked at the ingredients carefully, hoping that there would be nothing objectionable in them. The boy's face was expectant, waiting for my verdict. But I found what I was afraid of: gelatin and glycerine, two very questionable ingredients when a product carries no kosher supervision. "I'm sorry, Joey, but I'm afraid it's not kosher. I really am sorry." Joey looked at me. He saw my distress. "It's Okay, Rabbi," he said brightly, and flung the candy bar into the wastebasket.

That boy will have no trouble saying no to larger tempta- *Saying yes* tions as he grows up. He has acquired the power to say no to *and no* himself — and the realization that it is possible to do so and live through it. All the mitzvot, especially kashruth, can have a defining impact on a person's character.

D: But can an act so innocuous as eating have such an effect?

R: The point is that for the Torah, no act is innocuous. Just saying good morning to a person on the street can be fraught with all kinds of impacts — surface and profound — on the world. All things affect other things, just as each player in an orchestra has an impact on the entire musical output. He and his fellow musicians are not sitting by themselves. They are part of a unit, a whole.

So it is with eating. It's not simply a matter of taking food and inserting it into your digestive system, as we have seen. If one eats properly — and I'm not referring merely to table manners (though that, too, is a part of Torah) — it affects one's entire character and personality. Hunger is a basic instinct, and when we cannot indulge it without asking, "Is this permissible? May I eat this? Does it contain forbidden substances? Did I acknowledge God with the proper bless- ing?" — then we become conditioned to think before doing. When we do that long enough, in time our very instincts become sublimated and elevated, and instead of acting out of impulse, our behavior becomes measured and thoughtful. At that point we are on our way towards becoming conscious, sensitive beings, who do not go through life on automatic pilot, but take over the controls and becomes the captains of our daily actions.

This is the way of serving God: we become more Godlike. As He rules His world, so will we rule our world, and ourselves; and as He does nothing without thought, so, too, will we do nothing without thought.

D: You know, it occurs to me that all this can have some very beneficial side-effects. The thousands of weight-loss diets all have one thing in common: the need to curb the appetite. We ought to patent these Jewish ideas and put them on the market. "Religious eating — how to say no to that delicious but fattening dessert."

R: Even if it's kosher.

D: If we market it right, we could become rich.

R: Yes, but when we do become rich, it only means we will have a greater variety of things to say no to. Remember that King Solomon in *Proverbs* 30:8 prays that he be neither too rich nor too poor.

We are what we eat

D: Do you really mean that if I eat a pig, I become piggish?

R: The answer is yes, but that needs definition. Obviously, that is not to be taken literally.

D: And if I eat a cow, do I become cowlike? That doesn't sound too good, either. I wouldn't like to be either a pig or a cow.

R: Well, let's define things. You don't become a pig, you don't become a cow, or a turkey, or a crab, or a chicken, or a horse. What happens is that certain species of animals possess characteristics that the Torah does not want to see introduced into our systems, because eating these creatures influences us subtly to assume certain aspects of their natures. In a way, these qualities enter our spiritual bloodstream.

Let's take an example, based on the writings of the great Gaon of Vilna. A kosher animal has two identifying marks: it chews its cud, and its hooves are cloven, or split. These are more than mere physical signs. Cloven hooves indicate that this is not a beast of prey, that it is not a predator that tears its victims limb from limb. Chewing the cud — ruminating — symbolizes the concept of peace and contentment with one's lot; that is, the ruminant animal is content with whatever is already present in its stomach — instead of steadily hunting for more food or new victims. In a sense, it makes its food do double service.

The non-kosher animal may possess one of these signs, but never both. It either has claws instead of hooves, or it does not ruminate. That is, it either tears victims apart for its food, or it is not content with what it already has. The pig, which has cloven hooves, is not a beast of prey, but it is not kosher because the fact that it does not chew its cud symbolizes a lack of contentment, among other things.

Of course, not all questions about kashruth are answered by these very profound insights, granted, but they do provide an illustration of how some of the mysteries behind the commandments can be approached and somewhat clarified. Of course, as with all Torah laws, our limited and mortal intellects cannot fully plumb the depths of the mind of God.

D: A question on that insight. You are saying that certain animals are forbidden because when we fuse their flesh with ours through the process of eating and digestion, we become, deep within ourselves, susceptible and open to the undesirable characteristics of that animal: constant discontent with one's own life, and exploitation and violent behavior towards other creatures.

Let me grant you that foods can affect us spiritually — but why would the Torah single out these two qualities — discontent and exploitation — as being more harmful than other undesirable characteristics?

R: Good point. I don't want to go too far afield, but the last of the Ten Commandments, "thou shalt not covet," is in a sense fundamental to all the commandments. When do we begin to covet that which belongs to others? When we are not content with what we already have; and when this is so, we begin to exploit others so that we can obtain what they have and we think we lack. Ultimately, we might even end up getting it in some improper way, by stealing it from them, or even taking it by force. Nothing is as detrimental to our spiritual health as discontent within ourselves and the consequent exploitation and aggressiveness towards others. The Torah

Discontent and exploitation

does not want us to introduce these qualities into our spiritual selves, and from the Torah point of view, food has the capacity to do this.

There is one more point: when all is said and done, a person's discontent has its origins in a lack of real faith in God's providence. If you truly and fully believe that God is in charge, then what are you discontent about? I am not selling palliatives, but the fact is that the truly religious and believing Jew is satisfied and content and even joyous.

D: Then a cow is a religious animal and a horse is irreligious? Isn't that stretching things a bit? And didn't you say that God loves all His creatures equally?

R: You are extrapolating a bit. I am merely referring to the subtle symbols and the influences which they represent.

D: In any case, it is amazing that an instinctive act like eating can have so many implications. This may ruin my next meal — thinking of everything it represents.

R: On the contrary, if your next meal is kosher when you could have had non-kosher, it should make it even tastier when you realize that with every bite and swallow you are obeying God's law. I grant you, though, that the things we're talking about here could ruin a tasty non-kosher meal.

D: Is there such a thing?

Delicious but not kosher
R: Of course: we don't claim that non-kosher food cannot be delicious. As a matter of fact, the Sages tell us that the Jew is supposed to refrain from the pig — not because "it probably does not taste good anyway" or "it's not healthy." You're supposed to say, "I wish I could partake of it because it is probably very tasty, but the Holy One has forbidden it to me . . ." *Sifra, Kedoshim* 9, discusses this.

But let's get back on track. What I've really been getting at is something you raised a while ago about God being so concerned about details. As far as God is concerned, no action, to paraphrase Donne, is an island unto itself. Every deed affects every other deed — no matter how insignificant it may seem. It's like the proverbial pebble tossed into the middle of the pond: it causes endless ripples. A modern Jewish sage once said that a Jew in Jerusalem whose learning, piety and saintliness are beyond reproach has an impact on the ordinary behavior of a Jew he never met who may be living in Paris or New York. He was talking about spiritual ripples.

D: That is a very appealing concept with much spiritual resonance, but I'll have to let it sink in. Let me return to more physical matters. I have often heard that kosher food is more healthy, and that hygiene underlies all the kosher laws.

R: Kashruth may result in food that is cleaner and healthier, but that is beside the point. Ultimately, we do not serve God because of the benefits we may derive from it. Of course, everything in the Torah is beneficial, and God does not make demands of us that are harmful to us. The essence of God is goodness and love — this is not a term that Christianity invented — and therefore, the entire corpus of Jewish practice is "good for us," including kosher food. As King Solomon said of the Torah, "Its ways are ways of pleasantness and all its paths are peace" (*Proverbs* 3:17). But we should not stop there. The reason we perform the mitzvot is because this is a means of coming closer to God and expressing our allegiance and subservience to Him. God makes no promises that it will make us healthier, or more handsome or beautiful, or prevent wrinkles, or keep our teeth white, or make us popular, or restore our hair. For the Jew who truly loves God, there is pure delight in serving Him, regardless of whether or not it is convenient or comfortable. This is the ideal service of God.

Kashruth and hygiene

Admittedly, this is never easy, and not everyone attains this level of idealism, but it is something Jews strive for. That's what is meant by the verse in the *Shema*, "And you shall love Hashem, your God, with all your heart . . ." The Torah is not a mere health manual. It is God's overall blueprint for mankind, the guide that teaches us how to exist successfully, how to make our way through life with purpose and happiness and dignity — and sanity. Torah is concerned with the health of the body, yes, but it has other concerns as well: the spiritual health of the mind, the emotions, the soul, the heart, the character — every facet of a human being. To reduce the Torah's laws to good health directives is like saying that the most significant thing about an original

Rembrandt is the frame. We must be careful not to trivialize great things, nor to drag them down to our own level. We need to appreciate the big picture, not just its peripherals.

D: It all gets back to holiness again, doesn't it?

R: Precisely. It's almost as if God were telling us that we can serve Him not only in the holiness of the synagogue or the sanctity of the Jerusalem *Beit Hamikdash.* We serve Him even more meaningfully by sublimating our appetites, disciplining our instincts, channeling our hungers, harnessing our animal drives according to the dictates of the Torah. Not only are there laws about permissible and forbidden foods, there are regulations as to how permitted animals are to be slaughtered and made ready for the table. Even after they are prepared properly — which includes proper ritual slaughter, called *shechitah,* performed by a learned, pious and specially trained Jew who slaughters an animal only after reciting a prayer to God — they cannot then simply be eaten. There are further requirements which involve the removal of blood from the meat prior to cooking, plus several additional preparatory steps.

But even after it is prepared properly and is ready to eat, the Jew pauses for a moment and acknowledges God as the Creator of this food, and pronounces God's Name, and then expresses verbally — not merely by thinking or meditating — that God is King and that He has created this bread, this fruit, this meat, this vegetable, this wine, this water.

The world is not here only for man's carefree taking. It is here for man to utilize for his legitimate needs and enjoyment — and more, as a means for him to become aware of and appreciate God even as he utilizes His world. In that way, the world becomes truly pleasurable — and holy. You will recall our conversation on prayer when we talked about this.

D: Maybe all those food etiquette books I used to laugh at were making an important point after all. How we eat is significant.

R: How and what and why and when. The utilization of food — how we deal with all of our animal instincts — is an important litmus test of our humanity.

D: How do I respond when a friend asks me why I am observing kashruth?

R: The best answer is, "Because I am a Jew." Then you might add that you are maintaining an ancient and yet contemporary Biblical practice of our people. If you are pressed further, respond with some of the things we have discussed today: that, as is true of all mitzvot, we do not know the ultimate and hidden reasons that underlie kashruth. You can refer to the claws and the hooves, and then you can point to the very end of the kosher laws, where God says: "Thou shalt sanctify thyself and be holy, for I am holy . . ." (*Leviticus* 11:44). The word *kadosh* — "holy" — is utilized five times in these two verses: "For I am Hashem your God, and thou shalt be holy, for I am holy . . . For I am Hashem, Who elevates thee from the land of Egypt to be the God unto thee; and thou shalt be holy, for I am holy." And in *Exodus* 22:30 there is a similar connection between holiness and food: "Thou shalt be a holy people unto Me; torn flesh (the Hebrew word is *treifah*, about which we spoke before) from the field thou shalt not eat . . ."

And if that does not satisfy your friend's curiosity, mention that all this underscores the idea that when we discipline our appetites and refrain from certain foods, even though they may be tempting, we are on the way to becoming holy, to achieving a sense of *kedushah* — holiness — in life. We are on the road to becoming Godlike, in our own little way. That idea ought to keep your friend busy for a while.

D: These are all beautiful and lofty concepts. Do you mean to tell me that everyone who observes kashruth is aware of all this?

R: Of course not. People observe kashruth for all kinds of reasons, or for no reasons. Many were brought up on it, and they no more think about kashruth than they do about breathing. But even they should stop and think about it from time to time — which is what we're attempting to do.

D: But is it right to perform a mitzvah without thinking? Is serving God by rote such a good thing?

R: Rote service, without thought or feeling, is obviously not good enough. Of course, the ideal way of eating is to remember with each bite that God is the Creator of this food. The Torah does not insist on this ideal, however. It simply requires us to remember God through the blessings at the beginning and at the end of meals. That's because the act of eating *per se* is not a commandment. When we are performing a positive thou-shalt such as tefillin, or shofar, or prayer, rote service is an insult to God.

Practical aspects

D: Let me be honest. Much of what you say appeals to me intellectually and even emotionally. But I am frightened of the hundreds of practical details involved in maintaining a kosher home. Let's face it, for a beginner these details are a bit awesome. There are so many laws, so many do's and don't's, it is downright discouraging. In other words, I may be prepared intellectually, and perhaps in theory — but the practical side does worry me.

R: This is understandable. But keep in mind that the observance of kashruth today is greatly simplified by modern technology. Thousands of kosher foods are on the supermarket shelves — in fact, many supermarkets feature "Kosher Only" sections, and not only in the larger cities. The rules of the kitchen are easily learned, and in a very short time they become second nature. There is also a large network of support from those who already keep kosher and who have worked through your same problems. You can talk to rabbis, teachers and a host of people who will be more than happy to help you along the way until it becomes a part of you. There are also a number of fine handbooks that offer practical, how-to advice.

Granted, it is not easy at first. Habits of a lifetime do not let go; there will be some initial mistakes and frustrations. You will wonder why you need all this. But life is most satisfying when we break through barriers, when we climb to new levels. And just the knowledge that in this act you are fulfilling a Biblical commandment and maintaining a thirty-three-century tradition of our people; that you are part of a link in the chain going back to Sinai, infusing holiness into a physical act, and that you are doing something special for your soul (and probably for your body as well); that you are one of countless Jews who are doing this in our own day and who have done so in the past; that you are bringing into your life the rare qualities of self-discipline and self-control that distinguish you from the beast, and are beginning to move closer to the Torah's ideal of "a kingdom of priests and a holy nation" — and I could go on — all this should strengthen you whenever you begin to falter or have doubts.

And besides, you can always call me.

D: If I call you, do I have to listen to that same long sermon again?

R: Not the same long sermon; maybe a different long sermon.

ıɴterpersoɴaɭ
reɭatıoɴshıp– the jew
ɭoves hıs ɴeıghbor

David: It occurs to me that we have spent a great deal of time discussing our relationship to God. We've examined *Teshuvah*, Shabbat, Yom Tov, prayer, the idea of holiness, and the meaning of Torah — but so far we haven't really looked closely at the area of interpersonal relationships. Didn't you once tell me that while some of the mitzvot deal with the man-God relationship, others are concerned with the relationships between people?

Doing kindness **Rabbi:** You are quite right. Judaism has a great deal to say about this area — literally *bein adam lachaveiro,* "between a person and his friend." In fact, the Mishnah in

Avot 1:1 explicitly states that *chesed,* "lovingkindness," is one of the three pillars on which the world stands, the other two being Torah and Divine service. And the Talmud in *Yevamot* 79a suggests that doing kindness is one of the signs of an authentic Jew.

This theme is echoed throughout our classical literature. Psalm 89 says, for example, that *olam chesed yibaneh,* "the world is built on *chesed.*" God Himself is the very embodiment of *chesed,* and describes Himself in *Exodus* 34:7 as *rav chesed,* having an "abundance of *chesed.*" And the Talmud in *Sotah* 14a makes a very suggestive statement about God as a provider of *chesed,* pointing out that the Torah both begins and ends with deeds of *chesed:* in the very beginning, God Himself makes clothing for Adam and Eve, and at the very end, He Himself buries Moses. That is to say, *chesed* is the framework of Torah and of God's relationship to us. The Jewish mystical sages point out that God created the world because He wished to infuse the entire universe with His goodness, and that ever since Creation He has sustained us through this goodness. And everyone is familiar with the Talmudic tale in *Shabbat* 31a, in which the heathen asks Hillel to teach him the entire Torah while he is standing on one foot. Hillel responds: "What is hateful unto you, do not do unto your friend. The rest is commentary. Go and learn." Among the many things one can derive from this incident is the centrality of interpersonal relationships within Judaism.

When you get right down to it, *chesed* is one of the qualities which distinguishes us from the other creatures; it makes us a partner of God Who is the embodiment of *chesed.* So to say that interpersonal relationships is a major aspect of Judaism would almost be a gross understatement.

D: Well, all that is fine theory, but what about practical, ordinary, every-day relationships?

R: The Torah is the most profound book in the world, but *To mold us* it is also a very practical guide. It is replete with commandments whose purpose is to mold us into people who are loving, considerate, sensitive, and unselfish. Especially unselfish.

D: Why especially? Are you saying that selfishness is worse than being unkind and uncaring?

R: Selfishness — by which I mean qualities like pride, arrogance, self-centeredness — is the root of most of the problems which are destroying us as individuals and as a society. The notion that we have everything coming to us as an inherent right, that the world owes us this and that, that we are not required to give and share but rather may take and grab all that we can lay our hands on — this is destructive of everything: marriages, friendships, relationships. If there is room only for the "me," then every "you" is an unwelcome intruder. The self-centered person cannot do genuine *chesed*, because no one else but he matters in his little universe.

D: But isn't selfishness natural?

R: By now, you know that a genuine human being is not one who merely does everything that comes naturally. The fact that something is natural or instinctive is not reason enough for us to give it full reign. Society today is destroying itself because we have allowed the "natural" to dominate. Violence, drugs, fear for one's elemental safety are the hallmarks of contemporary life. In the world around us we are witness to ethnic cleansing, genocide, brutality, massive rates of abortion. The sacredness of human life has lost all meaning. Permissiveness is the order of the day, and as a result the weakest members of society are at risk: the unborn, the handicapped, the aged, the unemployed, the refugee, the poor, the infirm, the sick.

This represents a corrosion of moral values, and it is the inevitable result of a society living according to instincts that are unbridled and unchanneled.

D: I do recall that we have discussed this idea on several occasions. But I still don't understand how Torah combats this selfishness you describe.

Not just charming theory *R:* Bear in mind that matters like giving to the poor, or visiting the sick, or comforting the bereaved, or feeding the hungry, or tending the infirm, are not just charming theory in Judaism. They are specific commandments which the Oral Torah fleshes out with directives as to how to perform them —

with the ultimate purpose not only to help the other, but also to help ourselves — to make us less self-centered and more aware that there is an other. And there's another Other, with a capital O, with Whom we need to relate — and that's God Himself.

D: It's not really clear what one Other has to do with the other other.

R: Everything. Did it ever occur to you that arrogance and selfishness are the major impediments to genuine belief in God and worship of Him? This is because a human being tends to worship himself. This is another one of those "natural" characteristics we possess, and it is the ultimate selfishness — which is not just a character flaw but a serious barrier between us and God. As the Sages in *Arachin* 15b tell us, God declares that He and the arrogant person "cannot dwell in this world together." *Impediments to belief*

Let me explain. One of the key reasons we are unable to worship God fully is that we fail to recognize the unlimited good which God bestows upon us. The concept of *hakarat hatov*, "acknowledging the good" which others have done for us, is foreign to us. We tend to believe that everything we have is really our rightful due, and therefore we find it impossible to recognize that Someone is benefiting us. What prevents this recognition? Self-worship, self-centeredness.

D: But isn't it important to have a sense of self-worth?

R: There's a huge difference between self-worth and self-centered arrogance. The person who has a sense of self-worth is aware of his or her talents, and skills — but if he is a sensitive person, he will realize that these are all gifts from Above. A person who has self-worth can also be a selfless person. The self-centered, arrogant person, on the other hand, deludes himself into believing that skills and talents are of his own making, and such a person remains dedicated to himself alone. In brief, one realizes that God is the Giver, while the other thinks he acquired it all by himself. *Self-worth vs. self-centered*

Obviously, we all have a certain sense of pride and self-awarenesss, and I'm not talking about eliminating these but about controlling them and reducing their power over us. Like everything else we are born with, pride and ego can be used for good purposes if channeled carefully and intelligently: if we control them and they do not control us.

D: Fine. I've always wanted to become less selfish. How do I go about it?

Reducing selfishness **R:** The best way to reduce selfishness is through performing acts of *chesed*. These have the power to transform us. Even if we do them at first without the noblest of motives, the mere act of doing *chesed* has in it the power to transform and mold our feelings. If you know someone you don't particularly care for, try being especially kind to him. Over a period of time, your feelings towards him will change. This is because the external often controls the internal. For example, we normally view the act of bowing down during certain points in our prayers as an expression of inner submission to God. However, bowing also creates an actual sense of submission within us. Or take the matter of dress: when we wear casual clothing, we feel casual; when we dress in black tie or a long gown we feel more special and celebratory within ourselves. Externals affect internals. Similarly, reaching out towards others affects our feelings towards them. Selflessness is one effective way to reduce selfishness

Once we reduce this selfishness, we are able to recognize the enormous kindnesses constantly being showered upon us, and the natural result of this recognition will be to turn in thankfulness to the Source of all that good — which is God.

In other words, when we learn to reach out easily to others and to be sensitive to their plight, that very reaching out makes it more possible for us to reach out genuinely to the ultimate Other, God Himself. Serving others and serving God are really intertwined.

D: So why does everyone split Judaism into ethics on the one side and ritual on the other?

Ritual vs. ethics: a cliché **R:** The everyones who do the splitting are simply parroting discredited clichés. In fact, the structure of the Ten Commandments itself suggests this: the first five commandments deal with the man-God relationship, and the last five deal with interpersonal relationships. To observe one without the other is to observe only part of the Torah and to symbolically accept only half of the Commandments. That is, God wishes us to serve Him fully and passionately, but we need to understand that a major ingredient of being a true servant of God and a truly religious person is to be a good, ethical and moral individual.

In other words, service of God includes service of our fellow human beings, in whom His spirit also resides. Proper interpersonal relationships, the living of an ethical, caring, sensitive, actively good life, and interacting lovingly with our fellow human beings, is also service of God, and is as much a fulfillment of God's will as is the donning of tefillin or the observance of kashruth. To submit ourselves to God without simultaneously establishing a sensitive and loving relationship with others is to subvert the essence of Judaism.

Similarly, a person who observes only the interpersonal dimension in Judaism and ignores the human-God element, also subverts Torah. In a word, in Torah there are duties to God — *bein adam lamakom* — and duties to fellow human beings — *bein adam lachaveiro*. Both sets of duties emanate from God, and carry equal weight.

The fact is that without *chesed* we could hardly exist in this universe. People need people. For example, other than the death penalty, the severest punishment in criminal justice is to place someone in isolation, in solitary confinement. That's why *chesed*, which brings people together, is such a critical facet of Jewish law.

D: Let me bring up an issue that troubles me: this matter of having laws about interpersonal relationships. I try to be a good person, to be decent to others, to be kind and understanding. I may not always succeed, but I try. This type of thing, it seems to me, should flow naturally from within a person. You can't really legislate goodness, can you? What good is kindness if you're only doing it because you have to do it?

Legislating goodness

R: You are making too facile an assumption: that left to his own devices, man would be as concerned with the next person as he is with himself, and that all this would, as you say, flow naturally from within. This is not the assumption of the Torah. The Torah's point of view is that there are two conflicting impulses within a human being, the *yetzer hatov* and the *yetzer hara*, the inclination for good and the inclination for evil. Unfortunately, the inclination for evil, unless it is consciously fought, is at least as strong as that for good. The fact is that man is basically a creature of instinct, and the most natural instinct of all is to look out for number one — which often results in hurting others. When *Genesis* 8:21 says that "the inclination of man's heart is evil from his youth," it means to say that man, left to his own devices, is going to be selfish, greedy, and quite unconcerned about his fellow human beings. And *Job* 11:12 tells us that "like a wild ass is man born." When the Talmud in *Kiddushin* 30b states that the Torah is the antidote against the inclination towards evil, it means that without the leavening and humanizing influence of Torah, we would all be like denizens of the jungle.

The **D:** Let me interrupt: are you saying that without the Torah a
antidote person cannot be ethical or moral or any of these good
against things? But you and I both know that this is not so, that there
evil are some very moral and ethical people out there who happen
not to be believers.

R: You raise some crucial points. First, I want to say paren-
thetically that I am not at all certain that most self-styled
unbelievers are really unbelievers. There are millions of people who are religiously unlettered, or haven't really thought
about God deeply, or haven't read or studied very much in
this area, who take the easy way out and refer to themselves
by some fashionable label like "agnostic" or "unbeliever."
Often, when you scratch such people you find below the surface a strong residue of religious feeling.

But I won't belabor that point, and I will grant that there
are in fact true unbelievers (which for me is an oxymoron)
who are nevertheless very fine people. But let's define our
terms. How would you define an ethical person?

D: Someone who is, well, a decent human being, and doesn't
go around hurting other people.

Not yet **R:** From the Torah's standpoint, those traits, fine as they are,
ethical do not yet qualify that person as "ethical" or "moral." A
person who is decent and does not hurt others is merely some-

one who is not an evil person, not a bad person — but not yet ethical or truly good.

D: Well, I wish we had more people who were "not yet ethical or truly good" who at least didn't hurt others.

R: I agree. But from the Torah's standpoint an ethical person cannot simply be passive and avoid harming others. He is required to pursue good. We are told to go after justice and morality and ethics actively. *Deuteronomy* 16:20 says it specifically: "Justice, justice shalt thou pursue . . ." We may not simply sit around and avoid injustice; we have to run after justice and seek it out. And in *Leviticus* 19:16, for example, we find an explicit commandment which underscores that simply not doing harm is insufficient: "Thou shalt not stand aside while your fellow's blood is shed." That is, when your neighbor is in trouble, help him.

Here is the point: at the beginning of the Torah, Cain kills Abel. God asks Cain where his brother is. Cain responds: "Am I my brother's keeper?" It is an insolent retort. One might say that the entire Torah is an effort to respond to Cain's question, to teach us that the answer to that question is, "Yes, you are your brother's keeper." And the Torah sets out to teach us how we can develop into becoming our brother's keeper. *Your brother's keeper*

The fact is that Cain's retort is the natural, instinctive one: "I am only concerned with myself; since when am I accountable for someone else?" And what the Torah wants to do in this area — as in every area of its legislation and teaching — is to wean us away from the instinctive and naturally selfish view of life.

This is the answer to the question you raised earlier about legislating kindness. The Torah gives us specific commandments in interpersonal relationships, because the Torah in effect is saying that not only is the recipient of our kindness helped, but so are we, the givers. By the regular performance of these commandments, our very characters are affected and molded by living the life of *chesed* — by giving *tzedakah*, tithing, honoring parents, visiting the sick, taking care of the aged and infirm, burying the dead with care and respect, leaving the ends of our field unharvested, not even returning to pick up what may have dropped during our harvest so the poor can have it as their own; by helping arrange a dowry for a poor bride, by refraining even from taking revenge, by being truthful, by avoiding even the most tasty gossip — we ourselves become less instinctively self-centered and begin to understand that there are others who need our care, love, understanding, sympathy, and lovingkindness.

Not a
religion
of whim
If it were up to us, would we ever give ten percent of our produce away? We would say, as so many people still say today, "I worked for what I have, let the poor also work. Why should I take my hard-earned money and share it with them?" Or we would say, "Why should I lend him my rake — he refused to lend me his yesterday!" Or: "Why should I tell the truth when the truth might hurt me? Besides, nobody will know." Left to ourselves, we would never know the parameters of hospitality to strangers, or the requirement to express simple gratitude or appreciation for favors done to us, or how serious an offense it is to humiliate others. I wonder how many of those ethical unbelievers refrain from gossip at all costs, or truly understand the ramifications of honoring one's parents, or really know how to give charity or offer hospitality.

In Judaism, none of this is left to our whims. All of this is law. And its purpose is clearly to transform our baser natures into something more noble and more human — and yes, more Godly.

Hakarat
hatov:
gratitude
Take, for example, the matter of gratitude. Few people know that central to the Torah's ethical viewpoint is this concept of *hakarat hatov*, "acknowledging the good" which others have done for us — gratitude and appreciation for favors done — which we just discussed, and that without a sense of gratitude to God and to others, one cannot be truly religious.

One of the underlying reasons for the great stress on honoring parents, beyond the idea that they are the earthly representatives of our Creator, is this concept of *hakarat hatov*. We owe them a deep debt of thanks for all that they have done for us in our lifetimes, particularly when we were helpless infants and children. On a broader level, we are reminded by the Torah's ethical system not to forget what other individuals may have done for us, the assistance they may have provided, the friendship, the support in times of need. Such things tend to fade from memory unless we sensitize ourselves about the need to recall the good. And most important — and most often overlooked — is the need to remember with gratitude what God has done for us, in providing us with lifelong sustenance and protection. In fact, in *Deuteronomy* 32:6, Israel is castigated because of her lack of gratitude to God.

D: Nevertheless, we do see non-pious individuals who are in fact pursuing good — individuals like the secular humanists, for example.

R: Don't confuse being "nice" with what the Torah requires *From* of us. We have seen in this century how so-called decent *"nice" to* and nice people became savages. Decency was subjective, and *savage* could not survive real temptation. I keep thinking of Dostoevski's remark in "The Brothers Karamazov": "If God does not exist, everything is permissible." We have seen precisely that in this century: everything was permissible.

However, let us not talk in global terms, but about day-to-day life. How many non-pious people do you know who actually seek out the poor to help them? How many know about the dignity and respect which are the inalienable right of a dead person? How many of these so-called decent people refuse to engage in any sort of negative talk about others, refuse even to listen to someone else's gossip — let alone slander?

And if such a rare individual does exist, my contention is that this is only because religion through the centuries has left a residue of civilized behavior in the world. Though they may not be aware of it, such people acquire their basic values from forebears and from a civilization that once upon a time was fundamentally a religious one. I do believe that if, theoretically, there had never been any Judaism in the world, we would today rarely if ever encounter this phenomenon of people who call themselves unbelievers and yet lead relatively decent and moral lives. On the contrary, we would all be devouring each other.

D: Perhaps so, who knows?

R: I would nevertheless ask such people some serious questions. First, is an ethical life without a grounding in some higher standard — based on something other than that which I by myself consider to be right and moral and ethical — truly a solid ethics? Will it be able to survive all crises and challenges? During World War II apparently fine, moral and ethical people stood silently by as their Jewish neighbors were hauled out of their homes never to return — and these so-called ethical people quietly and without any pangs of conscience proceeded to occupy these homes.

You simply can't have an ethics which takes its guiding principles from what each individual feels is right. Hitler felt he was right. Murderers feel they are justified. Thieves have their own rationalizations. (The Talmud in *Berachot* 63a says that even a thief prays to God that his thievery should succeed!) There has to be some higher, universally binding system if ethics is to have any force or meaning.

Second, what about the offspring of self-induced ethical people? Will such offspring, who are cut off from the well-springs of ethics and morality which are based in religion, have the anchor and the roots to remain ethical and moral no matter what? Once you are disconnected from a higher, transcendent source of morality, you are skating on very thin ice — and ultimately you confront ethical and moral dilemmas that are not clear cut, that are marginal, and for which you must have some religious grounding in order to address them from a truly objective ethical standpoint.

D: Such as?

Abortion, **R:** Such as the following: without a ground belief in God and
euthanasia, therefore in the holiness and value of human life, how
dialysis does one approach the problem of abortion, or of euthanasia, or of suicide? Are all abortions murder, or only under certain circumstances? Are they all permitted upon demand? Is a mercy killing — whose sole purpose is to end someone's terrible pain — murder, or is it not? Are there circumstances under which ordinary killing is permissible? We must not lie, but are there situations where a "white lie" is ethical? When is heroic medical intervention required for a sick person who has been given no hope for recovery? When you have only one kidney

dialysis machine and two desperately ill patients who need it now, how do you allocate it? By what standards do you make your judgment?

Ethics cannot be simply an instinctive matter, something that you practice because you feel it is the "right" thing to do, because ultimately you will run up against situations where your personal feelings are simply inadequate to the task at hand.

D: These are all true, but the average person does not have to make such decisions or face such problems.

R: True. So let's put things on a practical, less lofty plane.

You find a lost object which you become very fond of. You suspect that the owner doesn't care about it at all. Can you keep that object and not bother to return it? After all, the owner doesn't really want it. Nevertheless, Jewish ethics requires you to return it in any case. Another common example: you are not permitted by Jewish law to borrow someone else's possession without his or her knowledge even if you know he won't miss it. You must request permission.

In general, there are always going to be times when you simply do not feel like bothering to be kind, or sensitive, or charitable — you're not in the mood, you're angry or upset — and then the ethical element in you tends to evaporate on the moment unless there is a solid anchor in God and His law.

Not in the mood for kindness

This is why Judaism presents an extensive system of moral and ethical law which sets up moral imperatives, not suggestions, and which endeavors to create within us a self-discipline which will in the long run make us instinctively good and not the reverse.

D: But I know many people who attempt to live by the ideals of "Love thy neighbor."

R: Really? That's hardly likely, because "Love thy neighbor" is one of the most complex laws in the Torah, and one of the most difficult to fulfill. "Love thy neighbor" is not just a slogan. It's a lifelong task. And, by the way, most people forget that this central commandment was not invented by Christianity, but is in *Leviticus* 19. More significantly, most people also forget that the passage concludes with the phrase,

"I am the Lord." This underscores the concept that you are to love your neighbor not because it is a nice thing to do, or because you want him to be good to you in return, or because you want him to realize what a fine person you are, or because you're in a good mood today. You are to love your neighbor through thick and thin — even when he is not so lovable, and even when you are too tired or distracted to do so — for one reason: it is God's wish that you love your neighbor, with all that that implies. In other words, Judaism has codified ethics and good behavior and placed them on a transcendent base. This makes it mandatory for a person to act with compassion towards his fellow man even when on occasion it is against his supposed self-interest to do so.

This whole matter of interpersonal relationships is crucial to our understanding of the Torah. We get an idea of its importance by the frequency of certain words in the Torah. For example, can you imagine how many times the word *mishpat*, "justice," occurs in the Torah? Over five hundred times! The word *tzedakah*, loosely translated as "charity," but which really means "righteousness," occurs over one hundred-fifty times. It is a manifestation of the most elementary social justice that I must concern myself with the needs of those less fortunate. *Leviticus* 25:35 leaves nothing to the imagination or to vague feelings of pity: "If thy brother becomes poor . . . thou must help him that he may live with thee." And the prophets are constantly stressing the fact that worshiping God and serving fellow human beings are the parallel duties of every religious person.

To perfect the world   This, by the way, is what Judaism means when it expresses the hope, in the *Aleinu* prayer which is recited at the end of every single service, *letaken olam bemalchut Sha-dai*, "to perfect the universe under the sovereignty of the Almighty." Ethics is a way of perfecting the world — by first perfecting one's own self. We believe that it can only be achieved "under God."

D: All that sounds noble, but what does it really mean?

R: What this means precisely, as well as the definitions of "help" and "live with thee," and "love thy neighbor," are worked out in great detail in the Talmud and in the law codes.

D: Are you suggesting that we simply look up matters of compassion and lovingkindness in the law codes? That sounds so heartless, so dreary and perfunctory. Is that the Jewish way to be a good person? Where do heart and emotion and feeling come in?

R: You raise some important questions. The best answer is the Jewish people itself. We are known as a charitable people even to this day. We are anything but cold and heartless automatons when it comes to our fellow human beings — the whole world recognizes that. And this is because of the very legislation in the Torah which has shaped and honed our national character for thousands of years. Our entire tradition stresses love and compassion. And the famous passage in *Micah* 6 says that God wants us to "love *chesed*" — not just to do it perfunctorily, but actually to love it. At the end of the daily *Amidah* prayer, we acknowledge God Who has given us *ahavat chesed*, the love of *chesed*. Jewish life is permeated by this concept.

D: I have heard that the lives of religious Jews are so circumscribed that they don't do anything before looking it up in the law codes.

"Look it up in the book"

R: This is poppycock. Granted, all that we do is based on God's will as revealed in the Torah and the tradition. But we are far from being automatons. There is enormous room for human decision-making within the parameters of Torah — for not everything can be spelled out. Interpersonal relationships are too subtle and too complex for that. In general, life is filled with ambiguities, and decision-making about behavior is not always a clear-cut matter. We have to strike the proper balance between love and justice, between pride and humility, between personal needs and altruism, between legitimate needs for self-actualization — fulfilling one's own potential — and self-surrender. We decide how much to give to whom, we decide to whom we grant our hospitality.

It is precisely because of the ambiguities of daily life that the Torah does not attempt to legislate all the details of interpersonal behavior, but instead provides us with broad principles such as "Love thy neighbor."

Two poor men   To illustrate what I'm saying, let me ask you a question: imagine a poor man going from door to door asking for bread. One person, who happens not to follow the Torah, gives him bread because he wants to help him. A second person observes the mitzvot and gives him bread because it is a commandment to help the poor, and because he wants to help him. In the eyes of Judaism, which is the preferable act?

D: I prefer the one who instinctively does the right thing
   He is not giving the bread because he is forced to do so by a directive from above, but because his own heart tells him to do so.

R: Which is the response most people give, and which is logical on the surface. But the Talmud in *Kiddushin* 31a says the reverse: *Gadol hametzuveh v'oseh mi-mi she-aino metzuveh v'oseh*, "Greater is the one who is commanded and acts, than he who is not commanded and acts." The one who gives the bread because it is a mitzvah to help the poor is more beloved in the eyes of God. There are many reason for this, but one of them is what we just spoke of: the Torah does not want our help to the poor to be dependent on our own personal whims.

D: I'll have to digest that, but apparently there's much more to loving thy neighbor than I thought. Let me now raise another question that has been disturbing me. What about supposedly religious people whose ethics leave much to be desired?

Are all observant Jews ethical?   *R:* I don't deny that such people exist, and obviously they are an embarrassment to religion. Someone once said that there are people who don't believe that God exists but who behave as if He did — and there are those who say they do believe that God exists but behave as if He did not. The fact is that if a person prays with tefillin every day, keeps a strictly kosher regimen, observes Sabbaths and holy days — and is nevertheless unethical in his profession, dishonest in business, or engages in slander or gossip, or is untrustworthy, or is unkind — that person by definition is simply not a religious person. He is observing only half of the Torah — which is the man-God half — and is not observing the other half, the man-

man half. And even his man-God service is severely tainted. Such a person is not considered by the Torah to be a religious person at all. He is in fact guilty of the most heinous sin of all, for which there is no forgiveness: the sin of *chilul Hashem*, the desecration of the Divine Name.

D: But what does it say about Torah if it can produce such people?

R: Listen — the Torah doesn't "produce" such people. You can't blame the Torah for people who distort it. There are people who commit evil in the name of law, science, medicine, or what-have-you. An idea is not responsible for the behavior of those who claim to follow it.

Yes, I do believe that a consistent, faithful observance of Torah — all aspects of it — will gradually transform us into better and finer human beings. I have lived with very traditional Jews in many different places, and I can testify to their almost universal caring and active concern for others. *Chesed* is pervasive in such communities. They don't do any posturing about it, because with them it's perfectly normal not only not to steal or cheat or speak ill of others, but actively to pursue *chesed* through generous giving, sharing, sensitivity, and profound decency — all of it done in a quiet and natural way.

D: You say that the Torah sets up a system of moral and ethical laws, and you even cited the frequency with which certain ethical concepts are used in the Torah. And yet, when you really get down to it, there do not seem to be many laws in the Torah dealing with ethics or interpersonal relationships. I mean, you find many more laws about the details of rituals — like, say, bringing a sacrifice — than you find about the details of lovingkindness.

R: Technically you are right. On the surface, there seem to be many more so-called "ritual" laws than there are "ethical" laws.

By the way, let me stress once again that I consider this popular "ritual-ethical" dichotomy to be a false one. The fact is that the mezuzah on the door is no more a ritual than the giving of tithes; and the giving of tithes to the poor is no more ethical than is the placing of a mezuzah. Each is done because of a commandment of God, Who wants us to learn how to serve Him as well as our fellow human beings. Don't fall victim to the old anti-Biblical canards that set up a dichotomy between so-called "prophetic Judaism" and "priestly Judaism," with the one concerned with ethics and the other with ritual. This is pure nonsense. The prophets were as concerned with the proper way to offer sacrifices — the ultimate "ritual" — as they were with morality, and the priests were as concerned with lovingkindness as they were with service of God. The commandments to love our neighbor and to feed the poor, after all, are in the same Torah and were not invented by the prophets.

Why so few ethical commandments? To return to your question: the fewer number of so-called ethical laws should not mislead us. Take, for example, the long and graceful narratives in *Genesis.* If the Torah is designed to teach us how to live our lives, who needs all these stories? True, they are magnificent; true, they are uplifting. But what place do they have in a book of laws?

I've just answered my own question: I said they are uplifting. That is to say, one of the underlying purposes of these exquisite narratives is to teach us by the example of our forefathers how to live and how to behave.

Abraham negotiates with God over the fate of Sodom, arguing that a just God would not permit righteous people to be killed with the wicked. Elsewhere, Abraham teaches us hospitality to guests — and the story teaches not only that hospitality is important, but how to go about it: the text gives us a vivid picture of ninety-nine-year-old Abraham, just three days after his own circumcision, rushing about to take care of his guests who, as far as he knows, are total strangers.

Proper burial is taught to us by the account of the funeral of Sarah, and God Himself is engaged in the burial of Moses and Aaron.

Judah, in the case of his daughter-in-law Tamar, demonstrates undeviating honesty and unflinching moral courage.

Tamar, on her part, teaches us about the requirement not to humiliate anyone.

Joseph, in the incident with the wife of Potiphar, offers us a lesson in holiness and heroic self-discipline.

Moses teaches us about self-sacrifice and courage on behalf of others, without a concern for his own destiny.

And throughout the Torah, God is the champion and defender of the weak, the orphan and the widow, and constantly warns us that if we attempt to take advantage of them He Himself will come to their aid and exact retribution from us. The Bible is filled with such admonitions against exploitation of others, against deceitful behavior, against taking advantage of another person or his property.

Morality and goodness and ethics cannot be left up to us alone, but neither can they be simply laid down as "thou-shalts." By and large, the Torah attempts to teach these qualities by example. Just as a parent teaches a child to be honest not simply by giving lectures on honesty but by demonstrating honesty in his own daily life, so does the Torah teach us certain things not only by telling us what to do and not to do — which it explicitly does in many instances — but it also shows us how our own Biblical fathers and mothers lived their daily lives in fulfillment of these tenets. *Models of behavior*

Another point: interpersonal behavior is so complex and so subtle that "thou-shalts" and "thou-shalt-nots" cannot possibly cover all of its ramifications. When we are commanded to place a mezuzah on the doorpost, or not to eat on Yom Kippur, that is clear-cut and objective. But when we are commanded to give *tzedakah,* or to be kindhearted, we become engaged in a subjective interplay between two individuals that is extremely delicate and sensitive: what are my motivations, am I receiving honor or benefit for this act, is my heart in it, am I doing this in the proper way, am I embarrassing someone instead of helping, am I doing too much or not enough?

This might explain why there are technically a smaller number of mitzvot dealing with interpersonal relationships than with the man-God relationship. Bear in mind, however, that "Love thy neighbor as thyself" is only one mitzvah on paper, but it is a cardinal principle of human relationships, and covers tens of thousands of possible scenarios and situations. Rabbi Akiva in *Bereshit Rabbah* 24 calls it "the great principle of the Torah," because through it we learn to emulate God.

D: Isn't that a rather tall order, to become like God?

God visits   **R:** The Talmud in *Sotah* 14b reminds us that just as God
the sick   clothes the naked (*Genesis* 3:21) and visits the sick
(*Genesis* 18:1) and comforts the bereaved (*Genesis* 25:11) and
buries the dead (*Deuteronomy* 34:5) — the acts we just spoke
of — so should we. This is the key to interpersonal relationships: to fulfill *Deuteronomy* 13:5, to "walk after God," to try
to follow His example.

D: I asked something similar before, but it still concerns me:
is it really possible to attain total selflessness?

R: Perhaps not, but most of us would do well to be partially
and occasionally selfless. Incidentally, we ourselves ultimately benefit from the *chesed* we do for others. First, there is
the deep inner joy we feel when we do good. This is because
we are satisfying the needs of our souls to reach out to others,
and to identify with the *chesed* of God. In addition, an act of
chesed which we perform for others on earth triggers parallel
impulses towards us from on high. That is, our compassion
towards others creates a Divine compassion towards us. This
may be what the Sages mean when they say that those who
have compassion for others are themselves granted compassion by Heaven. So *chesed* is ultimately for our own benefit —
which is just what God wants.

D: That's well and good, but why does the all-powerful
God allow poverty to exist in the first place? Surely
God could supply all the needs of the poor people in an
instant.

R: This is precisely the point. God could have created a
perfect world, but for His own mysterious reasons He chose
to have us become His partners in creating that perfection. The
weak are to be helped by the strong, the sick by the healthy, the
have-nots by those who have. God wants us to become His
agents. And, by helping God in His work, not only do others
benefit, but we ourselves benefit. And, as we said earlier, we
grow and develop into better people.

D: Ironic isn't it? *Chesed* ends up helping our own selves.
Does not that make it, in the final analysis, a selfish act?

R: Good point. The definition of selfishness is self-interest, while *chesed* is by definition "other-interest." If I am kind because of self-interest, then by definition I am not doing *chesed*. But if I am "other-interested," I have made myself into a better person even though I might be receiving accolades as a result.

The point is that the focus should not be solely on our- *To focus on* selves and how it might benefit us, but rather to concentrate *the other* on the other. This is the pure way of doing *chesed* — though I would not be too upset if people were to do wonderful *chesed* even if some selfish motives were involved. Ultimately, I have the faith that their motives would themselves become purified by the mitzvah that they are performing.

D: More and more, I am beginning to sense that there is a lot more to this Judaism of ours than I have been led to believe.

R: That insight alone is a major achievement for someone returning to the faith of his people. The tragedy is that so many of our people are convinced that Judaism and Torah and its practices and beliefs are superficial things: you light candles on Friday night, you eat gefilte fish, you fast on Yom Kippur, you have matzot on Pesach, you give to Jewish charities, and you try to be a nice person. What they are really saying is that Judaism is a glorified Boy Scout troop. Given the little that they know about God and Torah and Judaism, it is no wonder they reject it.

D: All of which means that you and I will simply have to continue talking with one another.

R: By all means. It's my way of sharing, doing *chesed,* and studying Torah at the same time. And as we said before, you are not the only one who benefits: I also benefit a great deal. So let's meet again.

jews and
non-jews – the jew
views the world

. . . in which is discussed . . . The historical separation of
the Jewish people from the
nations of the world / The purpose of Judaism / The Jew and
the Holy Land / Is chosenness racist? The covenant / The
Jewish mission / Missionaries / Judaism's relationship to other
religions / Conversion to Judaism . . .

David: Based on our discussions so far, one clear pattern
  is beginning to emerge. I detect one underlying motif
beneath many of the mitzvot, and that is an effort to ensure
that Jews remain different and separate from the rest of
the world. For example, our food laws certainly keep us apart
from other people. As you yourself said, if we can't eat
with others, that severely limits our social interaction with
them. We are forbidden to marry them, we do not pray
with them, we don't even share the same day of rest with
them. Almost every aspect of our religion sets us apart
from the rest of mankind. And, I must add, that's not too comfortable a feeling.

Rabbi: Your perception is quite accurate, as far as it goes. *Part of* Kashruth does in effect separate us from other peo- *the world,* ples, but that is not its primary purpose, as we discussed *but apart* during our conversation on that subject. Obviously, kashruth laws apply even in a totally Jewish environment where there is no chance of mixing with other nations.

But what you say is quite true: the Torah and its mitzvot clearly set us apart from the rest of mankind, deliberately so. Our enemies in particular have noticed this. Haman describes us as "a people dispersed among the peoples . . . their laws are different from every other people's . . ." (*Esther* 3:8) In *Numbers* 23:9, the heathen prophet Bil'am calls us "a nation that will dwell in solitude and is not reckoned among the nations . . ."

These are legitimate descriptions of the Jewish condition. God explicitly tells us in *Leviticus* 20:26, *va'avdil etchem*, "I have separated you from among the peoples to be Mine." And Abraham himself is called *Avraham ha'Ivri* in *Genesis* 14:13. That is normally translated as "Abraham the Hebrew," but *ivri* stems from a root word meaning "the other side." This is a geographic as well as a spiritual designation. Abraham does in fact come from the other side of the river, but the term is used throughout the Bible to designate a Jew. Thus we find Joseph, in *Genesis* 39:14 and 41:12, and the Prophet Jonah in 1:9, as well as others, also referred to as *Ivri*. The Torah is informing us that Abraham and his children stand on "the other side" of mankind, and represent a way of life different from the rest of the world.

Yes, it is part of God's overall plan for mankind that the Jewish people should remain separate. The fact is that to be a holy people in a world that disdains holiness means to be a separate people.

It's interesting that the world seems to recognize this *Jewish* Jewish differentness intuitively. Even the assimilating Jew — *otherness* who does not wear distinctively Jewish dress and does not practice anything distinctively Jewish, who is a citizen of the world and faithfully lives by the ways of the society around him — even he is nevertheless pointed to as a Jew, as some- one different from "the rest of us." This makes the assimilator very unhappy, but it probably makes God very happy, because Jewish otherness is all part of His plan.

D: But if religion is supposed to bring people together, why should Judaism consciously and willfully set us apart from the rest of the world? Instead of unity, it seems to promote divisiveness.

R: Let's get our definitions straight. First, being separate and having a unique mission is not synonymous with divisiveness. We are commanded to be a model for humanity, to help bring them closer to the truths of God and Torah. To fulfill such a mission, we must remain somewhat apart from the rest of mankind.

Despite this separation, Judaism has never persecuted people of other faiths, and has never initiated pogroms or forcibly converted others to Judaism. While the Torah prescribes the commandments as the proper way to worship God, to arrive at a state of closeness with Him, and to achieve a sense of sanctity in this life, the Torah nowhere even suggests that all human beings must be Jews or that we should try to convince them to be. The only restriction the Torah makes on any religion is that no one may worship an idol. Rather than being a divisive force, Judaism is a unifying force in the world of religion.

Bringing us and God together
Second, your assumption that the purpose of religion is to bring people together needs some sharpening. Surely you do not mean to imply that there should be some sort of lowest-common-denominator religion which will make all human beings feel comfortable and unthreatened. If the major purpose is to bring people together, we might as well abandon Judaism altogether, because every aspect of Judaism sets us apart. While this unity among peoples will come about in Messianic days, the immediate purpose of Judaism is to bring man and God together by bringing God into the daily lives of Jews.

The Noachide Code
Once this is achieved — and it will be a stupendous achievement — the sense of oneness and unity among all of God's creatures will fall into place by itself. The Prophet Zechariah speaks of the ultimate time of redemption in his fourteenth chapter: "On that day, God will be One and His Name One." Jeremiah in his seventeenth chapter is even more explicit: he foresees the time when the nations of the earth

will cast aside their false doctrines and will declare their fealty to the God of Israel and to the truths of His teachings — but even that does not mean that all human beings will become Jews. They won't. Instead, they will faithfully observe the Noachide Code. This has been in existence since the Creation and, rooted in *Genesis* 9, deals with worship of God, murder, theft, incest, sexual immorality, eating the limbs of living animals [which was added, according to Maimonides in his Laws of Kings, 9:1, in the times of Noah], blasphemy, and setting up courts of justice; they will acknowledge God as the Creator and Israel as His chosen people; and they will strive to help Israel remain the people of God and the bearer of holiness in this world.

Let me explain that last idea: we did not ask for our special role, but were chosen by God to represent Him on earth. He has assigned us a special mission: to bring His teachings to the world. This is a special role, and requires a special people to carry it out. If we lose our distinctiveness and simply fade into the background and become like everyone else — through ignorance, or marrying out of the faith, or other quick routes to oblivion — it is clear that we will never succeed at our mission. God would either have to choose another messenger, or, so to speak, give up on mankind. That's why uniqueness, otherness and separateness is an integral part of our being as a people. *Israel's special role*

Certainly unity and oneness are goals devoutly to be wished for — in fact, that's how the ideal world began, when all of mankind consisted of a single couple: Adam and Eve in the Garden of Eden. And, of course, unlike the ancient deities, God is not limited to a certain nation, to certain borders. He is One and He is universal, and some day He will be recognized as the One God of all mankind. But until that wondrous moment of unity comes about, the apartness of the Jew is part of the plan of God. If the Jew performs his mission properly, that paradisiacal state will eventually become a reality.

As you mentioned earlier, our mitzvah system in fact contributes to this. The mitzvot have many functions: they instill sanctity within us, they help us reach up towards God, they connect us with Jewish history, they provide a momentary glimpse into eternity. But in addition to all this, the mitzvot serve the purpose of preserving our uniqueness. They set us apart, just as a uniform sets a soldier apart from the rest of society. In essence I am saying that by keeping to ourselves, we guarantee that ultimately mankind will come together as one.

D: That's all pretty theory, but it's still not a very comfortable role to play — to be different from the rest of mankind.

Comfort and religion

R: As for its not being comfortable, several responses: First, if you will forgive me, so what? What does comfort have to do with it? You are assuming that anything that makes us uncomfortable is by definition bad. That is an incorrect assumption. It may not be comfortable to be a role model to students and disciples and to be aware that one's every word and deed is scrutinized and analyzed, but that model has the immense privilege of molding and elevating others. It may not be comfortable to give away ten percent of the product of your hands — after all, you worked hard for it — and yet that is what the Torah expects of you. (Besides, you do keep ninety percent of it!) It may not be comfortable to fast on Yom Kippur, and yet how very significant it is. It is not always comfortable to be honest, or moral — sometimes it's much more comfortable to cheat and lie and cut corners.

In all these cases, however, the uncomfortable way is the preferred way. One of the purposes of our Torah is to arouse people from their lethargy, to stir them up, to point out to them their duties and responsibilities — to God, to other people, to their own heritage, to their wives and husbands and parents and children and neighbors, to themselves. Being awakened from a deep slumber and shaken by the shoulders is not very comfortable. Again, so what?

When Abraham taught the idea of an invisible and untouchable God, that was revolutionary and went directly against the prevailing human superstition that oceans and skies and mountains and stars and heavenly bodies are divine creatures. It has never been comfortable to be the bearer of that message.

Fingerprints are not alike

But much more important is this: differentiation and distinctiveness are integral aspects of God's creation. No two fingerprints are identical. No two individuals are identical.

The universe is filled with a dazzling variety of creatures, on land, in the air, in the seas. Within nature there is a panoply of colors and sizes and shapes and functions. Each of the millions of stars is different from its neighbors, as are the countless species of plants and flowers. The differences and the variety in the universe are staggering in their infinity. Differentiation, not sameness, is built into the pattern of the world.

Note, for example, that at the very beginning of the Torah's Creation narrative, the fourth verse states that God separated the light from the darkness. A few verses later the Torah states that God separated the water from the dry land, and that He separated the upper waters from the lower waters. That very first part of the Torah uses the Hebrew term for separation five different times, and throughout that chapter the separation of species from species is found many more times.

The subtle message here is that we are not one homogenized universe. An even more important message is that through the process of separation, God creates order out of chaos.

This is part of the stunning beauty of our world: it contains such infinite variety. As a matter of fact, the *Havdalah* prayer that Jews recite at the end of the Shabbat is an acknowledgment of separation, and it blesses God "Who has differentiated between sanctity and profaneness, light and darkness, between Israel and the nations, between the seventh day and the six days of creation . . ." So it should not be surprising that the Torah in *Leviticus* 20:26 explicitly states that "I have separated (using the same term, *va'avdil*) you from the nations to be Mine."

Variety and beauty

Besides which, what is really so uncomfortable about standing out in a crowd? People often go to great lengths to do just that — in dress, in manner of speech, in literary style. In fact, leaders and stars in every field of endeavor cultivate their uniqueness. Certainly when it comes to religion, a person with a sense of self should wear his or her distinctiveness proudly. Especially since this distinctiveness has a higher purpose to it.

D: I ask the following question not out of a sense of discomfort, but in a totally objective manner. We have been around for thousands of years, and we have surrendered a

If Jews and Judaism disappear

great deal to be loyal and faithful to God's teachings and to spread His word to all corners of the world. Maybe that's enough. Maybe our mission is complete. Would it be such a tragedy for the world if Judaism were to come to an end?

R: Decidedly yes, because there is still a long way to go before we reach the top of the mountain. Mankind today more than ever is in need of the civilizing teachings of God. If we were to disappear, the conscience of the world would disappear, and gradually the ideas of holiness and Godliness which emanate from Judaism would vanish. That would be a tragedy — not only for the Jews, but the world itself. First of all, our mere presence on earth, in defiance of all the rules of history and logic, is itself a testimony to the presence of God. This is in fulfillment of God's covenant and a vindication of Biblical prophecy that Israel is an eternal people. He obviously wants us to exist.

D: Well, covenant or not, some of our people seem to be doing their best to help us disappear — by intermarrying in high numbers, by assimilating, by not studying any Judaism at all, by sheer ignorance. They're completely unaware of any special Jewish role in history, or of any Jewish destiny. I don't want to be unfair, but they seem to expend a great deal of energy trying not to be too obviously Jewish, and to become exact replicas of the people around them.

R: You're beginning to sound like me.

D: The dangers of too much exposure to a rabbi.

Functioning on another level *R:* I'm hoping that can never be "too much." In any case, Jews who assimilate are unfortunately very myopic. They have never learned about Jewish destiny, or distinctiveness, or about the Jewish role in history. For many of them, Judaism is identical with certain vague notions about social justice, ethics, and support of the State of Israel. If they were sitting in on our discussion here, they would realize that Judaism functions on a different level, and that we can never be a people like other people.

But there is one small consolation about those disappearing Jews. As we mentioned at our very first discussion, they are not deliberately and with forethought abandoning Judaism. They are just flowing out with the stream and following the crowd, doing what everyone else does. They are for the most part not consciously opposed to their Jewishness — just oblivious — and it all stems from Jewish illiteracy and ignorance. These are our great enemies today. If we don't begin learning who we are and where we come from, we could fade away from this world. By the same token, learning about ourselves as Jews will definitely bring us back — as it already has done for tens of thousands.

D: If it is God's promise that we will always exist, why worry about our future? We will never disappear, no matter what.

R: True, we will not literally disappear; how many Jews will remain, however, is up to us. If you read it in minimal terms, God's promise merely ensures that there will be a bare *minyan* of us, but there is not much point to Jewish existence if it is mere physical survival without any spiritual vitality. Even though we would be technically alive, in effect this would be the end. We would disappear not with a bang but with a whimper — which would be a really tragic ending to a glorious story. *Not with a bang but with a whimper*

But I am optimistic that it will not come to this. I think we are beginning to see a renaissance in Jewish life all over the world. We have already hit rock bottom — physically with the destruction of the Holocaust, and spiritually with the self-inflicted wounds of ignorance and illiteracy. We can hardly sink lower without disappearing entirely, and I think our people sense this. There is a slow, gradual turnaround taking place in our generation — imperceptible, almost invisible, but nevertheless real. We discussed this in our first meeting, if you recall.

D: How can you be optimistic in the face of all that is going on around us?

R: Because of the bottom line: the Jewish people are inextricably tied to God: as He is eternal and forever, so are His people. Somehow and in some way, we will remain. If we work hard and set our minds to it, we will not only survive — this in itself is not the crucial point — we will flourish and continue to be the true and faithful messengers of God, and bring His teaching and the fact of His existence and providence and sustenance to all of mankind.

To turn to your question once again: yes, it would be a profound tragedy, both for the Jews and for the world — and if I dare say so, perhaps even for God — if we were to disappear. For one thing, look at what the Jew has already contributed to the world. The idea of one God, the basis of all morality: these are Jewish ideas. Can you imagine what the world would be without them? And can you imagine what the world would be if the bearers of these ideas, the Jewish people, were to vanish?

But even more significant, the end of the Jewish people would end our opportunity to bear witness to God's existence. Our adherence to the principles of Torah, to a different and more stringent level of morality and ethics and commitment to God, are living testimony to God's presence. We have to exist in order to do this.

D: Some of the Jews I know don't quite fit this ideal portrait you are painting.

Bridge from heaven to earth **R:** Granted. We are far from being perfect, and there are those among us who fall short of the ideal. But no one can deny that historically as a people we have been faithful to God's covenant and have stubbornly adhered to Him despite everything.

What I mean by all this is that in a very real way, the Jewish people are the bridge between God and mankind. If the bridge is destroyed, if it ceases to exist, mankind will never be able to cross over towards God.

D: But cannot God come over towards man?

R: There are of course no limits on what God can do. But He so designed the world that Israel is the connecting link between Him and man. Without the presence of Israel, God's relationship with mankind must change radically. So the end of the Jewish people would be a tragedy for mankind in general.

Unbeloved conscience **D:** Most of mankind would give you an argument about that.

R: I'm sure they would. Some would be quite content to see us disappear, because we are the conscience of mankind

— which doesn't make us very beloved. We plead guilty as charged: we brought the message of monotheism to the world — and of morality and ethics and civilized behavior and personal discipline, and we persist in it. These are not very popular notions — and the Jewish people are not the most popular people on earth.

D: Wouldn't you agree that the Jewish desire for separateness has been a contributing factor to anti-Semitism?

R: Not at all. Anti-Semitism is not a rational phenomenon. It does not require reasons or logical underpinnings. The anti-Semite hates Jews because they are Jews and later appends a reason to his hatred: Jews are all communists, or all capitalists; Jews have no backbone, Jews are aggressive; Jews do not know how to fight, Jews are too militaristic; Jews are too separate, Jews are too pushy. And so forth.

D: Is there, then, nothing we can do about anti-Semitism?

R: I happen to think it is part of the condition of the world we live in, a contagious disease which infects every generation in one form or another. It has been around ever since we became a people, and before that as well. Esau hated Jacob, and in fact the Sages say that it is a "halachah, an incontrovertible rule, that Esau always hates Jacob." (See Rashi at *Genesis* 33:4, citing *Sifri* on *Leviticus* 9:10.) Remember that line in the Passover Haggadah? *Bechal dor vedor omdim aleinu lechaloteinu . . .* "in every generation they rise up against us to destroy us, but the Holy One Blessed Be He rescues us from their hands . . ." Pharaoh was fearful that we were multiplying too rapidly and would take over his government and his land. Haman hated us because our religion was strange. Throughout history there have been tens of thousands of variations of these prototypes. Hatred of the Jew is irrational and therefore there is precious little that we can do about it. I hope I am wrong, but in all likelihood it will be with us until the end of days.

Anti-Semitism and logic

Yes, I agree that we should not simply be fatalistic and not try to combat it whenever it rears its head — particularly in situations where our lives and property are at stake. But the best way to fight it is to become more learned and committed Jews. That way, we will at least know who we are and what it is about our beliefs which so enrages our enemies.

Holiness and the beast

There is one small comfort, however, that emerges from anti-Semitism. You can judge individuals or nations not only by their friends but also by their enemies. The greatest tyrants in history have hated Jews and Judaism and tried to blot us out. This is an oblique tribute to the elements of holiness and Godliness which they clearly sensed within our people — a holiness which enrages the beast within man and causes him to turn ferociously against those who first brought such teachings into the world.

D: Scant comfort.

R: Very scant. But think for a moment: as difficult as life is today, imagine what it would be like if there were no such thing as the conscience which the Jews provided to the world, and which, in theory at least, most people grudgingly accepted. If left to their own devices, it's pretty clear that mankind would long ago have chosen savagery over civilization.

D: Which is what the world seems to have chosen these days in any case. Evidently, the Jews are not doing too good a job.

R: We could be doing a better job, granted. But imagine this universe without the teachings of Torah and morality which have unobtrusively seeped into the consciousness of millions of people. At the very least, there is today a sense of what theoretically is right and theoretically is wrong. This is crucial, because when this basic line of demarcation disappears, all is lost.

In brief, a world without Jews and Judaism would be the poorer for it — although admittedly more "comfortable." I dare say that without Jews — which is to say, without Torah — civilization would come to a swift end. Perhaps that would please some people, but if the civilized world had any foresight at all they would do everything in their power to maintain us as a people. The problem is that no one likes a conscience, and that's what we are: the conscience of mankind. This is one of the facets of being chosen by God to bring His teaching to mankind.

D: This idea of chosenness is another uncomfortable concept for me. Which, I suppose, means that it's an important idea. *Are we chosen?*

R: Exactly. It is a core concept in Judaism.

D: I don't want to repeat what is obviously a cliché, but doesn't chosennness imply superiority? Do we actually consider ourselves superior to the rest of mankind?

R: That is another false supposition. Superiority *per se* is not an evil. Certain athletes are superior to others; certain musicians are superior to others; certain doctors are superior to others. They and everyone else acknowledge this. Is this evil? Superiority and inferiority are part of the human condition. Certainly a top-flight surgeon knows that his surgical skills are superior to that of the pharmacist, just as the pharmacist knows that his knowledge of various drugs is superior to that of the surgeon's. Awareness of one's ability or talent is not an evil in itself. It becomes an evil only when the individual forgets that what he has is a gift from God, when he thinks that he himself is the author of his talent. Then it becomes a vehicle for arrogance and overweening pride, and could be utilized to hurt the less superior ones, to oppress them, or to destroy them — as Nazi Germany attempted to do because it considered itself the master race.

The fact is that certain nations are superior to other nations in specific areas of endeavor. Yes, we believe that the Jewish people is chosen for its mission by God because it possesses certain God given talents: a clear vision and knowledge of God and how He wants mankind to live on His earth, and the ability to connect with God and with the sacred in life. The Jewish genius lies in its appreciation and yearning for God, its stubborn tenacity in maintaining that yearning and contact, its perception that religion and God-consciousness are not merely one compartment of life, but are in fact the summation and totality of all of life, and its willingness to give up everything in order to remain the instrument of God and spread that teaching and that sanctity to the rest of mankind.

Other nations may be superior in other respects: they may be more clever, more intelligent, more inventive, more athletic, more attuned to law or economics or science or music or mathematics or philosophy. Each nation has its own God-given genius. Who can match the contribution of the ancient Greeks in art and design and architecture? Or that of the ancient Romans in their understanding of governance? Or of the Phoenicians in their genius for commerce and trade? Or the Slavic peoples in their appreciation of music and dance?

The Jewish people was seen by God as having certain qualities — steadfastness, spiritual resilience, courage, faith, self-discipline — which made us the most suitable agent for bringing the concepts of God and holiness into the world. That is to say, our national character — which we inherited from the Patriarchs and Matriarchs — was most appropriate for carrying out God's mission: to introduce the qualities of His realm into this earthly realm.

A different destiny   The natural corollary of this assignment is that our destiny is different from that of the nations. They all function in this world of nature, while our destiny is to function on a super-natural level. Our very history confirms this. How is it, for example, that we have defied the usual laws of nations and of history and have not rolled over and died? What other ancient empire is still identifiable and vibrant today? We have achieved this miracle because we are essentially not of this world, and not subject to the mundane rules of history that say, for example, that when you lose your land and your holy places, and your populace is exiled in chains, you are finished as a people.

D: Has it all been worthwhile, this chosenness of ours, our isolation from the rest of the world? Look at how much we have suffered because of it.

R: Whether or not it has been worthwhile is beside the point, since we had no choice in the matter. Remember, we did not unilaterally arrogate this title for ourselves. For some mysterious reason of His own, God chose us as His instrument, to be His people and to be the bearer of His teaching to mankind. It all began with Abraham, whom God promises in *Genesis* 12, "I will make you a great nation," and it continues in *Exodus* 19:6, where God commands us to be "a kingdom of priests and a holy nation." We are commanded to

do an enormous job, to transform and help perfect the world
— *tikkun olam* in Hebrew — and, in the words of *Isaiah* 63:6,
to be a "light unto the nations."

We did not seek any of this out, and we do not know
for certain why we were chosen. In *Deuteronomy* 7:7, we do
find an important hint: "Not because you are the most
numerous among the nations did the Lord desire you and
choose you, for you are the least among the nations, but
because He loved you and maintained the oath He swore to
your fathers . . ."

To be sure, it is a great privilege, but it has also meant *Dominance*
obloquy and scorn from a world that did not want to be *and*
reminded about God, or personal discipline, or individual *servitude*
responsibility, or a universal morality, or integrity, or sanctity,
or peace, or justice, or love, and would rather be left to do
things and to live life without any "interference" from above.
In fact, Isaiah depicts Israel as the "suffering servant," the
people which suffers on behalf of mankind. But whatever we
have borne for God's sake has been eminently worthwhile,
because we have tried to fulfill His will and to bring His teachings into the world. We can well appreciate God's comment to
Israel as recorded in Tractate *Horayot* 10a-b: "You think I am
giving you dominion? I am giving you servitude."

Is this an important mission? Yes. Is it the most important
mission a nation could possibly have? Yes, because it is the
mission of teaching men not to be beasts, but instead to live
civilized lives together under God. That's why Jewish mystics
refer to Israel as the heart of the nations, and the nations as
the limbs. Neither can exist without the other. Just as the
heart pumps the blood, the vigor, the life-giving quality, so
Israel activates the humanity within the nations and cleanses
out the beastly. But just as a heart without a body has no life,
so Israel without the nations has no purpose.

Does it smack of superiority? Yes, in this one area of life.
Can you name any other nation that has carried God's word so
faithfully and for so long a time and at such great sacrifice as
has the Jewish people?

D: And with all this, you say that there is no concept of racial
superiority in Judaism?

R: I am saying precisely that. Of all the major religions, none
is more universalistic than is Judaism. The prophet Isaiah
in his fifty-sixth chapter, for example, foresees the time when
God's house "shall be a house of prayer for all the nations."
The Torah even contains the words of a non-Jewish prophet,
Bil'am. Search the Christian or Muslim Bibles and see if you
can find any Jewish prophet. Jonah's entire message of
prophecy is directed to the heathen city of Nineveh. And there
is one Talmudic view, in *Beitzah* 25b, that holds that Israel
was chosen by God not because it was the best of the nations,
but because it was the worst — an echo of *Deuterenomy* 9:6.
And, of course, it is not only Israel but all of humankind
which is created in the image of God.

Serious and Therefore, it is not surprising that there is no concept of
frivolous race in Judaism. Races all possess certain common features;
connections the Jewish people is not a race: there are dark-skinned Jews
from Ethiopia and Yemen, and Jews from India, and blond,
blue-eyed Jews from Scandinavia. Blood lines are not an issue
with us. Were we to believe in our "racial" superiority, we
would not accept converts from other peoples or races. But
the fact is that anyone, regardless of background or upbringing
or faith system, can become a Jew if he or she is serious about
joining our people.

D: What do you mean by serious?

R: A serious convert is ready to commit himself or herself to
our mitzvot, our Torah, and our God. He or she is ready to
stick with us through thick and thin, to suffer with us if need
be, and also to be joyous with us. Ruth in the Bible is the magnificent prototype of the classic convert. When her mother-
in-law Naomi tries to dissuade her from accompanying her to
the Holy Land and from becoming part of the Jewish people,
Ruth replies that she is prepared to accept Judaism in its
entirety: "Your people will be my people, your God will be my
God . . ."

She was a truly serious convert, and that is why she was
chosen to become the great-great-grandmother of none other
than King David. And when you consider that King David is
the forerunner of the Messiah, and that therefore the Messiah
originates in a convert, that gives you several surprising

insights: first, that hidden within Judaic teaching lies the ultimate unity of mankind; and second, when someone becomes a Jew, he or she is not a second-class citizen, but becomes an integral part of our people. Were we a racial society, no one could enter, not even serious converts. The Nazis did not permit strangers to become naturalized Germans, no matter how serious they were.

D: And what is a non-serious convert?

R: Sadly, most of the conversions taking place today in America fall into this category, because they are by and large devoid of any serious commitment to Torah practice or belief. Most conversions being done today are of the quickie, convenient variety, usually motivated by the desire to paper over an intermarriage, and by and large they are presided over by rabbis who themselves do not believe in the Divine origin of the Torah and who do not practice its mitzvot. Such rabbis can hardly create converts who are committed to anything Jewish beyond supporting Israel and giving to the annual appeal, lighting Chanukah and perhaps Friday evening candles, attending synagogue on the High Holidays, and accepting some amorphous notions of social justice. When they don't inform such potential converts that Halachic Judaism does not accept the validity of such conversions, these rabbis are not leveling with innocent people who know no better.

D: Why don't we make serious efforts to convert mankind to our way of life, just as other religions do? If we possess the true perception of life and of reality, why don't we share it with the world? Don't we want everyone to be moral and ethical and God-fearing, and holy? In fact, are we not being selfish and thus immoral when we do not share the wonders of the Torah?

Jewish mission-aries?

R: Excellent points. Let's approach them from several perspectives. First of all, the Torah does not ask us to be active missionaries to the world. We are required to live by the Torah and to live as complete Jews, and by so doing to bear testimony to the existence of God. Second, when various religions engage in missionary activity and try to convert others to their faith, they are doing so because they believe that unless one believes in their faith, one is eternally damned. This is particularly true of classical Christianity, and is the thrust behind the hundreds of millions of dollars they spend in trying to win converts. They believe that they need to "save" souls from eternal damnation.

Judaism does not believe that everyone must be a Jew, or that unless one is a Jew, he or she is eternally rejected by God. On the contrary, we believe that any non-Jew who follows the basic laws of Godliness, as embodied in the Noachide Code we mentioned earlier, is entitled to his eternal reward. In fact within classical Judaism one finds great admiration for the righteous among the nations. *Tosefta Sanhedrin* 13 explicitly says that "the righteous of all nations have a share in the World to Come." And *Tanna d'bei Eliyahu Rabba* 9 states clearly: "I call heaven and earth as witnesses: any individual, whether Gentile or Jew, man or woman, servant or hand-maiden, can bring the Divine Presence upon himself in accordance with his deeds."

Thus there is no religious need for us to save the souls of others. They please God when they live by the precepts of belief in God and the fundamental principles that flow from that belief. Therefore we do not send missionaries to the gentiles, and we do not proselytize or try to persuade others to join us.

D: But shouldn't we at least make some efforts to bring all the nations under the Noachide Code? Since it too stems from God, why do we leave it just to chance?

R: There is in fact a point of view within our tradition, though it is not a majority view , that we ought to be doing precisely that. Maimonides seems to allude to it in his Laws of Kings, 8:11. But our history of wandering and persecution has left us precious little opportunity for such activities. Our energies are fully expended in trying to bring our own Jews back into Judaism. (I always suggest the following to Christian missionaries who try to convert us: why don't you expend your energies on converting your fellow Christians? Let them learn to live by Christian teachings, and implement love in their lives, and learn to turn the other cheek. Why waste such huge resources on converting the Jews when so many of your own co-religionists remain unconverted to your way of life?)

Our only mission is to remain faithful to our God and His Torah, and thus bear witness to His existence and to the veracity of His covenant with our forefathers; to demonstrate that man is not a beast, that he can transcend his baser nature and can live a life of holiness even on this earth; and then in God's own time He will bring about His dominion over all the peoples of the earth. We do accept converts who come in of their own volition and who genuinely want to be part of our people, but the initiative must be theirs.

Objectively speaking, there is something mysterious about the continued existence of this strange people. It's as if God were holding us on high for all mankind to see, and pointing to us as proof that His covenant is still in force, that we are His people and that He shall never utterly abandon us — and, by the way, that He Himself is still Master of His universe.

This mysterious people

D: It's an obvious question, and perhaps has an obvious answer: where does this staying power come from?

R: We continue to exist only by virtue of our loyalty to the Torah. This has been our energizer and our unifying force. And remember that in His covenant with us, God promises to be our God and we promise to be His people. The covenant, the *berith*, is the eternal, binding contract between God and us. It was first made with Abraham, and cut into his flesh with the sign of circumcision. The covenant was then reaffirmed with his son Isaac, and then once again with his son Jacob, and yet again at Sinai. In it, we pledge mutual loyalty to one another. God promises to multiply us as the sands of the sea and the stars of the heavens, to give us His holy land as a dwelling place; He promises to protect us and maintain us, and never utterly to abandon us. We are given strict marching orders, so to speak, and are placed under strict accountability to Him.

This covenant is pervasive throughout Judaism. In fact, the Torah itself is called "the Book of the Covenant" in *Exodus* 24:7. The Shabbat day is the covenant between God and Israel in *Genesis* 17:7. And the word *berith*/covenant appears in the Bible about *four hundred* times.

The covenant   Despite the stern conditions of this covenant, we are assured by God Himself that He will never utterly abandon us. The twenty-sixth chapter of *Leviticus* contains the most dire prophecies about the future of the Jewish people if we abandon God and His teachings, but at the end of the fearsome litany we are told that despite everything ". . . I will not destroy My covenant with them . . ." The reason for this is that just as God Himself can never cease to exist, so can His people never cease to exist, for we are inextricably bound up with Him. In the third chapter of *Malachi* — the very last chapter of all the prophetic books — God says: "I the Lord have not changed, and you the sons of Jacob are not destroyed . . ."

Who is a Jew?   **D:** Since I'm asking obvious questions today, let me ask one more. Who exactly is considered a Jew according to Jewish law? I had heard that anyone who claims to be Jewish is considered Jewish.

R: Not exactly. Saying it's so doesn't make it so. Technically, a Jew is someone who is born of a Jewish mother, or, if he or she is born outside of Judaism, who accepts the God of Israel, His Torah, and His practices, and undergoes the halachically prescribed rituals of conversion.

D: Is someone born of a Jewish mother considered a Jew even if the father is not Jewish?

R: Yes, the child is halachically a Jew, since according to Jewish law the religion of the child follows that of the mother. And if the father is a Jew and the mother not, the child is not a Jew.

D: And the name "Jew," what is its origin?

R: Very likely from the tribe of Judah, which was the surviving remnant after the destruction of ancient Israel's homeland. Therefore we have names like "Judaism" and "Jew." Note, by the way, that the first three letters of the Hebrew name for "Jew" — *yehudi* — are the same first three letters of the Ineffable Name of God.

D: If, as you say, we have this special mission in the world, does not this very fact create a rather tense relationship with other faiths? How do we view other religions?

R: Every monothesitic religion has a place in the Divine scheme of things. As for idolatrous religions which do not have a monotheistic base, we have no relationship with them at all and do not consider them to be valid religions, because one of the seven universal Noachide laws expressly forbids idol worship. In a way, Christianity and Islam are offshoots of Judaism and still retain the monotheistic nature of the mother religion. We respect the adherents of these faiths (although from the Jewish point of view some of the icon-worship within classical Christianity is perilously close to idolatry) and we encourage them to follow their monotheistic ways.

D: Don't all religions try to do the same thing? Aren't they all trying to make people better, and to lift them up towards more Godly and more spiritual ways?

Judaism and other faith systems

R: They may be trying to achieve certain noble ends, but neither the means nor the ends are identical in the world's great monotheistic religions. They each approach life and God and people in different ways. Even though Judaism respects the teachings and the adherents of the monotheistic faith systems, respect is not to be confused with saying that we are all alike. There are many differences in outlook and in practice, and these should not be swept under the rug. In one of our earlier discussions, we talked about how Judaism and Christianity differ in their approach to the physical — how Christianity historically was never quite able to deal with it and attempted to ban it, or suppress it, or deny it, and how Judaism has attempted to elevate it and press it into the service of God. For example, we do not consider sex intrinsically evil, or marriage to be a concession to the baser nature of man.

That's one major difference. There are others: in Judaism there is no concept of damnation or salvation. We do not believe that we are all born in sin and unable to escape this eternal damnation unless we accept the lordship of the founder of Christianity. We do believe, however, that man is born selfish and greedy and concerned only with his own needs, and that one of the purposes of the Torah is to wean him away from his inborn self-centeredness so that he can begin to think of others around him, and the Other above him, and thus give his life some meaning and purpose.

Another distinction between us and Christianity is that we believe that the way to elevate the human heart towards God is through the performance of the commandments, and that belief and dogma by themselves are insufficient. While we do have dogmas and beliefs, they are but the first step in the performance of mitzvot, because ours is primarily a faith of action. It's how one implements his belief that is significant.

We believe in a life after death, and that the soul is held accountable for its deeds and midsdeeds on this earth, and that this soul returns to its Creator after death and ultimately lives in bliss and peace in the Presence of the Almighty. But we hold life to be extremely precious, not for its own sake but because the real purpose of living — which is to serve God fully and truly — can take place only in this world and not in the World to Come.

Has Judaism been displaced? And, of course, Judaism categorically rejects Christianity's claim that Judaism has been displaced by Christianity, which calls itself the "New Israel." We are still a vital, dynamic faith, and are still quite alive, thank you, and we believe that our role in history is far from played out. That a State of Israel could emerge after thousands of years of exile and dispersion, that it ceases all governmental work on the Jewish Shabbat and Yom Tov, that it is today the generator of intensive and dynamic study of Torah and intense Jewish living — this of itself should give pause to those who claim that Jewish history came to a halt nineteen-hundred years ago with the destruction of the Temple and the Jewish dispersion. In fact, it does give pause to the thinking theologians in the Vatican and elsewhere.

There are many more differences in the way we practice our respective faiths. For example, in Judaism the rabbi is not the intermediary between man and God, as is the priest in classical Christianity. The word "rabbi" simply means "master" or "teacher." No one, for example, confesses sins to the rabbi. This can be done only directly before God, without any intermediary. There are no special laws that apply only to the rabbi. He is encouraged to marry and raise a family, just like the layman. He is in fact a layman himself, and during worship, for example, wears no special priestly garb nor pronounces any special prayers. His primary role is that of teacher of Torah — but of course in the traditional Jewish community that is the most honored of all professions.

Over and beyond all this, perhaps the greatest demarcation line between us is the Christian belief in a Trinity, in Immaculate Conception, in the concept of a son of god who is also divine. We do not ascribe divinity to any being other than God Himself. The Torah in *Exodus* 2:1 takes great pains to inform us that even our greatest prophet, Moses, had a normal father and mother, and that he was conceived and was born in a normal, natural way. In fact, the burial place of Moses is deliberately kept unknown ("and the place of his burial is not known until this day" — *Deuteronomy* 33:6) so that his grave not be turned into a shrine of worship. There are many other differences between Judaism and Christianity, but the doctrine of the son of god is the great abyss that separates us.

Now, all this is not to deny that there are many points of commonality between the two faiths. However, the differences are quite striking and should not be overlooked in an attempt to be tolerant or ecumenical. One can respect other faiths without falling into the trap of saying that we are all alike.

D: And Judaism and Islam - are they not much closer?

R: In one sense, they have a greater affinity in that this great abyss we just spoke about is not present; that is, Islam does not worship anyone other than the One God Whom Jews worship, albeit in a much different manner. They do ascribe great powers to their prophet Mohammed, but they do not worship him as a deity. Of crucial importance is that neither of the other two faiths accepts the binding nature of the commandments, and neither of them has anything like our overarching halachic system of Jewish law and practice. Nor does either of them have as the great, all-encompassing purpose the sanctification of the world and of mankind. And, of course, neither of them lays claim to a public Divine Relevation; this is uniquely Jewish.

Jews and infidels   At the same time, Islam likes to trace its origins back to Abraham, considering itself to be of the descendants of Abraham's son, Ishmael. Although chronologically it arrived on the world stage some sixteen centuries after Judaism and six centuries after Christianity, it thinks of itself not as the last of the three monotheistic religions, but as the first and the only true religion. "The religion of Allah is Islam," says the Koran in the words of Allah (*Sura* 3, v. 19). Islam considers Adam to be the first Islamic prophet, as well as Noah, Abraham, and Moses. The final aim of Islam is to see the entire world as "the realm of Islam." In fact, both Jews and Christians are defined as inferior and as infidels by Islamic law, which openly prevents Jews and Christians from participating in the life of the Islamic state on a parity with Muslims. Many Islamic states even today are "Judenrein" within their borders.

The sad fact is that Judaism and Jews have suffered much indignity, hatred, persecution and killing under both Christian and Islamic regimes throughout history. This is not a very proud or happy chapter in the history of religions, but we will have to leave that subject for another time.

D: We spoke earlier about the covenant and how the Land plays a crucial role in it. And yet you say that Israel's vocation is supernatural, and is not dependent upon earthly matters. How do you reconcile this? Is not the Land an earthly matter?

The Land of the Jews   *R:* Literally speaking, yes. But our concept of the Land is also unearthly and reflects supernatural things. The Jewish relationship to the Land is different, say, from the relationship of the Irish to Ireland or Italians to Italy. For one thing, the Land is the locus of His *Shechinah,* the Divine Presence on earth, and the indwelling of His Holy Presence is centered in the Holy Temple in Jerusalem. So the Land is a geographical entity, yes, but also much more than that.

This accounts for the incredible and unprecedented fact that despite the loss of our Land and the exile of our people, we did not disappear by assimilating into the dominant culture. Of what other people can this be said?

For one thing, we never forgot the Land of Israel. We have always recalled it daily in our prayers, we maintain days of fasting and mourning over its destruction, and through our wanderings from country to country we have kept alive the hope that some day our people will return to that special Land. Our literature, both sacred and profane, has been centered on the Land for millennia.

The Torah refers to it as *eretz chemdah, eretz tzevi, eretz tovah* — a "lovely," "beautiful," "good" land. In *Deuteronomy* there is a loving description of its rivers and streams and valleys and hills (8:7), and God declares that His attention is focused on the Land from the beginning of the year until the end of the year (11:12). The vision of it remained always an integral part of the daily life of the Jew — through facing towards Jerusalem in our prayers, through the various days of mourning in which we remember its destruction, through leaving a certain area of the Jewish home unfinished in remembrance of that destruction, and through the numerous references to it in our daily prayers, blessings, and studies. In fact, Rashi, the classical expositor of the Torah, devotes his very first commentary in *Genesis* to the significance of the Holy Land in God's eternal plan.

Throughout our history, there has been this mysterious relationship between the One God, the one people and the one Land. Although we wandered from land to land in our dispersion, that one Land always remained the focal point of our existence: *Eretz Yisrael*. Not only did we carry its memory with us through the years of the Exile; there has actually never been a time when at least a minimal number of Jews were not dwelling in the Land, even during the worst period of our dispersion, even when they had to conceal their identity and live in mortal danger of discovery. *God, people, land*

We should not take lightly our dwelling on this Land today. It is an astounding fulfillment of the Biblical promise that some day we will return from the Exile to the Land — a theme that pervades the prophetic books. Did you ever read the thirty-seventh chapter of *Ezekiel*, about the dry bones coming to life? In today's events you see the embodiment of this prophecy — not only in the rebirth of the Land, but in the remarkable resurgence of Jewish learning and intensity in the Land.

It is obvious that there is a profound bond — really a supernatural connection — between the holy people and this holy place. The Sages in *Berachot* 5 repeat an ancient tradition that says that God gave three great gifts to the Jewish people: the Torah, the Land of Israel, and the World to Come. This loving relationship of the Jews to the Land has been compared to a betrothal where the groom is carried off by enemies just prior to the wedding. That is to say, the Jewish people was betrothed to the Land but was forced into Exile, and the Land has remained faithful to its betrothed, refusing to accept any other suitors until her beloved returns to her. All those other conquerors of the Holy Land during the past millennia — do you think they could not make the desert bloom because they were bad farmers, and that only the Jews could do it because they are good farmers?

D: If, God forbid, we should lose Israel today, would this be the end of the Jewish people?

R: Having said all that I just said, my answer may surprise you: even though the Land is an integral part of God's covenant and promise, and even though the Land plays a central role in our relationship with God, and even though we would be severely handicapped without it, and even though the Land is the only place where genuine service of God can take place, and even though it is the only place where we can completely fulfill our spiritual potential, the fact is that it is possible to have a Jewish people without the Land. Our very history has demonstrated this.

A people of time   That's because we are a people of Time rather than a people of Space. Our program and our function are not dependent entirely on earthly things, not even on a very special and beloved Land. We do not depend on the normal trappings of nationhood: flags, armies, parliaments, commerce, language — even land. We are a people not by virtue of these things, but by virtue of the Torah. We can exist without those external trappings — and have in fact done so for two thousand years of Exile. What we cannot exist without — is the Torah. Jewish communities who have attempted to exist without it have ceased to exist, period.

D: Are you saying that the modern State of Israel is not important? That sounds like heresy, Rabbi.

R: I warned you not to be surprised. No, I am not at all saying that. It is of crucial importance to our lives as Jews that modern Israel be maintained and developed to its full physical and spiritual potential. And it is wondrous and miraculous in this last half of the twentieth century to have a living, vibrant state in our ancestral home, to have a physical and spiritual haven, to begin rebuilding our spiritual resources, for it is only in the Land that the Jewish people can realize its complete spiritual growth. It would be a major catastrophe if we were, God forbid, to lose it. But it needs to be kept in historical perspective. All I am saying is that the Jewish people, if it maintains the Torah, would survive the catastrophe, just as it did for the past nineteen centuries. I pray that we will never have to witness that moment.

D: Would it not be ironic if, now that we have the Land, Judaism were to disappear from it?

R: Not only ironic, but tragic. I dare say that it is even more tragic that there are Jews who would like to see this occur. They find the Torah and its constraints too restrictive for contemporary times. They would like Israel to be just another Mediterranean country. If they have their way and succeed in removing Torah from the mainstream of Israeli life, they will simply create a Diaspora within the State of Israel, with a mentality which takes its cue from the nations, and whose primary ambition is to be accepted as an equal by the nations of the world — all the time unaware of its own vast resources of spiritual power. And the historic irony would be that after waiting two thousand years to return to the Land, a return that was in a major way effected by adherence to the Torah and the tenacious belief in its promises, we would reject that Torah and its Author. If that were to happen, God forbid, I believe that ultimately the Land would follow into oblivion. The Land is a gift to us, and we have to be worthy of that gift.

Just another country?

D: Do you really think that God would exile us once again from the Land?

R: I would pray that He would not, but I cannot speak for Him. Remember, the Land has a life of its own. When the Torah warns us that if we follow the immoral ways of the

Canaanites the Land will spit us out, that is not merely vivid poetry. Like any living organism that cannot sustain foreign and harmful elements within itself, so the Land rejects that which is foreign to its essential sanctity.

Spiritual facts of life   So when the prophets warn Israel not to follow the ways of the idolaters or the immoral practices of the Canaanites lest the Land vomit us out, they are not simply being dramatic. They are in reality informing Israel of a spiritual fact of life, of a cause and inevitable effect; namely, that a sacred land cannot tolerate profane behavior. That fact of life is still operative today, and those living in modern Israel have an awesome responsibility to preserve the Holy Land from destruction. After all, the reason God gave us the Land in the first place is because it is the best place from which to reach out to our Creator. This is specifically stated in *Leviticus* 25:38: "I am the Lord your God Who brought you out of the land of Egypt, to give to you the land of Canaan, to be God unto you." If we turn away from God in His own Land, we deny the very purpose for which we were given that Land.

But I hasten to add my conviction that those who want to deprive Israel of Torah are committing a major historical error, and they will not succeed. The fact is that Torah commitment, Torah living and Torah study in modern Israel are very strong, on a level of depth and breadth that has rarely been seen in the past two thousand years, and it grows stronger by the day. At the same time, those Jews who have abandoned Torah — whether in Israel or in the Diaspora — are seeing the tragic results before their very eyes, as their children and grandchildren disappear from the Jewish screen.

For the rest of us, it is scant comfort to be vindicated in one's beliefs at such a price, for we as a people can ill afford to lose what we are losing to assimilation in the West — and what we could also lose in Israel. I pray that before it is too late, the obvious dangers will help shock these drifting Jews into returning to the ways of our people, before total eclipse sets in. As always, I am optimistic, and there are signs of movement in this direction, as we discussed in our very first meeting.

D: But is it such a sin to want to live a normal life, and not to be an outcast among nations? *A normal nation?*

R: To want to live a normal life is perfectly, well, normal — depending on how you define "normal." Cannibals and drug lords have their own codes of what they consider normal behavior, but I don't think you would choose their definition for yourself. Some day, in God's own good time, the Jewish people will be seen to be a normal people, and those who reject God to be the abnormal ones.

But bear in mind that one of the great sins in the eyes of the prophets is this so-called normal Jewish desire to be a nation like all the nations, *kechal hagoyim.* As a matter of fact, if our attachment to the Land is based on the wish to become like the other nations, that very attachment is Jewishly inauthentic. This may be a natural desire, but as you have certainly surmised by now, to be a Jew is to transcend the merely natural and to operate on a different level — where the natural things are sanctity and awareness of God.

D: Normal and above normal; sanctity; awareness of God; chosenness; Jews and non-Jews — this may be a good place for us to pause today. I certainly have much to think about.

R: Good. We all need to do more thinking. Our mystical writers say that when we fill our minds with important matters, foolish things have no room to get in.

D: I certainly hope they're right, because in my case I've always had trouble keeping them out.

epilogue – the jew goes and learns

Rabbi: We have come a long way since our very first meeting.
For me at least, and I hope for you, it has been an exhilarating journey. We have looked at some of the essential areas of Torah, and uncovered, if I may say so, some new insights. But I think we have come to the point now where we should pause, take stock, and consider what we have done and where we'll go from here — sort of regroup.

David: Are you saying that this is going to be our last session? The end?

R: The last session for a while, yes — but not really the end.
I would prefer "the beginning," because now that we have discussed some of the essentials of Torah and Judaism, we can more intelligently begin to examine ourselves and our personal values and performance.

D: Certainly we have covered a lot of territory and seen a lot of new places. It has been an exciting adventure. And most important of all, I am more confident and less fearful about the Torah and its ways. They somehow seem less foreign to me now, less threatening. For me, this has truly been a journey of discovery.

R: To quote what you like to say to me: are those mere words, or have you really discovered something?

D: Primarily, I have discovered aspects of Judaism that I never knew existed. I feel almost ashamed at not having explored these basic matters much earlier in my life. But I'm puzzled: now that I know a bit more than before, what am I supposed to do with all this information?

R: I hope you realize that subjects like Torah, and covenant, and our relationship to God are something more than the mere gathering of information.

But in any case, what you do is up to you. The fact that *Judaism is* you have been exposed to it means that some of it has surely *not* entered your spiritual bloodstream, so to speak — which is a *theoretical* good beginning in itself. You now possess it, it is already yours to do with as you please, or to do nothing with. At the very least, you emerge from these discussions a somewhat more intelligent and conscious Jew — which in itself is an achievement, especially at a time when Jewish ignorance is the norm.

But should you want to follow things up, one of the things you should try to do, besides continuing to read and learn, is to experience some of what we have studied. It's one thing to theorize about Shabbat, for example, and learn all about the sources and philosophical underpinnings of the thirty-nine categories of creative labor; it's quite another actually to experience a living Shabbat day. The same holds true for everything we have touched on. Judaism is an experiential, not just a theoretical, way of life.

D: The truth is that, after all our discussions, in many ways I feel relatively more ignorant now than I did at the outset. There is so much more to know.

R: That is proof positive that you have learned something. Only a truly ignorant person thinks he knows everything.

You've been asking me questions all along. Let me turn the tables on you: throughout all the various talks we have had, what single aspect of Judaism most surprised you?

D: That's not easy to answer, but I would say that Judaism's understanding for human weakness and fallibility and vulnerability; its recognition that we are only flesh and blood; and the fact that it makes no demands on us that are irrational or that are impossible to fulfill — these are the things that most surprised me, and pleasantly so. Judaism is a rigorous way of life, of that there is no question, but it is also realistic and it understands human foibles. (I guess one should expect that from our Creator, Who knows us best.) Judaism doesn't deny our humanness or the fact that we are earthbound creatures. Its major thrust, I now realize, is to try to transform us into the best kind of human being possible.

I was also surprised at the intellectual depth and breadth of Judaism, something I never knew existed. As for most Jews, Judaism for me consisted of a few isolated practices like candle-lighting on Friday nights, fasting on Yom Kippur, having a Seder of sorts, giving to Israel, being a decent person, and believing in some sort of vague way in the existence of God. That was all there was to it. It never occurred to me for example, that "love thy neighbor" was much more involved and complicated, or that interpersonal relationships were covered by specific Jewish laws, or that the mitzvah system creates the bridge between God and mankind.

R: And what was it that most affected you personally, that most touched you as an individual?

The door is open *D:* I think it was the idea that no matter how far we wander away, God's door is always open to us. It's like one's own home: you can go home again. Of all the things we discussed, that idea of *teshuvah* is really the most electrifying, and means the most to me as a human being.

R: If you had to find one overarching theme, one thread that runs through Judaism, what would you say that is?

D: There is one concept that seems to stay with me, and that's the way Judaism handles the difficult problem of the physical versus the spiritual. Through the concept of sanctity, the Torah attempts to raise up the physical rather than try to stamp it out, to elevate it, and transform it into the realm of spirituality. The entire idea of holiness within the marketplace — that sanctity is not some fairyland idea but a very practical, down-to-earth concept seems to run through everything.

And there are other concepts that startled and moved me. One that kept popping up no matter what we discussed was the idea that we are not God, that we are not the Master of the universe, that there is Someone above us Who is always involved and to Whom we are subservient. Whether it was Shabbat, or prayer, or sanctity, or kashruth, this idea kept surfacing over and over again. This, plus the idea that although we are central in God's plans, we as individuals are not the center of the universe, and that there are others in the universe beside ourselves.

Well, where do I go from here?

R: In any direction you choose.

D: You're not going to direct me?

R: Not unless you want me to.

D: Not even going to try to persuade me to live a certain way?

R: With all the new ideas you've picked up, I don't have to persuade you of anything; they are bound to touch you in some way. These ideas seep into your bones and become part of you. In one way or another, you are affected by them. As to what action or behavior they will lead to, one of the principles of Judaism is that of free choice.

D: These sessions have impressed one crucial idea on me: *To be* in Judaism, one can never be static. You once told me that *or* a *tzaddik* is a person who not only is, but constantly becomes. *to become* We always have to be on the move, striding forward, climbing upward. A person is expected always to become something more and better — more holy, more connected with God, more of a human being, more connected with other human beings. We have to strive to pray better, to learn more, to think more rigorously, to become more independent of the misconceived clichés of the society around us.

But let me ask you one last question: now that we have made this journey together, what central ideas should I be taking away with me? If you had to choose, what concepts would you expect me to keep always in mind?

R: Well, I suppose my difficult question to you deserves your difficult question to me. You have already touched on some of the basics in your own response. I would add the following in order to round out the picture:

Fad vs. genuine
One of the cardinal teachings of Torah is that it wants us to be able to make distinctions: between right and wrong, good and evil, the holy and the profane. You may remember that I pointed out that at the very beginning of the Torah, God engages in acts of separation and distinction. Towards the end of the Torah, in *Deuteronomy* 30:15, God says to Israel: "See, I have set forth before you this day life and good, or death and evil." And a few verses later we read that God presents to us "life and death, the blessing and the curse, and you shall choose life so that you and your seed shall live."

We once discussed the *Havdalah* prayer that Jews recite at the close of Shabbat. In it, we acknowledge God who "separates between holy and profane, between light and darkness, between Israel and the nations, between the seventh day and the six days of creation . . ." In order to choose intelligently, one needs a sense of discernment, and this is one of the things Torah does for us. It gives us the ability to distinguish between the phony and the faddish on the one side, and the real and the genuine on the other. It would be a major blessing for you if you were to emerge from our discussions with this sense of *havdalah.* When that becomes part of you, you are no longer tempted to follow the mob, and instead you learn to look objectively at the vapid and empty silliness which pervades our existence today.

And I would underscore the one idea which must emerge from any study of Torah: the realization that the utter mystery of the universe, its awesome power and majesty, is far beyond our human understanding. Modern man does not comprehend that this is how it should be: we are finite — here today and gone tomorrow — while God is eternal and everlasting and the Author of all things. Just as God's world is not fathomable to the human mind, so too His conduct of the universe, His treatment of individuals and societies, His Torah, and His commandments are also not fathomable. As great and as magical as the human mind is, there are powers still greater than human reason. In other words, not everything has to "make sense" to us — not in life and not in Torah.

That's why I think that the single most appropriate symbol of the human being is our dual ability to stand erect and simultaneously to bow the head. That is to say, to be proud that though we are mortal, we nevertheless have the capacity to reach up to God and fill our souls with the awe and mystery of His universe, His people, His Torah.

I would also ask you to remember that our relationship with God is a two-way avenue. He communicates with us, sort of sending us love notes, by way of the Torah and the perspective it gives us on existence. And we communicate with Him by sending Him our little love notes, through prayer and through the mitzvot. *We send Him notes*

Through it all, one overarching idea emerges from all of our discussions, which is that while our souls apparently yearn for sanctity, there is a very powerful attraction within us towards godlessness, evil, and license. Against all this stands the Torah, and representing the Torah is the Jewish people. The Torah is the last barrier that prevents mankind from toppling over into the abyss. So we Jews have a pretty heavy responsibility — and privilege.

Finally, I would like you to keep in mind the very first question God asks to Adam, back in *Genesis*: "Where are you?" That is not only a question, but a challenge from on high. It's a question we always need to ask ourselves: Where are we — as human beings, as children of God, as members of the holy people Israel? Our lives should be an attempt to respond to that Divine challenge.

By the way, may I suggest that whatever you do, please maintain our regular meeting time as before, as if I were there. Use it for your own study and reading, but don't squander it. With all the fine and challenging material available today in English translation, you can set aside a regular study period — preferably with a friend — in which you can examine the weekly Torah portion or the Prophetic books in depth. Or begin some study of post-Biblical material such as Mishnah and Talmud. Become involved with an ongoing and serious learning group. And try to acquire the rudiments of Hebrew reading and some basic knowledge of the language.

D: Typically Jewish, this suggestion you're making. Don't I even get a small vacation? After all, you have loaded me up with so much that I need a respite.

Step by step ***R:*** Okay, but when you return to a regular schedule, take this practical advice: first, as you continue moving towards Jewish learning and Jewish observance, don't try to absorb too much at one time. Set reasonable goals for yourself. The Torah is a bottomless ocean of wisdom and knowledge and cannot be mastered overnight. Don't get discouraged. Step by step you will learn the rudiments and the basics, and then you will advance gradually into new challenges. Remember, no one knows everything. Our task, as we once discussed, is just to make a serious, honest effort. Try as hard as you can, and — this will surprise you — relax. Have patience with yourself, just as God surely has with us. He is on your side, and He will help you progress. Trust Him.

My second suggestion is even more practical. A Jew who begins to return to Jewish moorings, and begins to study more and practice more, occasionally represents a challenge to those who know him — including even members of his or her own family — who are still perfectly comfortable with their own lack of Jewish learning or living. Suddenly a person like you appears, and you are attending Jewish classes and perhaps beginning to observe more mitzvot. It could make those around you uncomfortable and a bit nervous.

Challenge or threat Sometimes the discomfort serves as a challenge and a prod, and such people are roused out of their lethargy when they see a living being striving to live more Jewishly. As a result, they too may end up going to a rabbi and having a series of discussions with him. But occasionally their discomfort is translated as a threat, and you may be accused of being insincere, or of being weak-minded, or of having hidden motives, or of having lost your mind altogether. Returning Jews are usually strong enough to withstand such pressures and not take them seriously — were they not strong to start with, they wouldn't be seeking a new kind of life — but I didn't want you to be taken by surprise either by the challenge or by the threat which some folks may see in you.

As a counterweight, you will find the Torah-observant community to be open and accepting — very hospitable, very friendly, very warm. You may lose some old friends (if they drop you because of your sincere quest, their friendship was skin-deep to begin with) but you will gain many new ones.

Whatever transpires, strive to be honest with your God, your Torah, your people, your heritage, and with yourself; and to be patient, tolerant, and accepting of everyone around you, both your new friends and those who feel left behind by your new quest. Things will surely fall into place.

It's time to say farewell for now — you know you can always give me a call as issues arise — but I do pray that you will continue to grow as a Jew. If you let things fade away, all the time we have invested in our own discussions could easily dissipate into nothing more than fuzzy memories and vague good feelings. And always bear in mind the Talmudic tale in *Shabbat* 31a that we once mentioned — what Hillel replied to the Gentile who wanted to learn all of the Torah while standing on one foot: "What is hateful unto you, do not do unto your friend; the rest is commentary. Go and learn." *The rest is commentary*

We have touched only on some of the basics. The rest is up to you.

Go and learn.
And think.
And absorb.
And review.
And ask.
And experience.
But most of all, go and learn.

index

index

m

maariv 90
Maimonides 73, 97, 99-
  100, 105, 110-111,
  198, 211, 261, 274
manna 178
marriage 132, 186, 214,
  240, 277
matzah 130, 150, 197
measure for measure
  53
Megillah 217
melachah 172, 179,
  182-184
Messiah 212-213, 225,
  260, 272
mezuzah 76, 98, 104,
  130
mikveh 112, 130, 162
minchah 89
mind 104
  —Torah and 109
miracles 196
Mishkan 180-181, 184
Mishnah 99-100, 106,
  113, 291
mishpatim 142, 144
missionaries 274
mitzvot 35
  —adding to 186
  —and God 141
  —and man 141
  —negative 162
  —positive 162
  —subtracting from
    186
  —surrendering life for
    151

—uniqueness and
  261
mo'ed 192
Mohammed 279
moon 192, 203-204
morality 39
Mordechai 217
Moses 53, 89, 99, 169,
  215-216, 239, 254-
  255, 279, 280
mourning 106, 194,
  198, 200, 207,
  281
murder 151-152
musaf 190
music 183
mystery 53-54, 59

n

Nachmanides 73
Naomi 272
natural 223, 227, 240
Noach 280
Noachide Code 274
non-believer 38, 244
non-kosher 232

o

observant 148, 156
Omer 199, 172, 193
Oral Torah 98-99
Oral Torah 115, 201,
  208, 240
order 140, 263

p

pagans 55, 126-127
Paradise 47, 175, 221-
  224

Passover 88
Pesach 191-196, 199-
  205
physical 118, 121, 169,
  206, 224, 277
physics 158
pilgrimage 191
pleasure 23, 122, 154,
  167, 173-175
  —pursuit of 19
practice, vs. study 107-
  108
prayer 16, 52-54, 61,
  96, 134, 153-162
  —Amidah 75-76
  —and fear 68
  —and humility 88
  —and prophecy 78
  —as music 79, 81
  —avodah 64, 73-74
  —blessing 83
  —change of mind
    88-89
  —commandment 72
  —communal 65-66,
    80
  —concentration 69,
    76-77, 82
  —daily 84
  —essence of 84-85,
    87
  —heart 69, 74, 85
  —language of 86, 90
  —laws 74, 82
  —lonely 65
  —maariv 67
  —minchah 67
  —mind 69
  —musaf 67